I0810392

Images of Modern America

SEDALIA

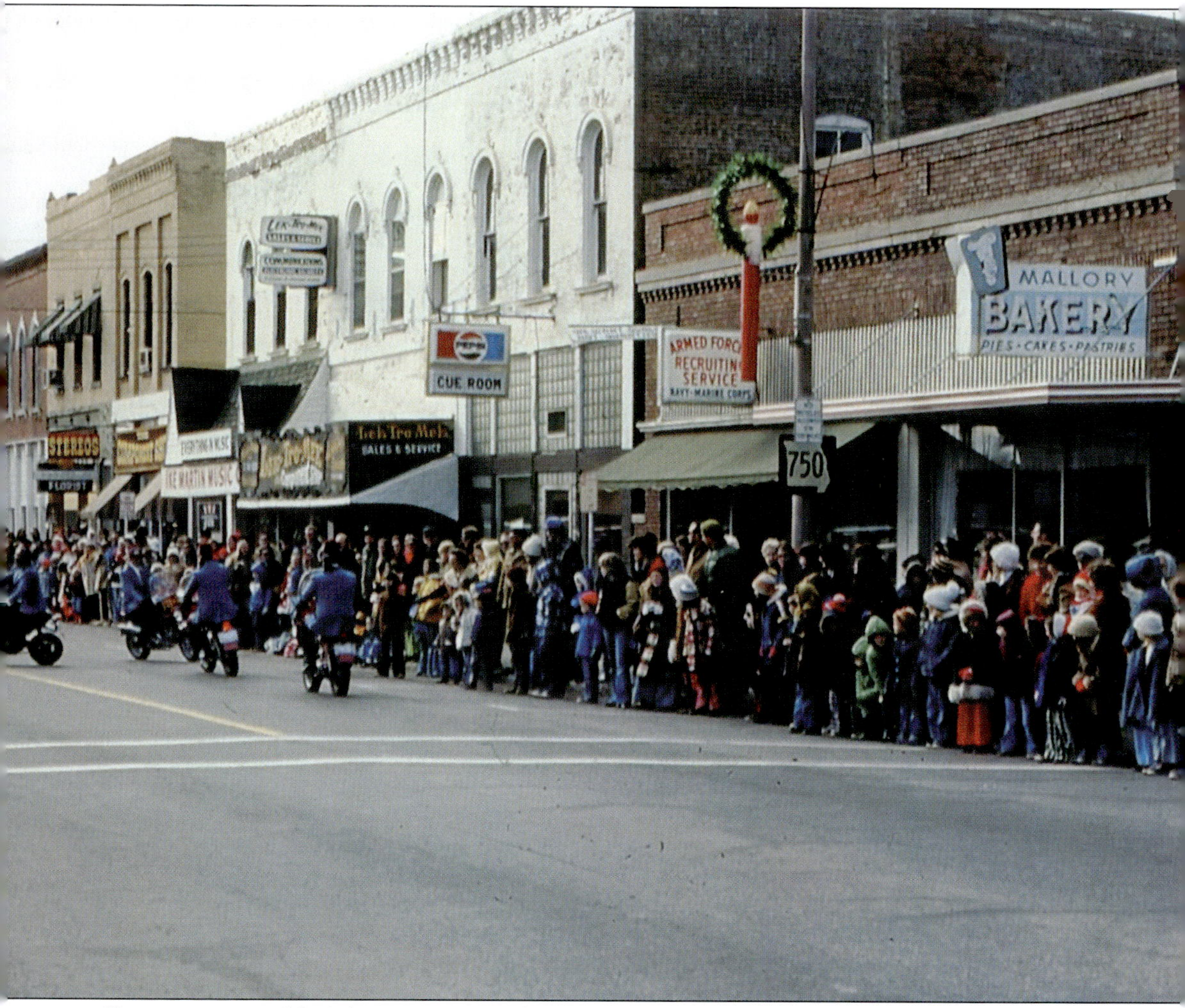

Few memories of Sedalia are sweeter than a parade, and such memories become even sweeter when coupled with the aroma of Mallory's Bakery (right). Marvin and Eloise Mallory opened their bakery at 600 South Ohio Avenue in 1954. The bakery is pictured during the 1976 Sedalia Chamber of Commerce Christmas Parade. (Courtesy of Dr. Steve Carr.)

FRONT COVER: The Wheel-Inn Drive-In (Courtesy of Tom C. Taylor; see page 65)

UPPER BACK COVER: The covered bridge over Flat Creek (Author's collection; see page 91)

LOWER BACK COVER (FROM LEFT TO RIGHT): The 400 block of South Ohio Avenue (Courtesy of the Sedalia Public Library; see page 9), State Fair Shopping Center (Author's collection; see page 63), Lamy Manufacturing Company billboard (Courtesy of the Sedalia Public Library; see page 74)

Images of Modern America

SEDALIA

Rebecca Carr Imhauser

ARCADIA PUBLISHING

ISBN 978-1-4671-2432-4

Published by Arcadia Publishing
Charleston, South Carolina

Printed in the United States of America

Library of Congress Control Number: 2016949502

For all general information, please contact Arcadia Publishing:
Telephone 843-853-2070
Fax 843-853-0044
E-mail sales@arcadiapublishing.com
For customer service and orders:
Toll-Free 1-888-313-2665

Visit us on the Internet at www.arcadiapublishing.com

To my mother, Betty Wasson Singer, who gave me a love for the Sedalia area, where our ancestors settled in 1826

Contents

Acknowledgments

This retrospective look at Sedalia could not have been produced without the generosity of those who shared photographs. Their names appear throughout the book along with the images they shared. Thanks go to Pam Hunter, Larry Melton, Arlene Silvey, John Simmons, and Angie Thomas, who provided access to invaluable archives and publications. Unless otherwise noted, all images are from the author's collection.

A thank-you goes to those who have walked with me through this and previous books. I cannot imagine writing without the encouragement of Mary McLaughlin, who introduced me to Arcadia Publishing, and support from Anna Lee Bail, Millicent Hale, James Keck, and Jane Harris Yount.

Two of my favorite Sedalians—Gerald and Helen Cecil—passed away while this book was being developed. A thank-you goes to their son Greg for sharing family pictures and memories. While an intern for the City of Sedalia Economic Development office in the 1970s, Greg developed a photo documentary of downtown Sedalia. Several of those pictures appear in this book.

Thanks go to Becky Bingaman Munson for not only sharing pictures from WEB & Sons but also for providing a tea party when we met at her house to discuss the book. Becky's thoughtfulness is another reminder of why I love Sedalia.

My ongoing appreciation goes to Randy Kirby, Sedalia's ever-present, always enthusiastic photographer. I value his expertise in representing historic sites as well as recording history-making events. Randy's influence will be invaluable for future history books.

I extend a special thank-you to fellow author and historian Tom C. Taylor. He offered his vast photograph collection for this book, as well as his expertise gleaned through a distinguished journalism career. When I first mentioned this project, Tom immediately mailed me a packet of images, including the picture of the Wheel-Inn Drive-In that appears on the cover. I appreciate Tom's many contributions to preserving and communicating his hometown's history.

Finally, my deepest thanks go to my writing partner and mother, Betty Wasson Singer. Now it's your turn, Mom, for your next book.

INTRODUCTION

When George R. Smith borrowed money to buy 337 acres of treeless prairie in 1856, his neighbors questioned his sanity. They wondered why he would leave the then Pettis County seat of Georgetown to start a new town. Smith was convinced his prairieland held the promise of becoming a railroad terminus, an asset he had been unable to secure for Georgetown.

Smith persuaded the Pacific Railroad to locate a depot on his land in 1859. The arrival of the first passenger train to Sedalia in 1861 was considered the beginning of the city, despite the fact that Sedalia had officially been founded a year before. Smith's image—and that of the new town—then began to change.

Sedalia was named the Pettis County seat in 1864, shortly before the Civil War ended. While the Civil War put Sedalia's growth on hold in some respects, it benefited the young city in others. According to I. Mac Demuth, troops stationed in Sedalia included "shrewd and observant men" who saw the new city's potential.

The end of the Civil War signaled the beginning of Sedalia's phenomenal growth. Several of those who had been stationed in Sedalia during the war returned to open businesses. The Missouri-Kansas-Texas Railroad (MKT, or the "Katy") established shops in northeast Sedalia in 1870. In 1872, the Pacific (later Missouri Pacific) Railroad established shops in east Sedalia. Railroads sustained the town for nearly a century. Sedalia was also a railhead for cattle drives and host to flourishing stockyards.

The 1873 city directory applauds Sedalia's status: "It is now the chief agricultural, commercial, manufacturing, and railway centre—the chief metropolis of this portion of the state—containing over 8,000 of as enterprising, public spirited, energetic, and intelligent inhabitants as can be found in any city of its size in the United States."

Sedalia constructed a new $100,000 courthouse in 1885, and additional multistory brick buildings soon followed. By the end of the 1800s, towering brick buildings had replaced the city's decrepit wooden structures. Sedalia's downtown district was a center of commerce and culture.

Optimism prevailed as Sedalia closed the 19th century. Downtown's growth was grand, but Sedalia had higher aims—to be the capital of Missouri. The Capital Removal Project, as Sedalia's initiative came to be known, spanned two decades. Despite the best efforts of leading Sedalians, a statewide vote in 1896 determined the Missouri capital would remain in Jefferson City. Sedalia lost its bid for the capital but gained the Missouri State Fair in 1899.

Sedalia grew immensely through the early part of the 20th century, largely due to railroad expansion. Its population increased from 15,231 to 21,444 between 1900 and 1920. The city entered the Roaring Twenties with a literal blaze, as a fire destroyed its courthouse in 1920. A new courthouse was dedicated five years later.

Then came the Depression. Three out of four downtown banks closed within a three-month period, from November 1931 to January 1932. Two officers of those banks committed suicide during the same period. *Life* magazine declared Sedalia the city second-hardest-hit by the Great Depression in the entire United States.

Despite the hardship, Sedalians were united in their quest for better times. World War II continued to bring the city together through bond drives and support for soldiers stationed at the nearby Sedalia Army Air Field in Knob Noster, Missouri.

The postwar era brought the greatest changes to Sedalia since its founding. Businesses and services began moving outside the downtown core. Dr. A.J. Campbell Jr., a longtime Sedalia physician, succinctly summarized why he moved his office from downtown Sedalia to a new single-story structure near Bothwell Hospital. "Stairs, stairs, stairs," he said. His office, and that of his physician father before him, had been located on the second floor of 312 South Ohio Avenue. Dr. Campbell noted that the stairs became an informal stress test for his patients. Patients' ability to climb the two flights of steps was a measure of their wellness.

Automobiles also brought wide-scale change to Sedalia. After World War II, automobile production increased, along with the size of vehicles. The tail-finned behemoths of the 1950s were no match for downtown parking, which had been designed for horses and carriages. Historic downtown buildings were razed to provide parking lots.

The advance of automobiles collided with the decline of the railroad industry. Passenger trains had provided the main transportation to and from Sedalia for nearly a century. They arrived at Sedalia's two depots near downtown, which fueled the hotel and restaurant economy. That changed when automobiles began depositing passengers at motels, initially known as tourist cabins, along Broadway Boulevard and South Limit Avenue. Broadway (now US Highway 50) and South Limit (now US Highway 65) soon replaced downtown as Sedalia's main business corridors. Thompson Hills Shopping Center, which opened on West Highway 50 in 1964, and State Fair Shopping Center, which opened on South Limit in 1965, further drew people away from downtown.

The railroads' demise was offset by manufacturing and industry that swelled after World War II. Town & Country Shoes, Parkhurst Manufacturing, Rival Manufacturing, and the Pittsburgh Corning Corporation rose in Sedalia in the 1940s and 1950s. By the time the railroad shops closed, other industries had moved to town to support its economic base. Alcan Cable, Duke Manufacturing, Kelsey-Hayes, Gardner-Denver, Waterloo Industries, and Payless Cashways became major employers.

Through the years, a myriad of people have helped transform George R. Smith's prairie town into a bustling hub of central Missouri. A new generation of visionaries is reviving culture and commerce in the historic district. Countless others are leaving their distinctive marks on the community. Smith envisioned a city that would provide opportunities for his family and those who came after them. His dream lives on through the people who continue to call Sedalia home.

One

Downtown

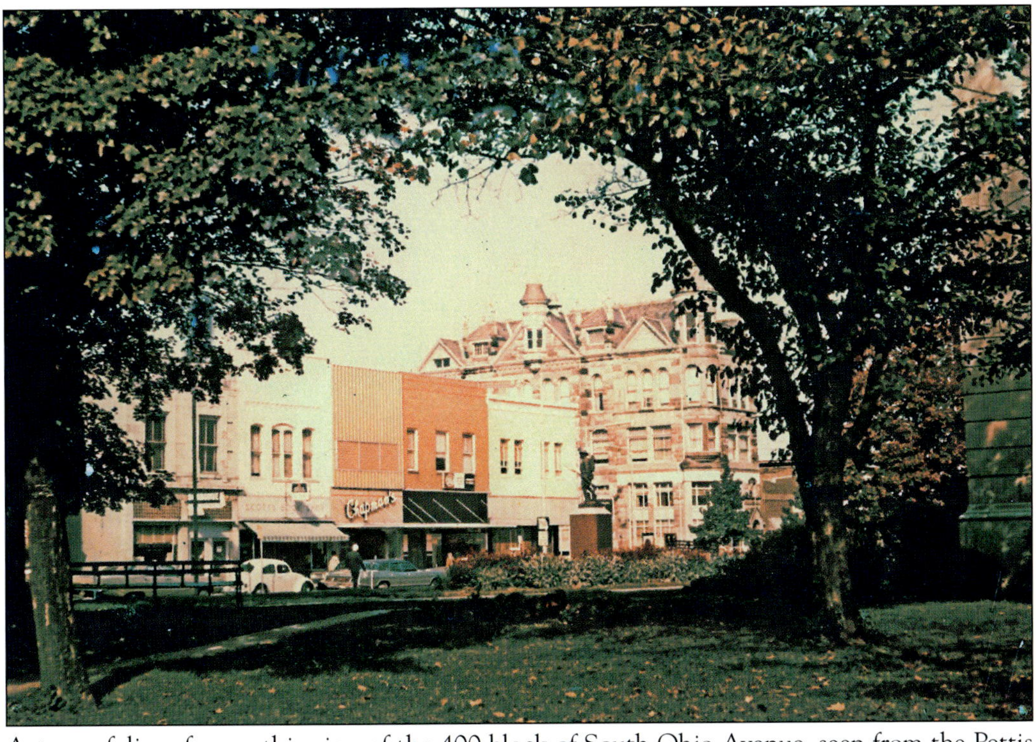

Autumn foliage frames this view of the 400 block of South Ohio Avenue, seen from the Pettis County Courthouse lawn in the 1970s. Businesses include, from left to right, Donohue Loan & Investment, Scott's Book Shop, Chapman's Clothing, and Missouri Public Service. The iconic Sedalia Trust Building is at far right. Different businesses now occupy the buildings, but for many, this view *is* downtown Sedalia. (Courtesy of Sedalia Public Library.)

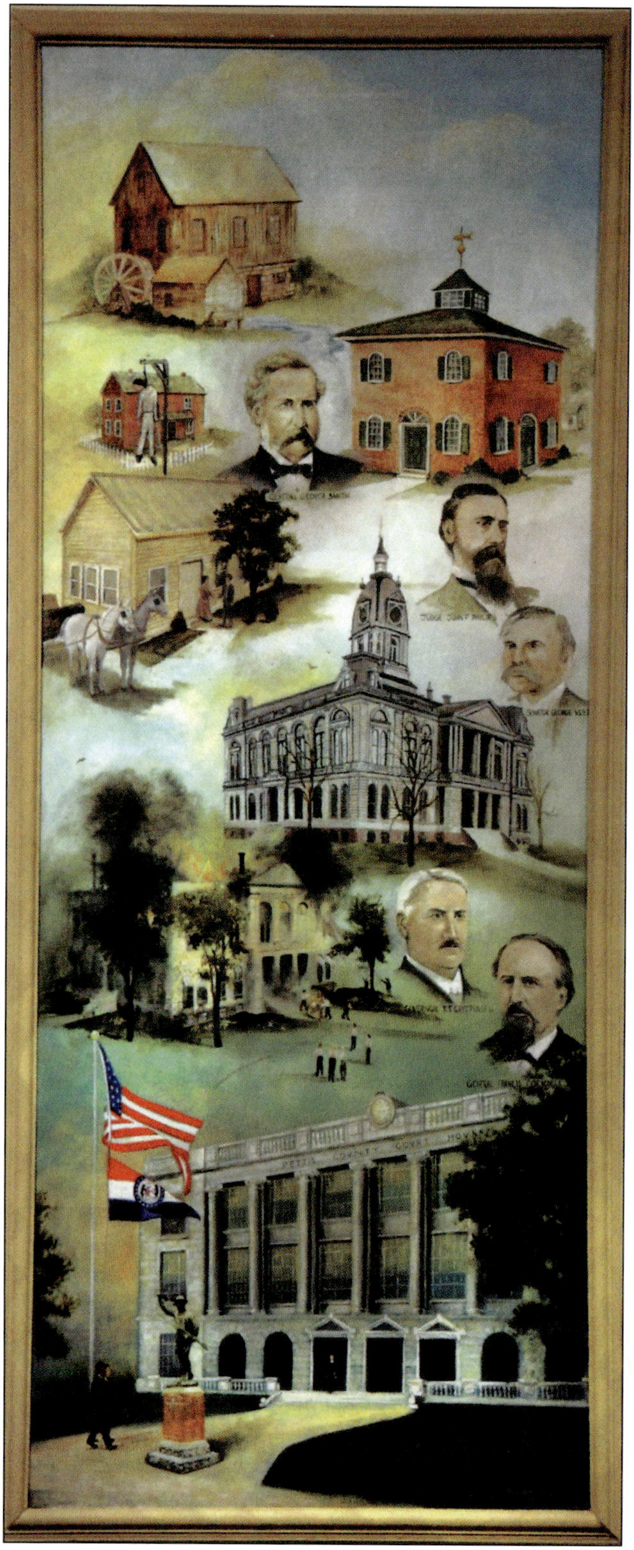

This is one of 36 murals in the circuit courtroom of the Pettis County Courthouse, a project initiated by Judge Donald Barnes in 1997. Barbara Manes Campbell completed painting the murals in 2002. Each panel illustrates a specific subject in chronological order, starting at the top with the earliest history. This mural depicts Pettis County's seats of justice, beginning in 1833 with a mill Thomas R. Wasson erected at Pin Hook (top, left). In 1837, Georgetown became the county seat, where a brick courthouse (top, right) was erected. The county seat moved to Sedalia in 1864. The first courthouse on the present courthouse square is illustrated in the middle of the panel. It was completed in 1885 and destroyed by fire in 1920. The current courthouse, completed in 1925, is shown at the bottom of the mural. (Courtesy of Randy Kirby.)

After a fire destroyed the Pettis County Courthouse in 1920, three sets of its limestone bases and capitals (right) were discarded on the grounds of Sedalia Water Works. John Simmons was alerted to the location of the remnants 75 years later. Simmons monitored the masonry for nearly a decade, bringing it to the attention of Meg Liston. In 2010, Liston expressed interest to the Pettis County Commission and the Courthouse Steering Committee in preserving the pieces in a public display. John Beykirch selected the monument for his Eagle Scout service project and became project co-coordinator with Judy Parkhurst. The memorial on the southwest lawn of the Pettis County Courthouse was dedicated in 2012. It was 100 percent privately funded, with design services donated by Robert Rollings Architects, LLC. (Right, courtesy of John Simmons; below, courtesy of Randy Kirby.)

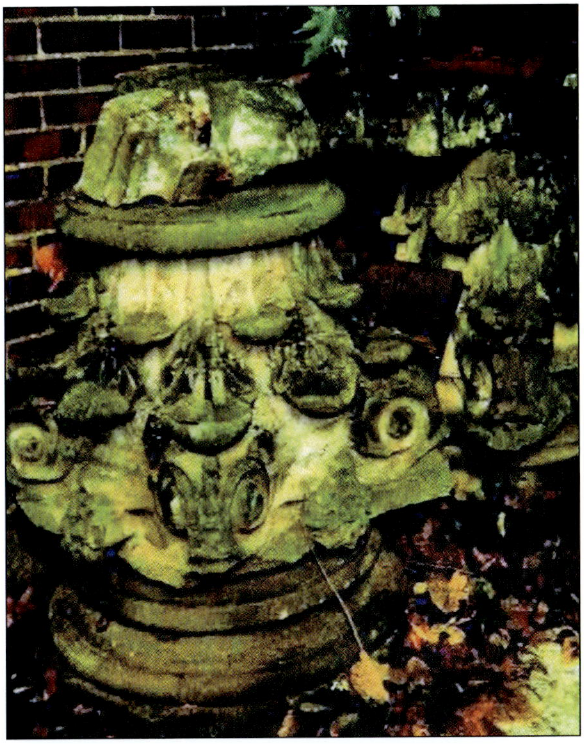

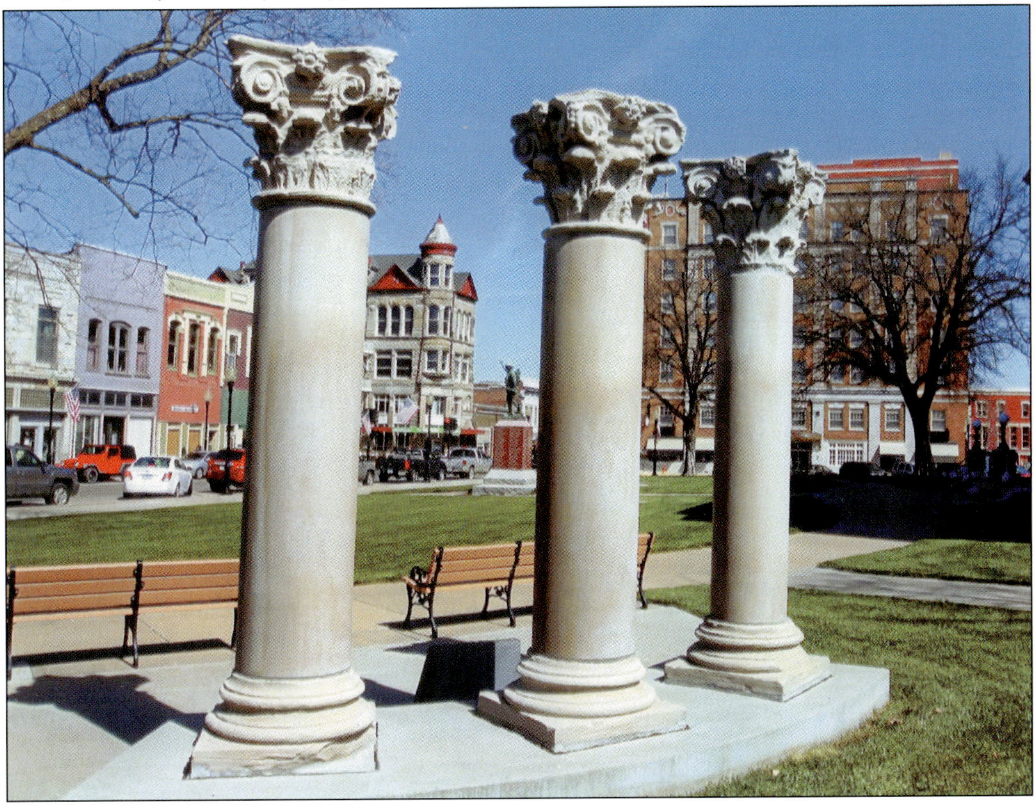

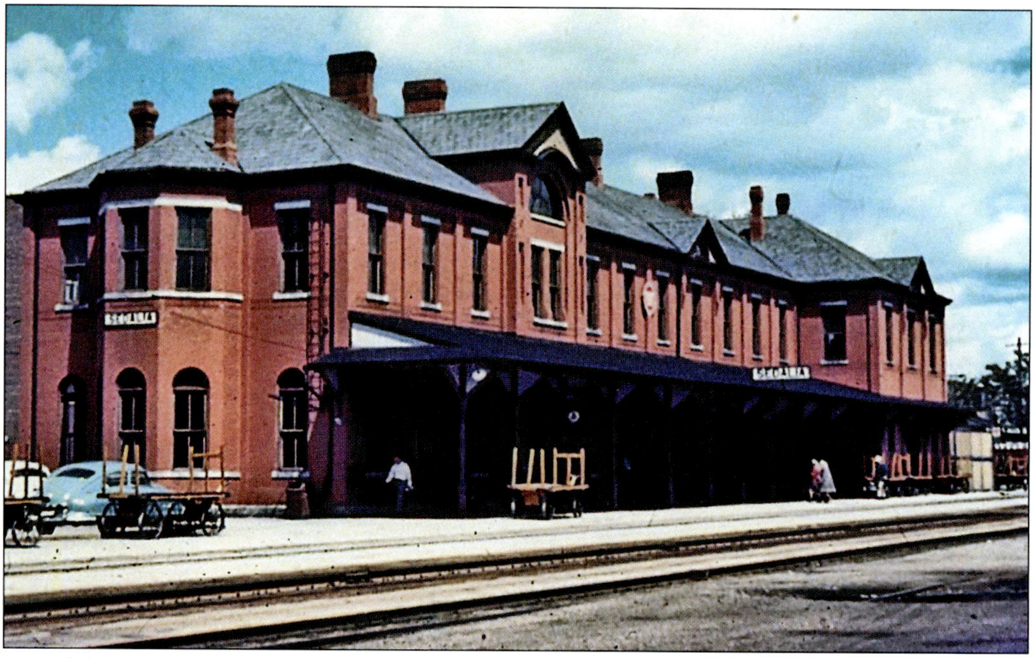

In Sedalia's early days, many people caught their first glimpse of the town from the Pacific (later Missouri Pacific) depot. The two-story structure at West Pacific Street and North Osage Avenue was completed in 1886. The first floor included the passenger lobby, telegraph office, and freight and baggage areas. Offices were located on the second floor. (Courtesy of Jane Harris Yount.)

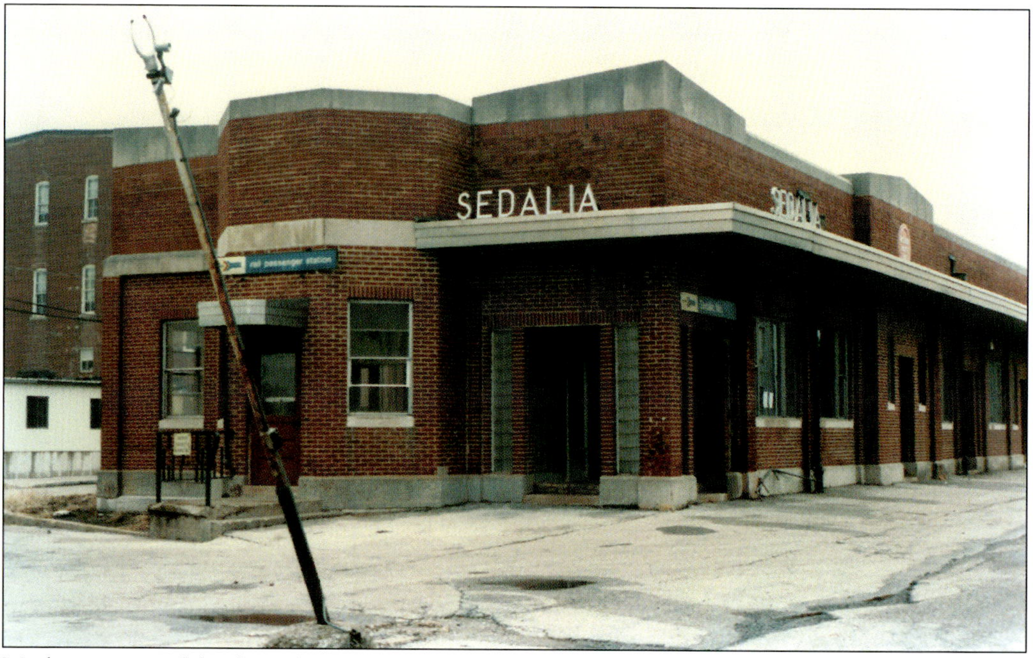

Modernization of the depot began in May 1950. Workers removed the second floor and renovated the exterior. The interior of the remaining ground floor was gutted, leaving a ranch-style building in keeping with the era's fascination with Western motifs. More than 1,800 people attended an open house at the station in March 1952. (Courtesy of Tom C. Taylor.)

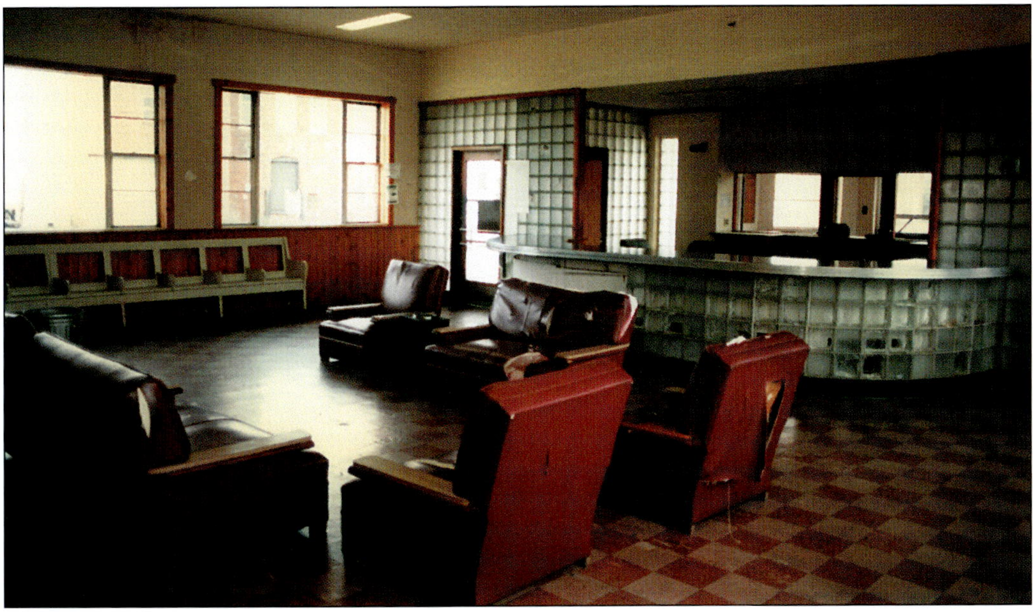

Railway travel experienced a steep decline in the 1960s, as did the Missouri Pacific depot. Vandalism made Sedalia a less-than-desirable stop along the route. This photograph shows the Missouri Pacific passenger lobby when torn upholstery, spray-painted graffiti, and broken glass blocks dominated the scene. (Courtesy of Tom C. Taylor.)

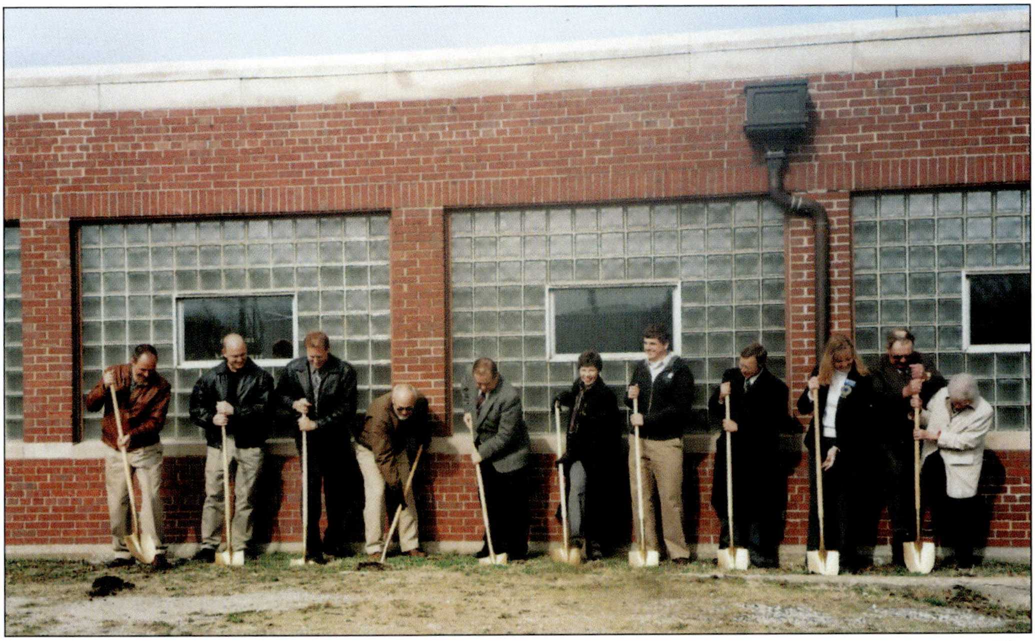

The 2008 ground-breaking ceremony kicked off a $1.5 million renovation project supported by federal and state grants and private contributions. From left to right are Randy Beem, Dion Knipp, Brian Smith, Dan VanDyne, Bob Wasson, Meg Liston, Travis Tindall, Jeff Kormann, Dianne Simon, Don Reed, and Nora Belle Bottom. The depot is now a multimodal transportation center, accommodating Amtrak, OATS (Older Adults Transportation Services), and Sedalia Downtown Development, Inc., offices.

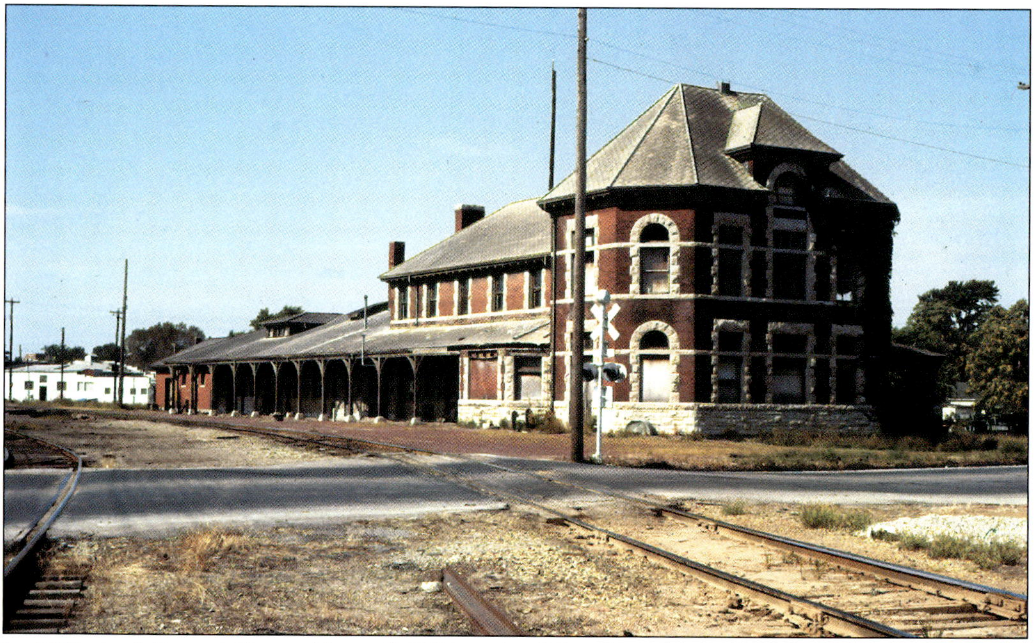

In 1870, the Missouri-Kansas-Texas (MKT, or the "Katy") established shops in Sedalia. By 1876, the railroad had employed 203 men in the shops and 60 men in its Sedalia offices. The $40,000 Katy depot was erected at East Third Street and Thompson Avenue in 1896. By 1988, the once-bustling station had been abandoned by the railroad and acquired by the Missouri Department of Natural Resources. A $3 million restoration and build-out began in 1998 and was completed in 2001. The Katy Depot Historic Site is a year-round visitor destination, serving as Sedalia's welcome center that includes an exhibit gallery, gift shop, and event space. (Both, courtesy of Tom C. Taylor.)

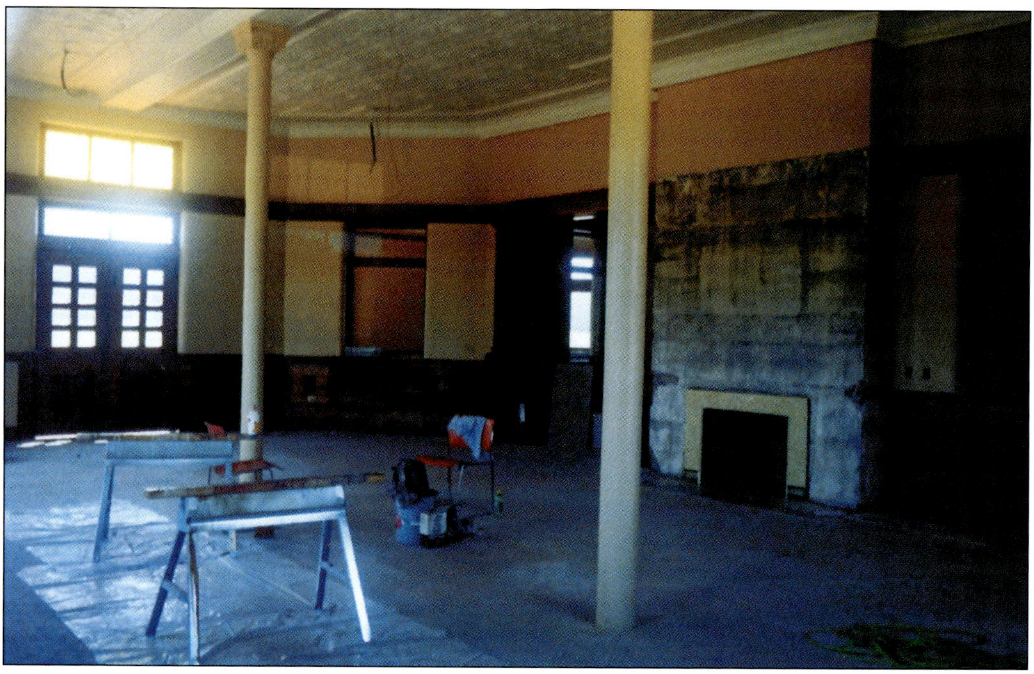

Sedalia City Hall is featured on this annual report for the City of Sedalia, designed and illustrated by Leslie Hall in 1949. Completed in 1875, city hall provided space for offices, the market house, city jail, and engine room. Proposals to replace the building were repeatedly defeated, until voters approved a 1 percent city sales tax in 1970. (Courtesy of Marty Lange.)

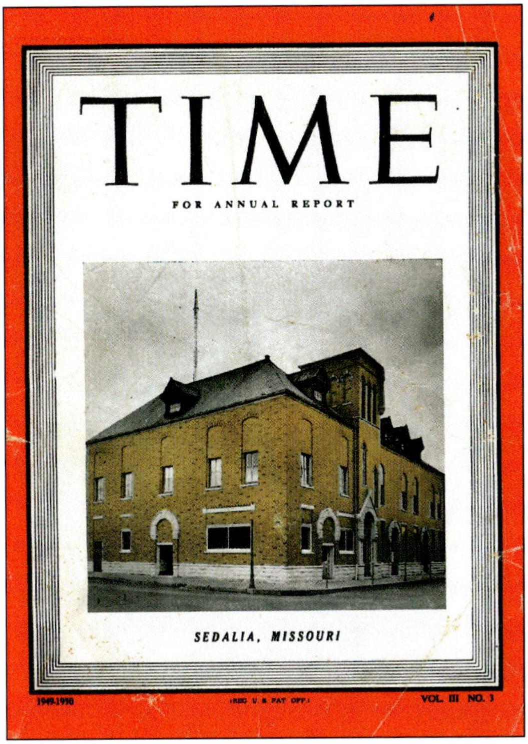

Sedalia's new municipal building was dedicated in November 1973. Located on the site of its predecessor city hall, the $750,000 structure initially provided space for city offices, the police station, city jail, and OATS office. The Smith-Cotton High School band is pictured during the dedication. (Courtesy of the City of Sedalia Archives.)

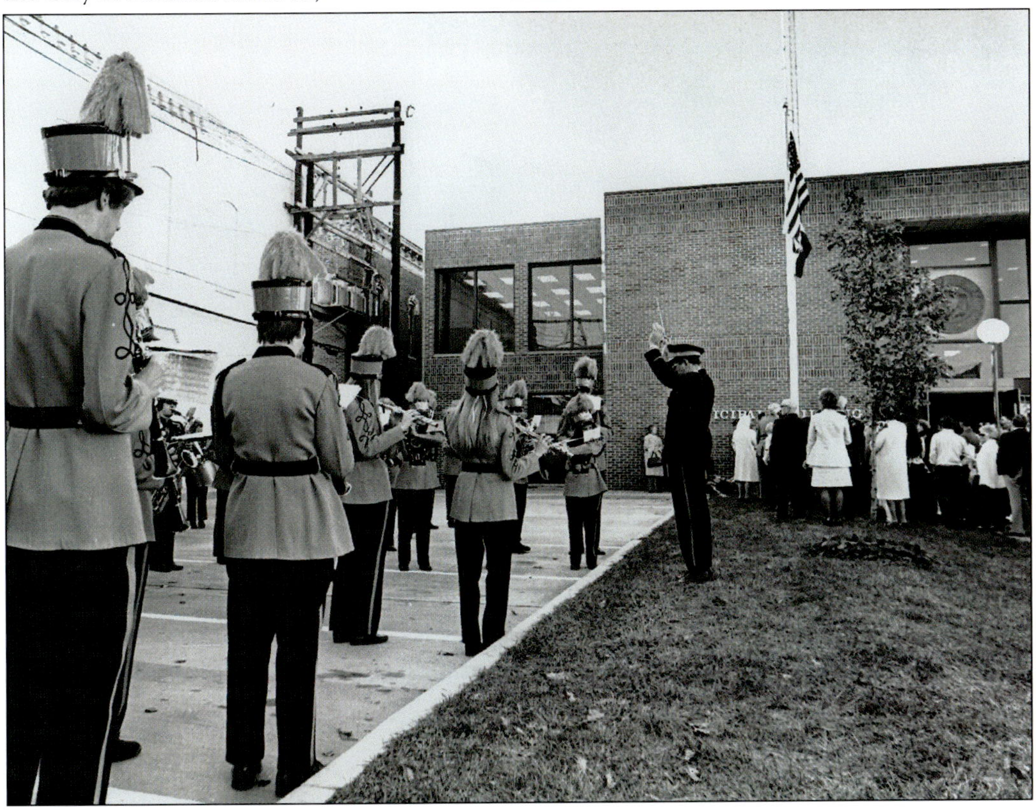

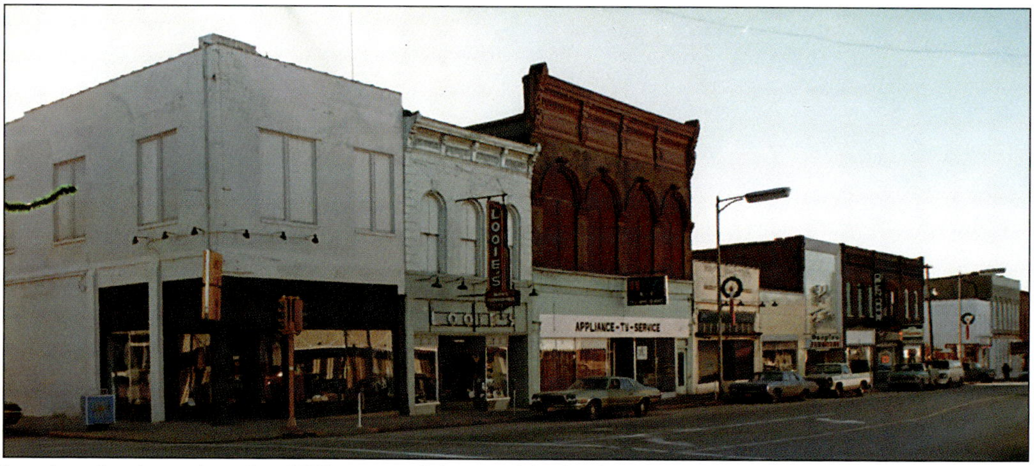

Landmarks abound in this 1970s view of the 100 block of West Main Street. The corner building, erected in 1872, was one of several structures with the upper floor(s) removed during the Great Depression to reduce real estate taxes. To the right (west) is Looie's Clothing, opened by Louis Isgur in 1932. The third and tallest building is the site of Smith's Opera House, built by Sedalia's founder, George R. Smith, in 1868. (Courtesy of the City of Sedalia Archives.)

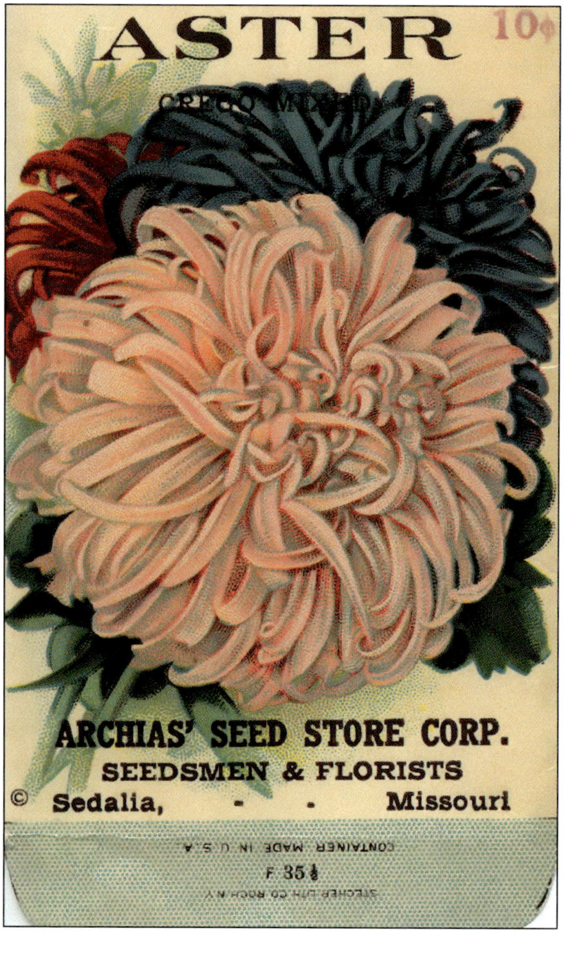

Leon Henry Archias established the Archias Seed Company in 1899 and operated a retail store at 106–108 East Main Street for nearly a century. In 1910, Archias purchased greenhouses at West Fourth Street and Park Avenue from Joseph Gelvin and founded the Archias Floral Company. Archias also helped found the Florists Telegraph Delivery Association (FTD) and Missouri State Florists' Association.

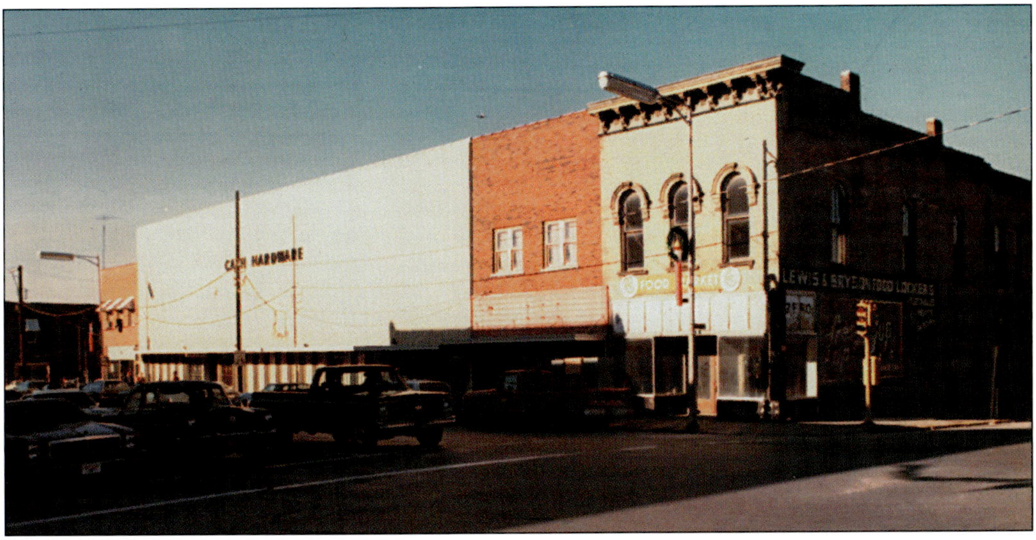

William Cline Cain founded Cash Hardware at 106 West Main Street in 1927. The adjacent buildings housed a variety of other businesses, including the longtime Bard Drug Store. Cash Hardware expanded through the years, eventually occupying five storefronts by the time it closed in 1987. Charles T. and Millie Curry purchased the buildings and opened the Maple Leaf Tea Room and Antique Mall. (Courtesy of the City of Sedalia Archives.)

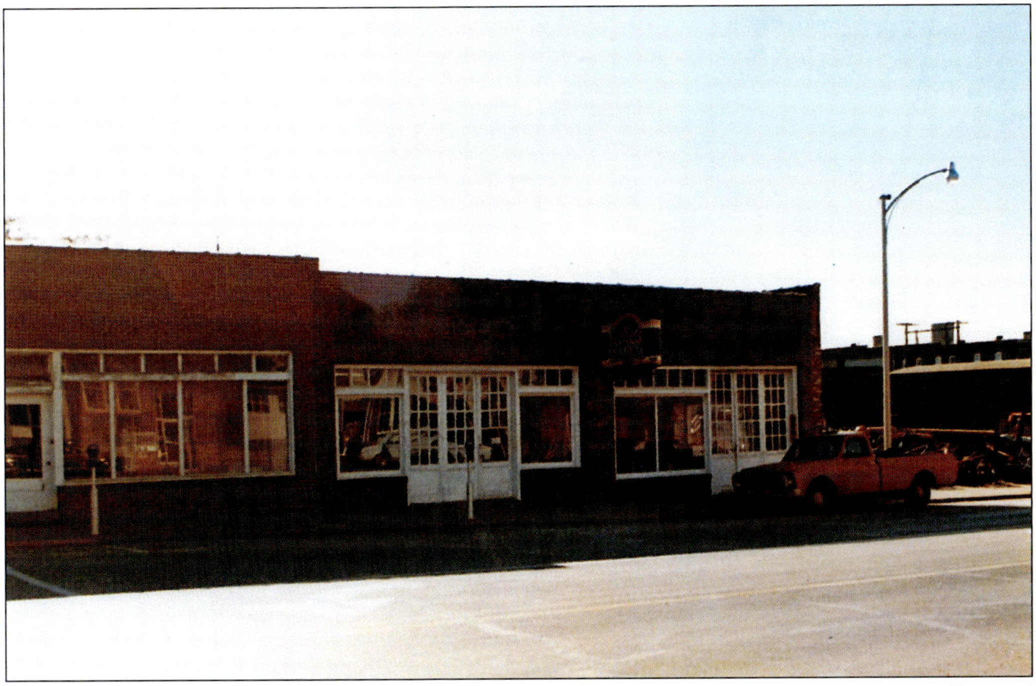

The Harvey Brothers Implement Company, owned by John and Paul Harvey, operated at 305 West Main Street for more than half a century. While the Harvey brothers were known for selling farm machinery, the Harvey sisters were recognized for entertainment. Anna Lee Harvey Bail and Ruth Harvey Ray, daughters of Paul Harvey, won contests for their song and dance routines. (Courtesy of the City of Sedalia Archives.)

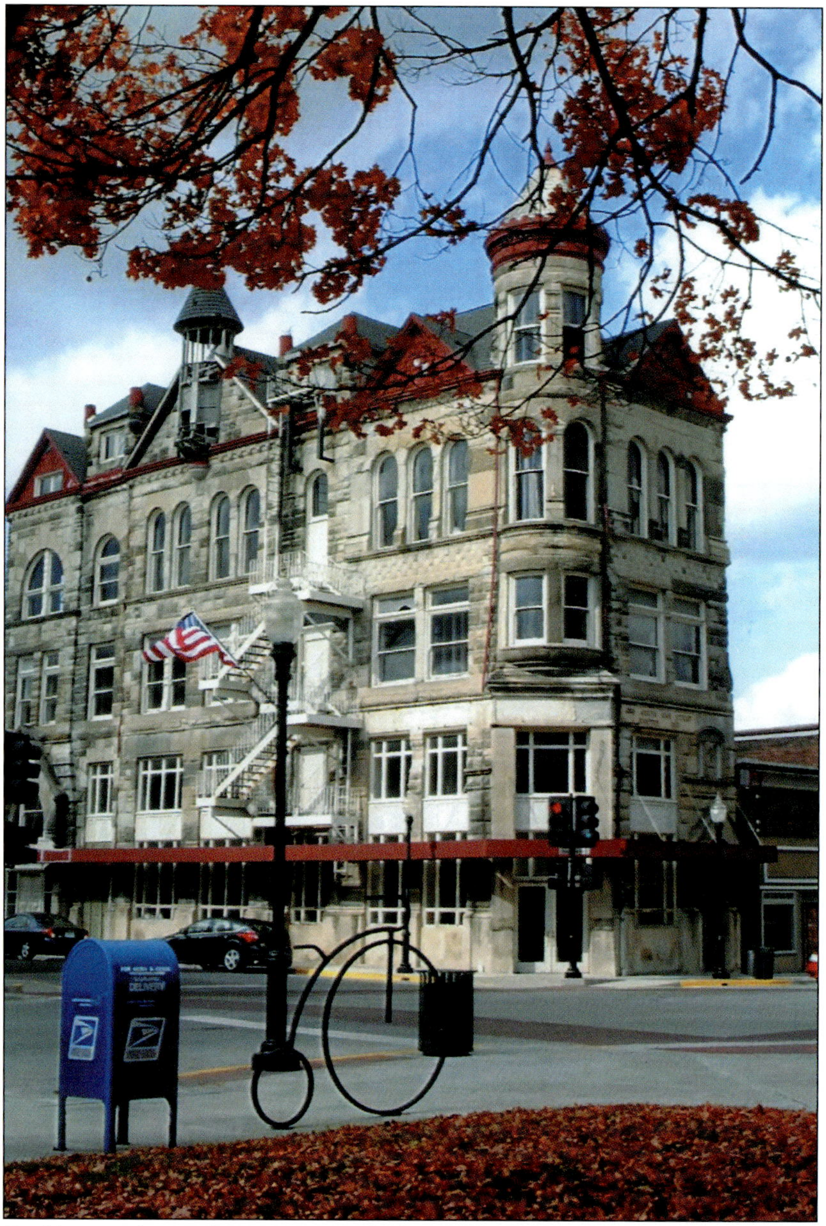

The Trust Building at the northwest corner of Ohio Avenue and Fourth Street is downtown's most distinctive landmark. Not only is it the most ornate and photographed structure, but it also has the most tumultuous history. The building was erected for the Missouri Trust Company in 1888, and beginning in 1901, it housed the Sedalia Trust Company. The Sedalia Bank & Trust moved to the site in 1934 and became the scene of one of Sedalia's most sensational bank robberies in 1935. The building then led a rather sedate life as an office and professional building until being converted into an upscale hotel in 1997. Four months after the hotel opened, two successive fires caused more than $500,000 damage, adding the word *arson* to the building's history. In 2014, the Friends of the Sedalia Trust (FRoST) was incorporated as a nonprofit organization and assumed ownership of the vacant building. FRoST is managing repairs to market the building for the next chapter of its history. (Courtesy of Bob Walters.)

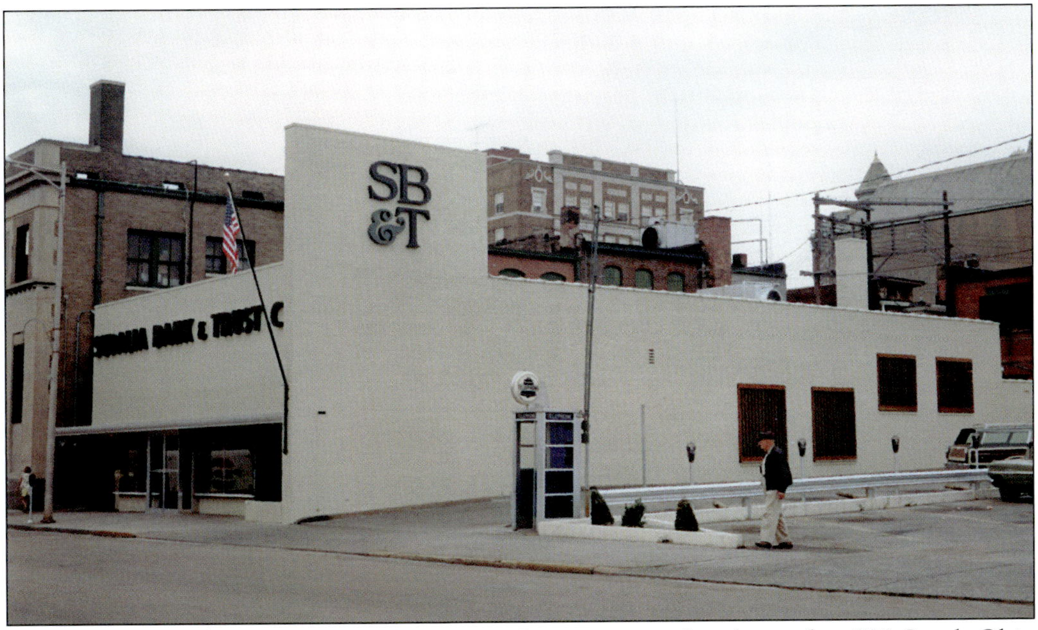

Founded in 1932, the Sedalia Bank & Trust Company was first located at 300 South Ohio Avenue. It moved to the Trust Building in 1934. In 1948, the bank erected a new facility at 111 West Third Street (pictured). It became Mercantile Bank in 1975. The Open Door Service Center occupied the site from 1997 to 2016, when the building became the new home for Landmann Title Company.

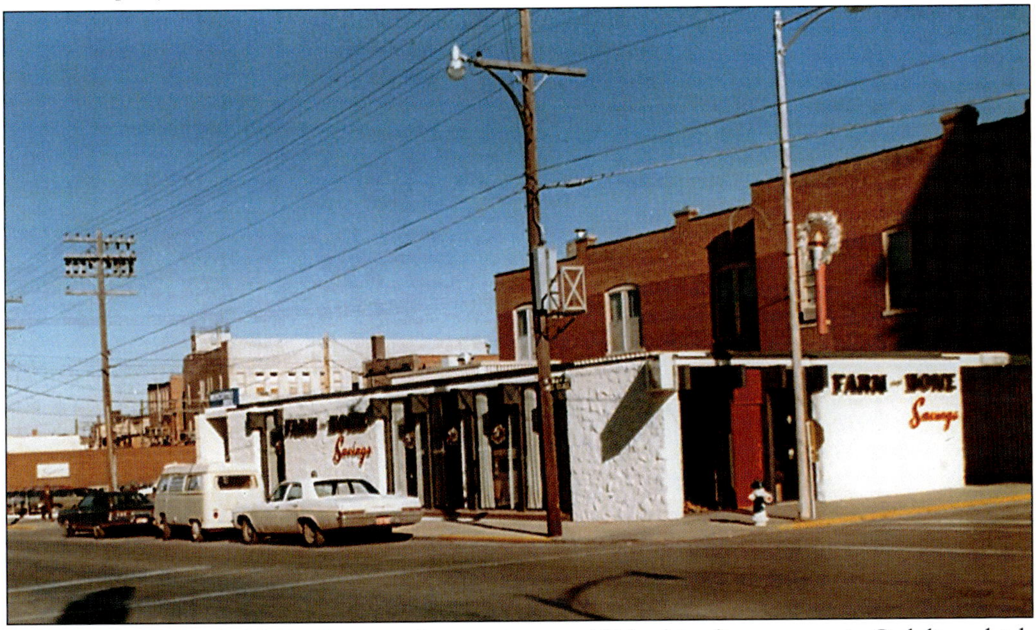

In 1896, the Farm & Home Savings Association established its first agency in Sedalia, which was represented by the Van Wagner family for many decades. The company built a new $100,000 facility at Fourth Street and Osage Avenue in 1965. The 2,400-square-foot structure featured heated sidewalks and a small garden area at its entrance. USBank now occupies the building. (Courtesy of the City of Sedalia Archives.)

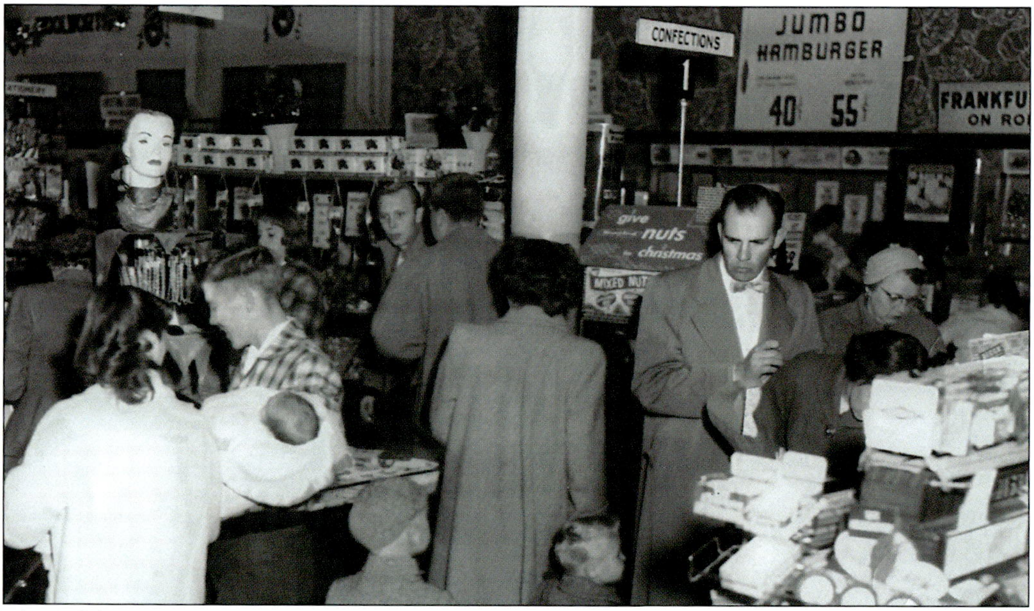

The *Sedalia Democrat* described shoppers at the July 1907 grand opening of the F.W. Woolworth Co. store at 230 South Ohio Avenue as a "sweltering mass of humanity." Air-conditioning eventually cooled the store but not Sedalians' appreciation for its discount prices and snack bar. This 1950s photograph includes, in the foreground, Helen Cecil (center, back to camera) Christmas shopping with her sons, Gerry (left) and Greg. Woolworth's closed at 224 South Ohio Avenue in 1969. (Courtesy of Greg Cecil.)

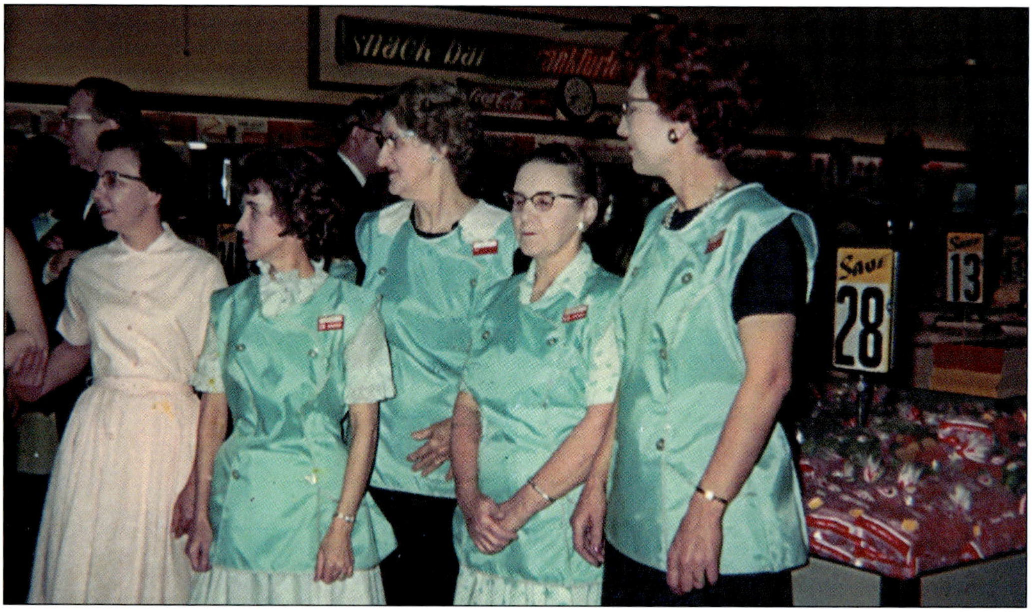

Jupiter Discount Store employees are pictured when the store opened at 306 South Ohio Avenue in May 1966. Jupiter replaced the S.S. Kresge Company, which had been located at the site since 1914. The remodeled building featured a bright-yellow storefront and added a delicatessen to its popular soda fountain. Pictured are Ann Carier, Susie Thomas, Beverly Embree, Flora Witt, and Hazel Chancey. (Courtesy of Duane Furnell.)

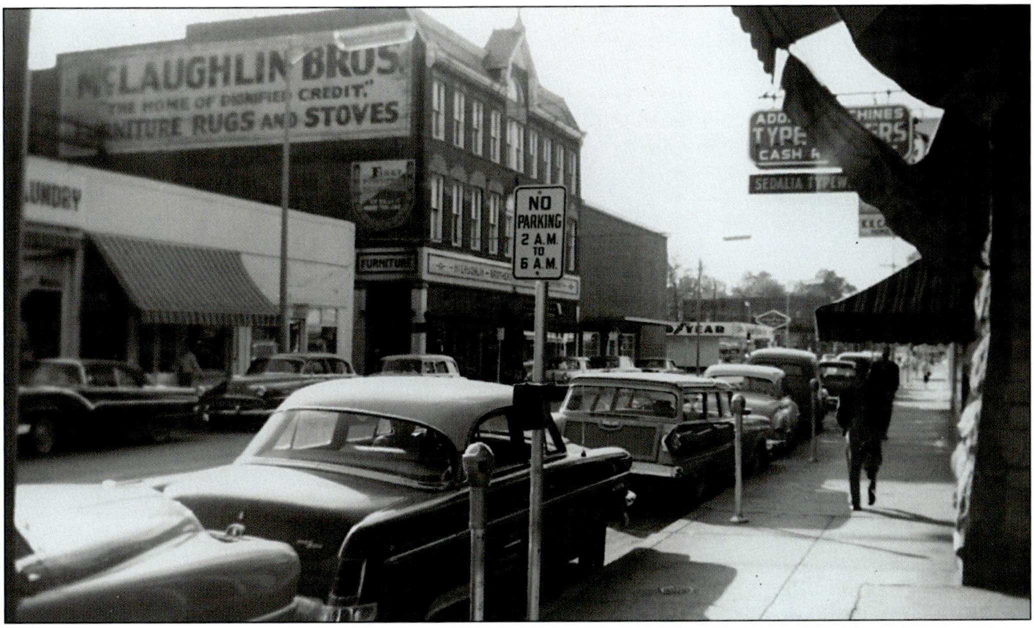

McLaughlin Brothers furniture store was a downtown landmark at 515 South Ohio Avenue from 1890 to 2009. George McLaughlin founded the business in 1880 and formed a partnership with his brother John in 1883. The McLaughlin brothers also owned a funeral chapel. Now under the direction of Jason and Bethany Weiker, the McLaughlin Funeral Chapel at 519 South Ohio Avenue continues the McLaughlins' tradition of service with dignity and respect. (Courtesy of Mary McLaughlin.)

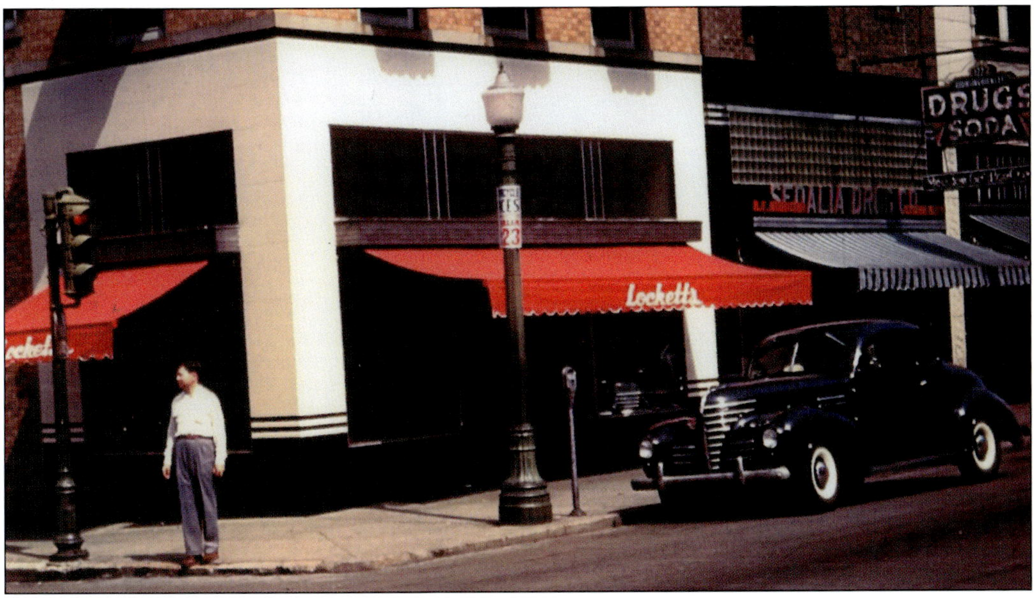

George and Elaine Lockett opened Lockett's Ladies Shop at 124 South Ohio Avenue in 1941. Their daughter Sally Lockett carried on the Locketts' tradition of happy, bustling boutiques in Sedalia until 2014, with shops named Lockett's and Fig Leaf. In addition, their daughter Lynne Lockett Hyatt opened Lockett's of Columbus in Indiana, a lovely downtown boutique carrying on the Lockett family tradition for the past 27 years. (Courtesy of Sally Lockett.)

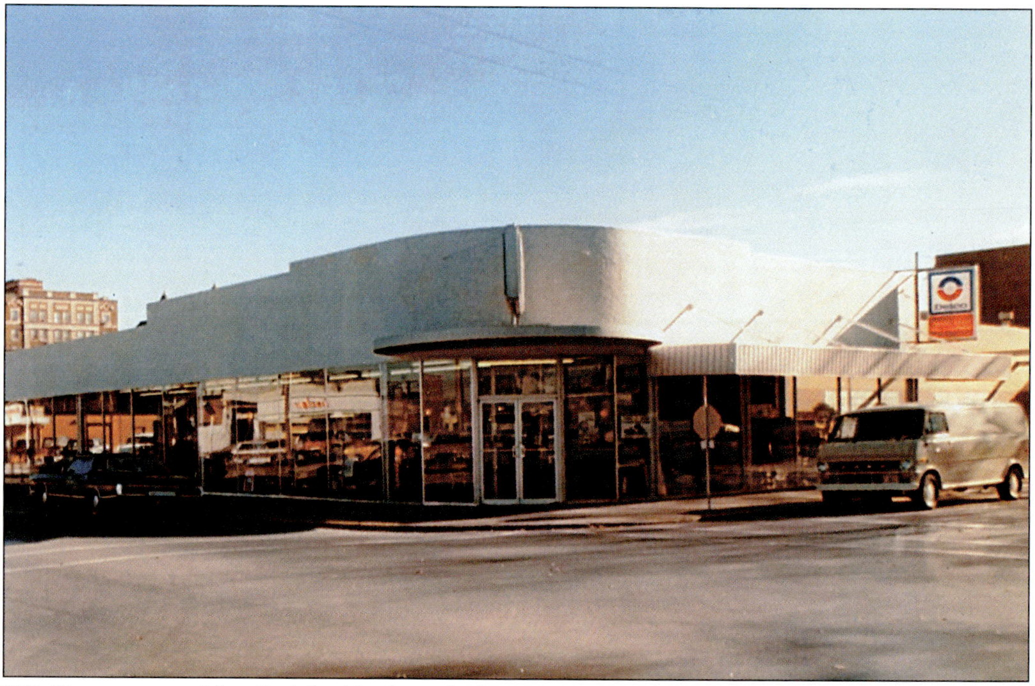

E.B. Brown opened his Sedalia blacksmith shop in 1918. He moved to a new building in 1922, by that time operating a blacksmith and machine shop, and expanded the structure in 1930 for his automotive clinic. This building at 219 West Third Street was completed in 1947, offering automotive and industrial parts and supplies. E.B. Brown's four sons, one daughter, and other family members operated the businesses. (Courtesy of the City of Sedalia Archives.)

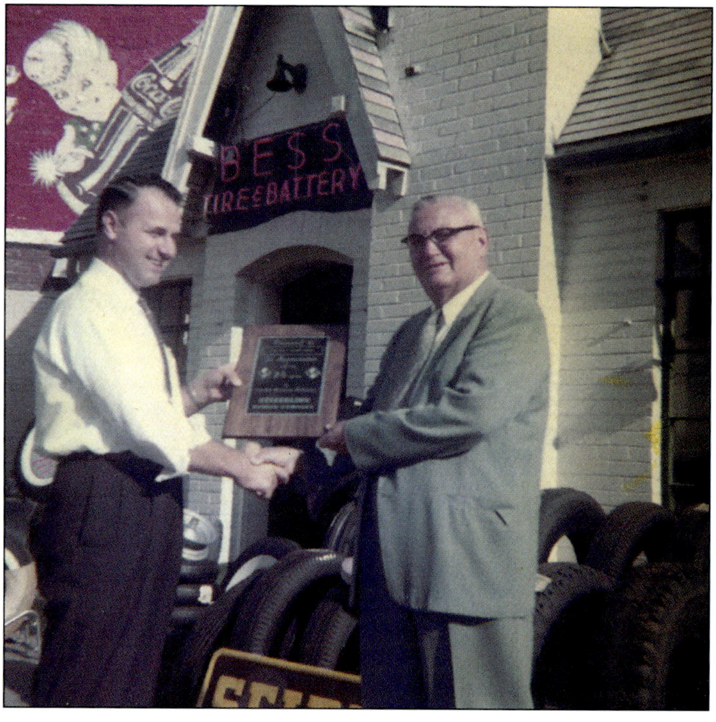

Burl B. Bess (right) opened Bess Tire & Battery Co. at 312 West Second Street with an investment of $228.84 in 1933. When he purchased his first electric sign, he said he thought he was "broke for good." Bess was not broke; in fact, his business steadily increased. He moved to Second Street and Osage Avenue (left) in 1949. Bess, an ordained Baptist minister, passed away in 1962.

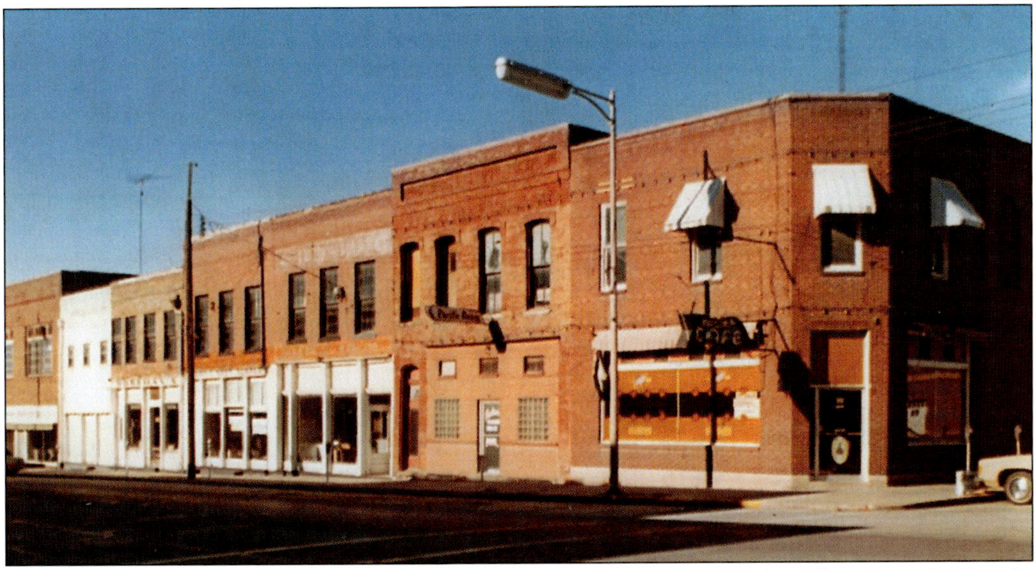

In 1917, Herman Kirchhofer purchased the Missouri Pacific Restaurant, later known as the Pacific Café, at 202 West Main Street. By the late 1920s, the café reported it served 640 cups of coffee every 24 hours. Roy "Dutch" Kirchhofer also managed the restaurant, adding its popular framed photographs of famous baseball players in 1944. The café is pictured at far right in this 1970s view of West Main Street. (Courtesy of the City of Sedalia Archives.)

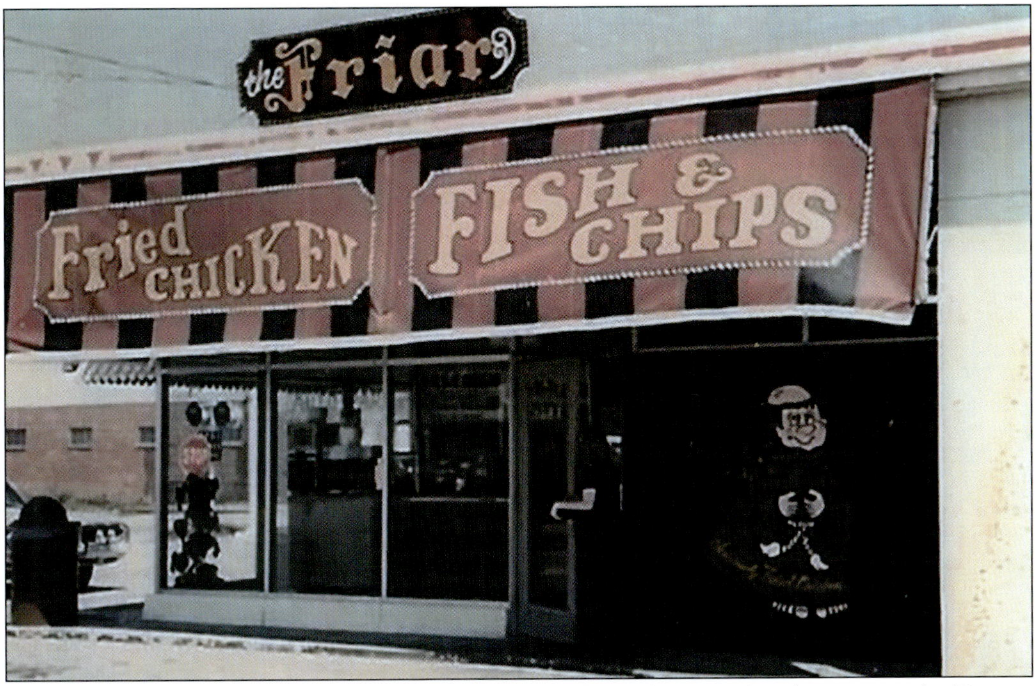

A monk design on a cookie jar inspired the Richard "Dick" Esser family to open the Friar, a fast-food restaurant at West Main Street and Missouri Avenue, in 1973. The restaurant's name, a play on words, highlighted its fried chicken, fish, and shrimp. Dick Esser's sons managed the Friar. The Essers also owned several package liquor stores, laundries, and a car wash. (Courtesy of David Esser.)

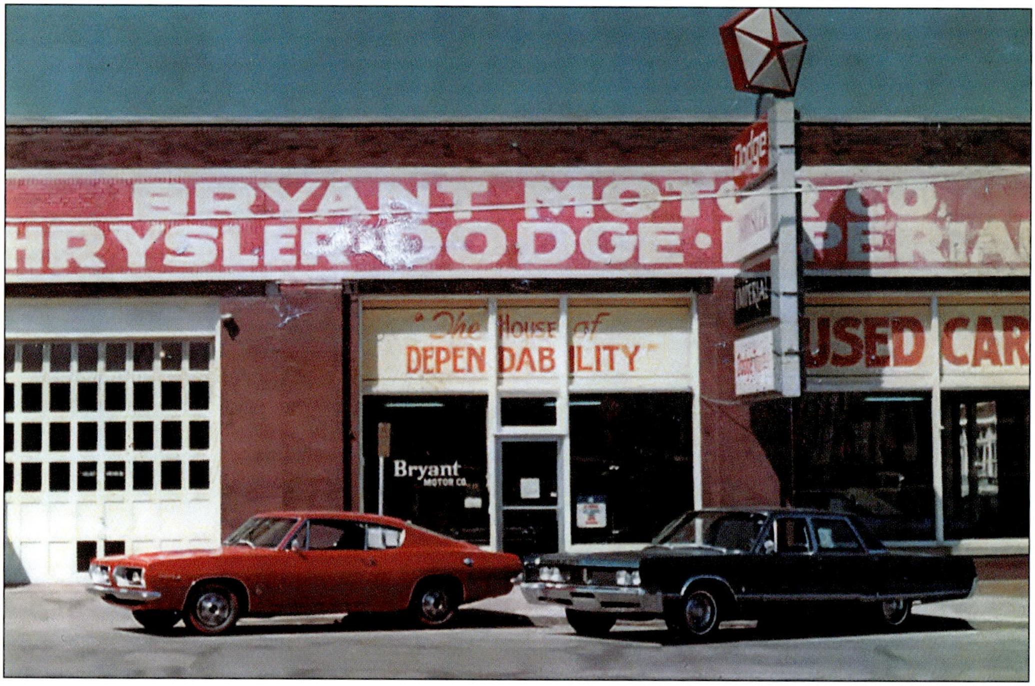

Bryant Motors, Sedalia's oldest automobile dealership, was founded in 1936 when Frank Bryant and Ben Robinson purchased the Mid-State Motor Company. They named their Dodge dealership Bryant Motors. In 1937, Dan Robinson began working as a garage mechanic for his brother Ben, and Dan purchased Bryant Motors in 1959. Dan's sons Jack and Mike sold the dealership to Kyle Herrick and partners in 2012. (Courtesy of Jack and Mike Robinson, Bryant Motor Company.)

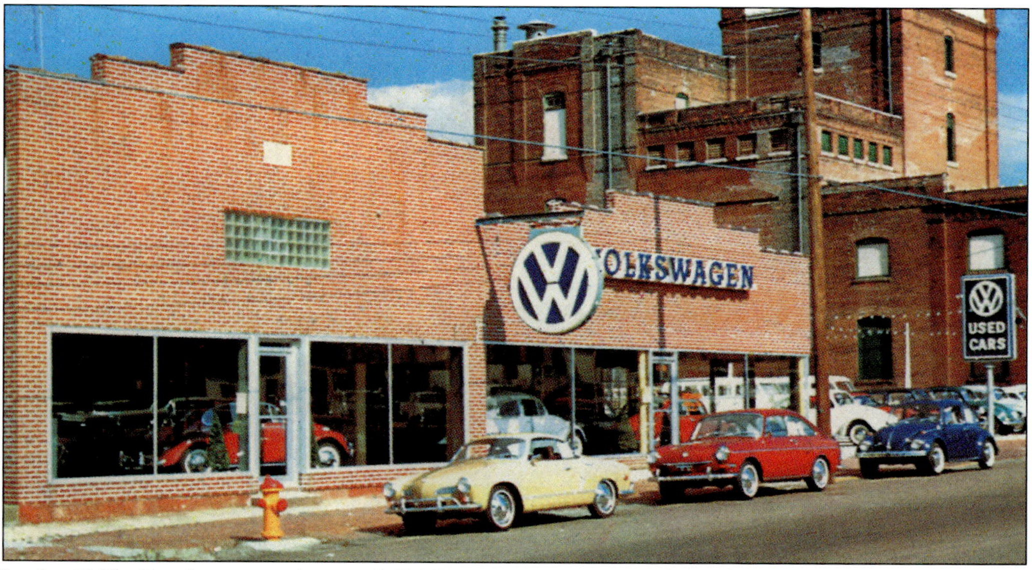

In the 1960s, Beetles scurried around 620 West Main Street, Sedalia's headquarters for the popular Volkswagen automobiles. Carlin Pruitt opened Pruitt Motors, a VW dealership, in 1961. Richard "Fitz" Fitzwilliam purchased the business in 1963, and it became known as Fitzwilliam Motors. Bill Lowman acquired the dealership in 1973 and operated it as Volkswagen Sedalia, Inc. (Courtesy of Sedalia Area Chamber of Commerce.)

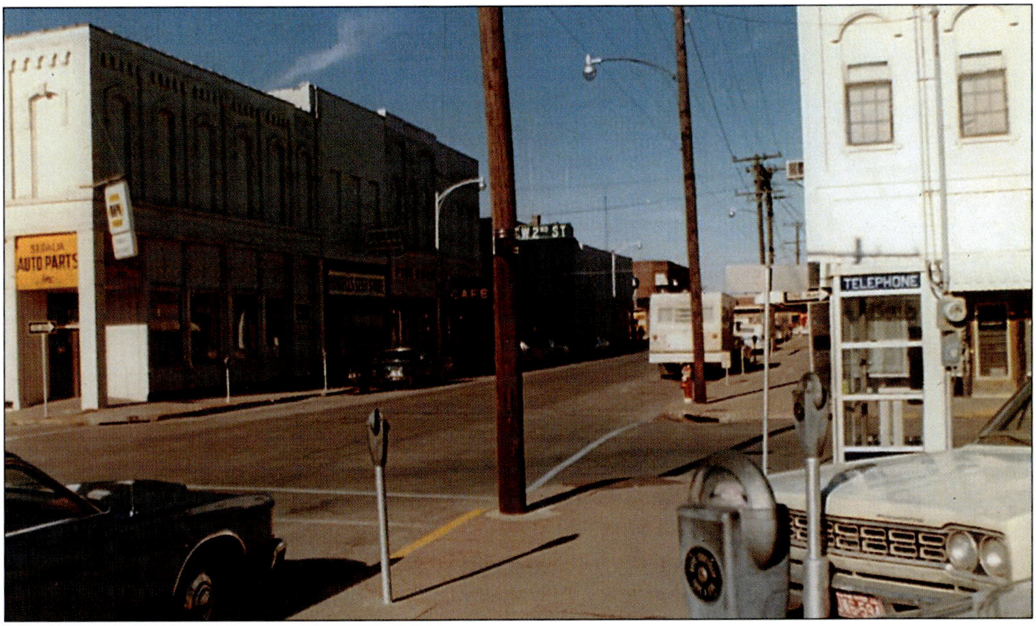

Parking meters are prominent in this view of South Osage Avenue and West Second Street. Installed in 1941, the meters created instant controversy. Some business owners resisted "feeding the meter" on behalf of their customers and paid the cost of parking. Attorneys and merchants—and the newspaper reporter who wrote about parking meter laws—were among the first to be ticketed for illegal parking. (Courtesy of the City of Sedalia Archives.)

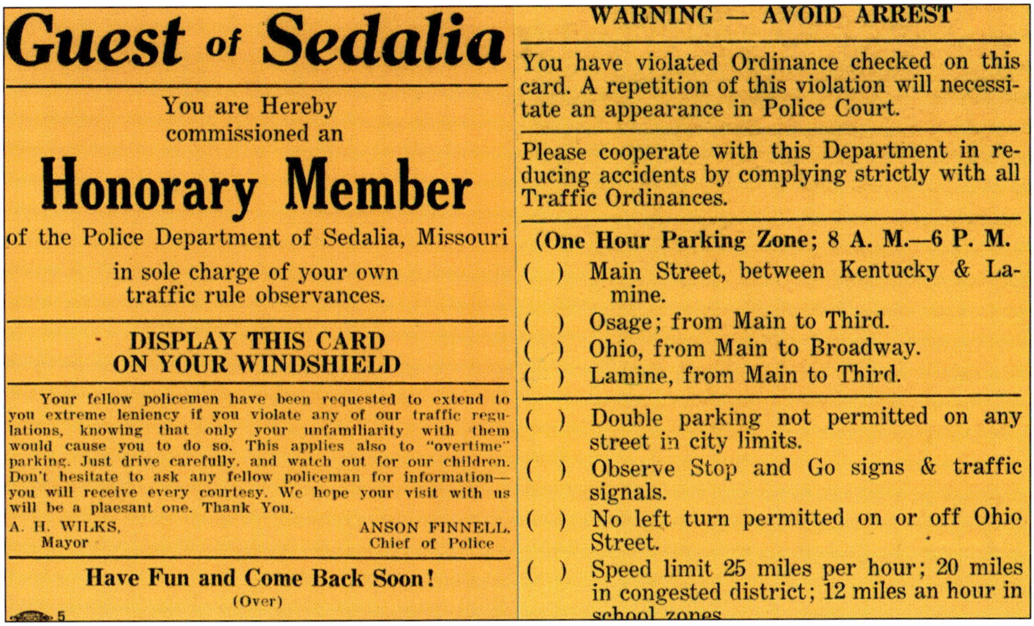

Guest of Sedalia

You are Hereby commissioned an

Honorary Member

of the Police Department of Sedalia, Missouri in sole charge of your own traffic rule observances.

DISPLAY THIS CARD ON YOUR WINDSHIELD

Your fellow policemen have been requested to extend to you extreme leniency if you violate any of our traffic regulations, knowing that only your unfamiliarity with them would cause you to do so. This applies also to "overtime" parking. Just drive carefully, and watch out for our children. Don't hesitate to ask any fellow policeman for information—you will receive every courtesy. We hope your visit with us will be a plaesant one. Thank You.

A. H. WILKS, Mayor

ANSON FINNELL, Chief of Police

Have Fun and Come Back Soon!

(Over)

5

WARNING — AVOID ARREST

You have violated Ordinance checked on this card. A repetition of this violation will necessitate an appearance in Police Court.

Please cooperate with this Department in reducing accidents by complying strictly with all Traffic Ordinances.

(One Hour Parking Zone; 8 A. M.—6 P. M.

( ) Main Street, between Kentucky & Lamine.
( ) Osage; from Main to Third.
( ) Ohio, from Main to Broadway.
( ) Lamine, from Main to Third.

( ) Double parking not permitted on any street in city limits.
( ) Observe Stop and Go signs & traffic signals.
( ) No left turn permitted on or off Ohio Street.
( ) Speed limit 25 miles per hour; 20 miles in congested district; 12 miles an hour in school zones.

In response to the meter outcry, the police department issued complimentary parking passes for visitors to Sedalia. However, parking passes, and even free parking during special events, could not compete with shopping centers that advertised "acres" of free parking. Parking meters were removed from downtown in 1980 but returned a few years later—when they were for sale in antique shops. (Courtesy of the Sedalia Public Library.)

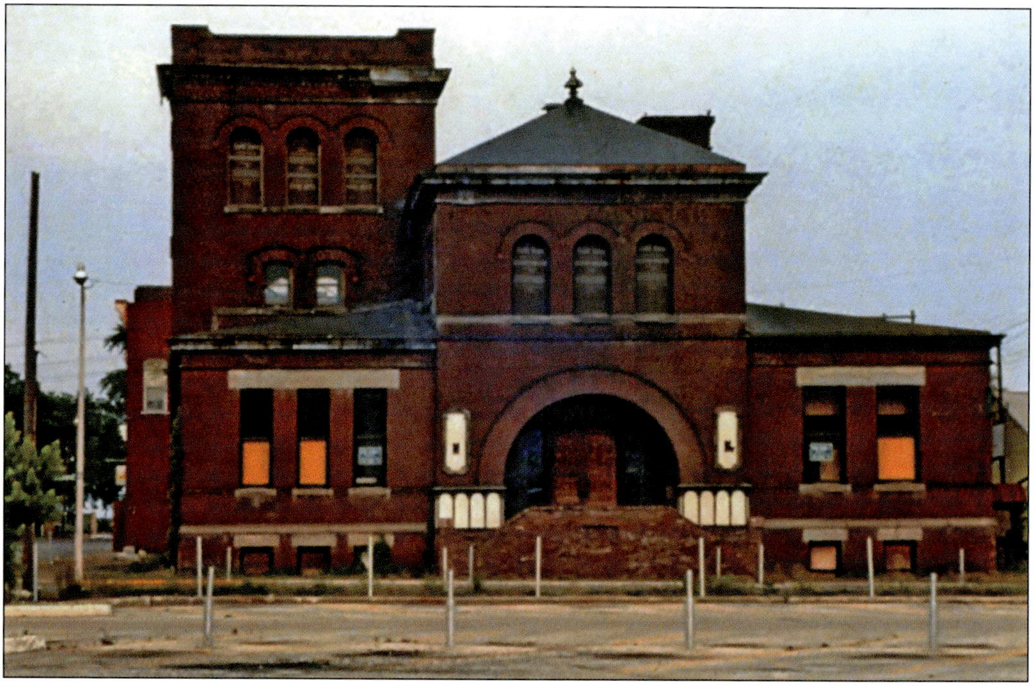

Sedalia's first post office was established in February 1861, just in time for postmaster A.T. Hodge to join the Confederate army. In 1891, construction began at 201 South Lamine Avenue on Sedalia's first building erected specifically as a post office (above). Postmaster H.C. Demuth drew an annual salary of $2,600 in 1892, the year the post office opened. The post office remained at this site until it moved two blocks south in 1931. The former post office building remained vacant and deteriorated until being torn down in 1988. Sedalia dedicated a new post office (below) at 400 East Fifth Street in 1968. This location, Sedalia's third building erected specifically as a post office, featured "electric eyes" that opened and closed doors as patrons entered and exited. (Above, courtesy of the Sedalia Public Library.)

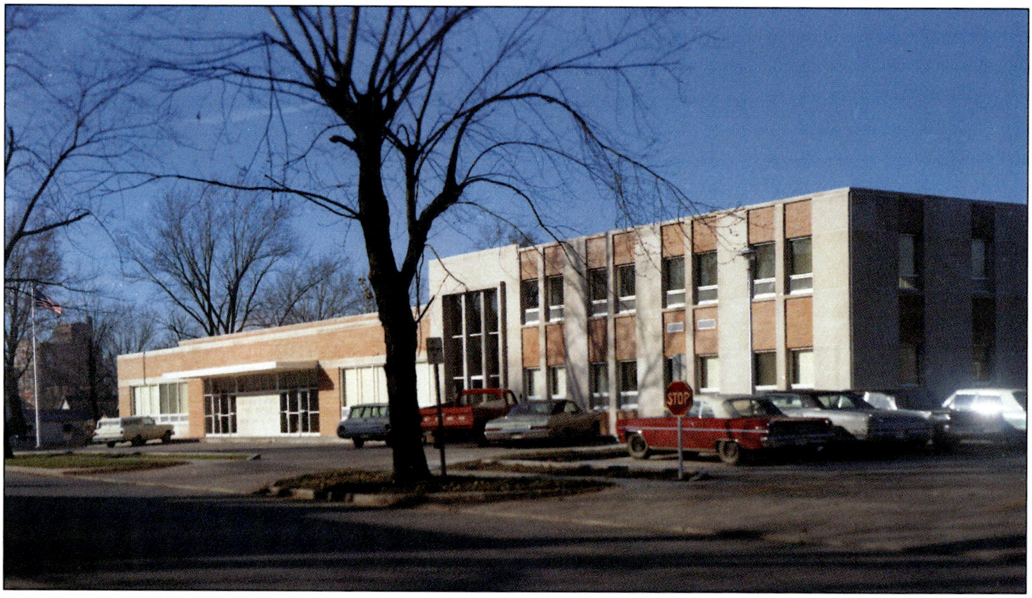

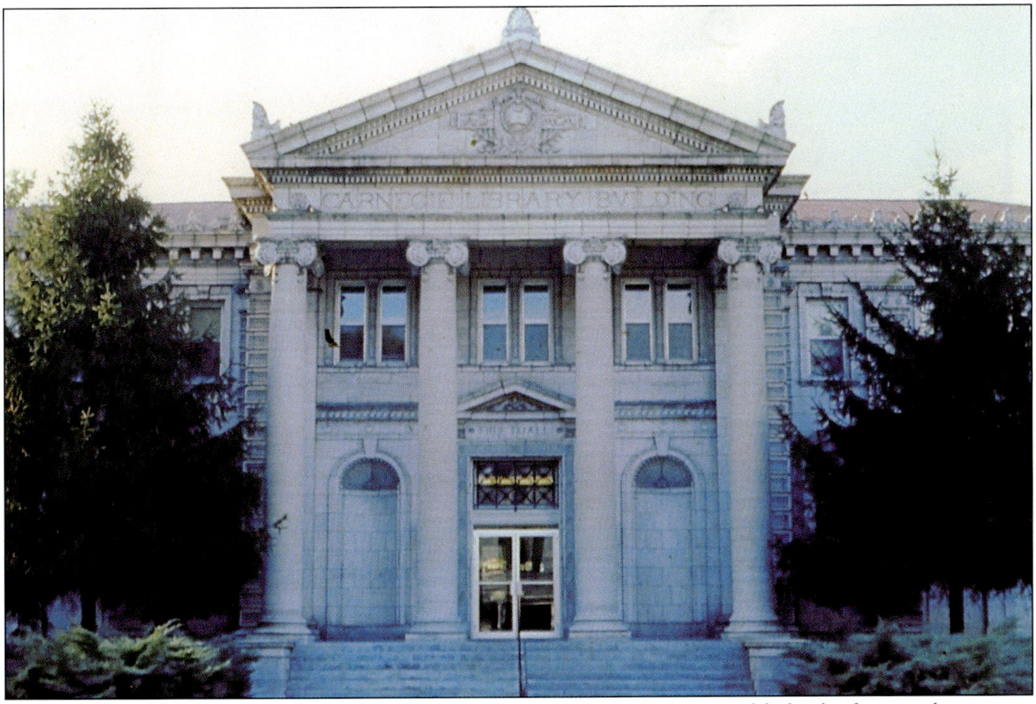

Sedalia's first library opened in 1871 when the Library Association established a free reading room at 115 South Ohio Avenue. Founded in 1895, the Sedalia Public Library was initially located in the basement of the Pettis County Courthouse. In 1899, Andrew Carnegie awarded Sedalia a $50,000 grant to construct the present library. Sedalia was the first city in Missouri to receive such a grant. The library was dedicated in 1901. (Courtesy of the Sedalia Public Library.)

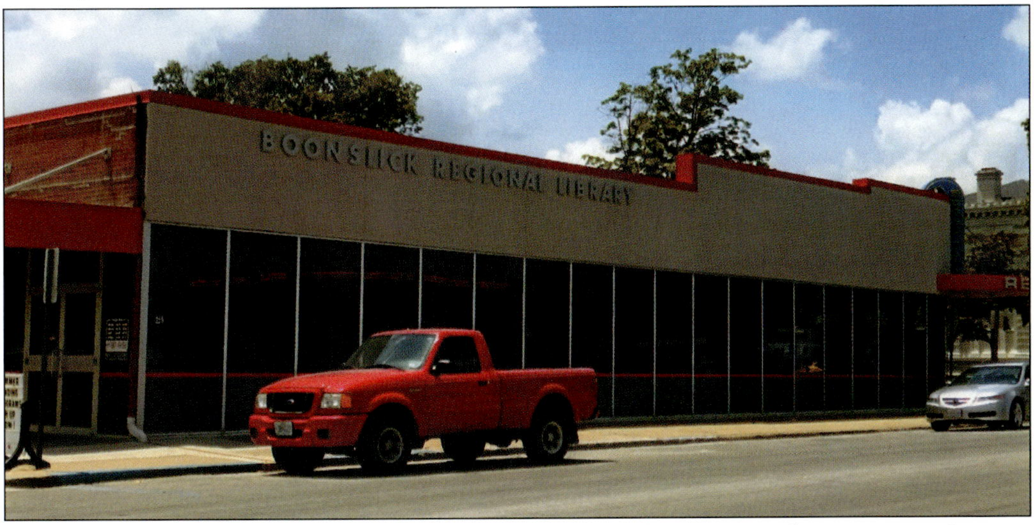

The Boonslick Regional Library was established in 1953 and now serves three counties: Benton, Cooper, and Pettis (excluding the city of Sedalia, as of the 1965 city limits). Originally located in the Pettis County Courthouse, the library moved to 602 South Ohio Avenue in 1954, and a new library was built at 201 East Sixth Street in 1961. In 1992, the library purchased the Brown Automotive building at 219 West Third Street. Sedalia serves as Boonslick's administrative headquarters. (Courtesy of the Boonslick Regional Library.)

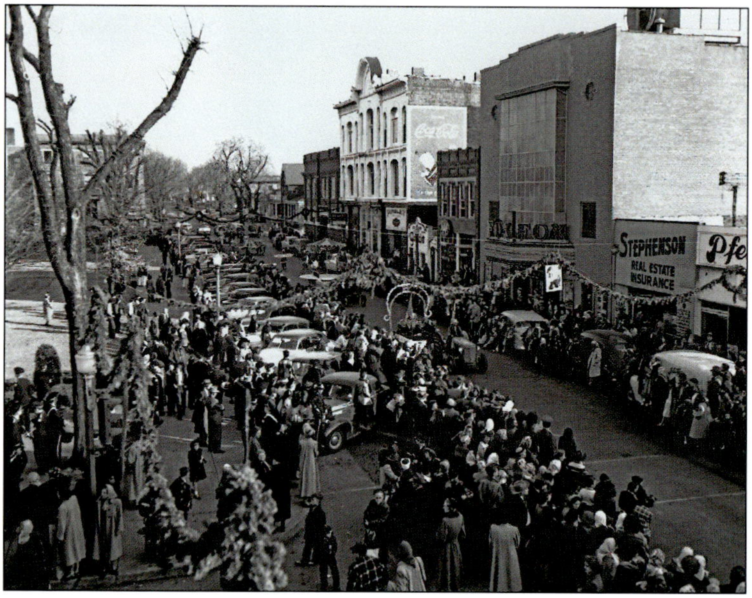

Sedalia's annual Christmas parade is one of its most cherished traditions. The Jaycees sponsored this 1950 parade, which included 18 units from the nationally known Earl F. Hammond show. Hammond, who also supplied units for the Macy's parade in New York, brought live reindeer to Sedalia to pull Santa's sleigh. The parade is pictured on East Fifth Street, moving west toward Ohio Avenue.

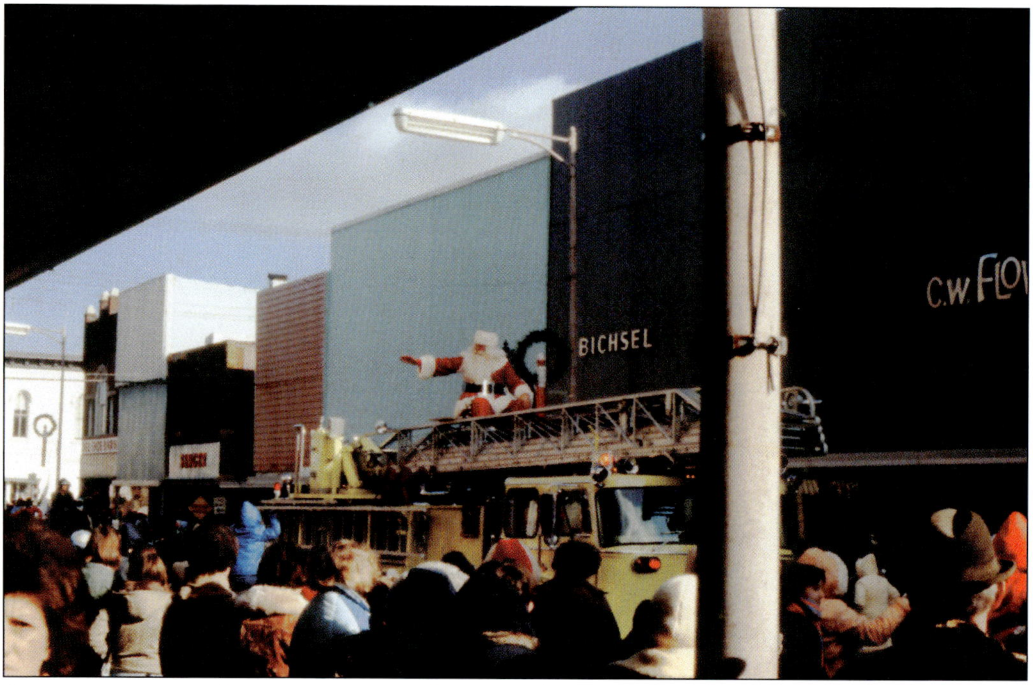

Santa waving from a fire truck traditionally signals the end of the Christmas parade. The tradition took a twist in 1976 when Santa rode in Sedalia's first yellow fire truck. Many cities switched from red to yellow fire trucks in the 1970s, as yellow was said to improve visibility. Sedalia's new truck cost more than $117,000, prompting a newspaper editorial to note that "a gold-like shade" seemed appropriate for its price tag. (Courtesy of Dr. Steve Carr.)

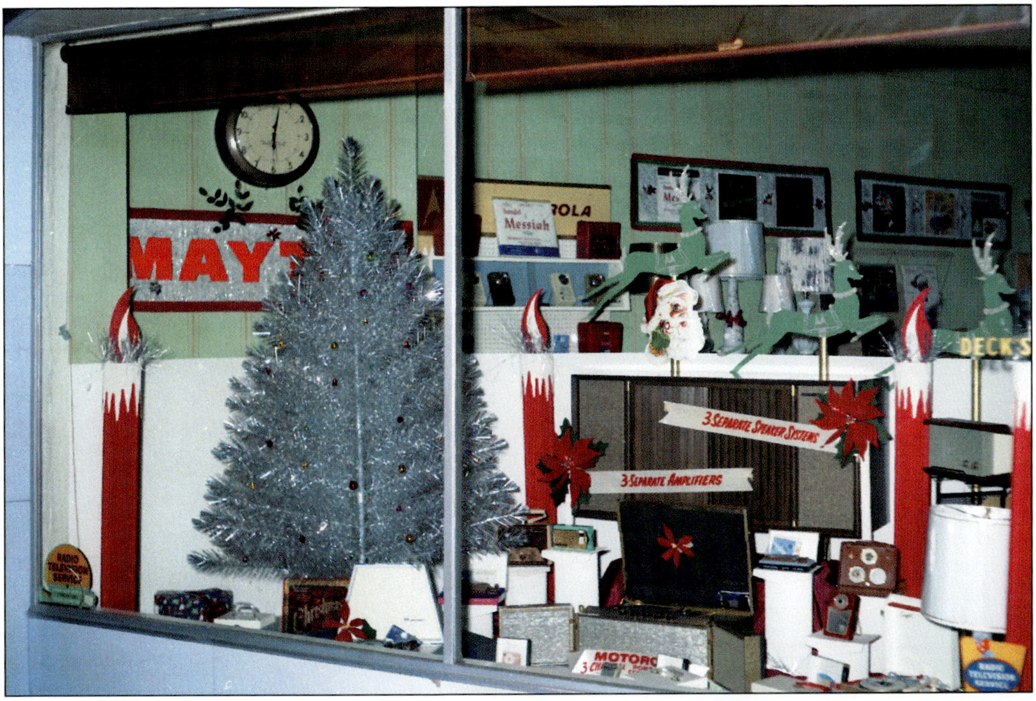

Deck's Appliance at 512 South Ohio Avenue was decked out for the holidays in 1959. The store also featured "Living Windows," when real people posed as mannequins in its window displays during the holiday season. Deck's inventory included refrigerators and freezers, electric ranges, sinks, food waste dispensers, steel kitchen cabinets, electric water heaters, radios, and televisions.

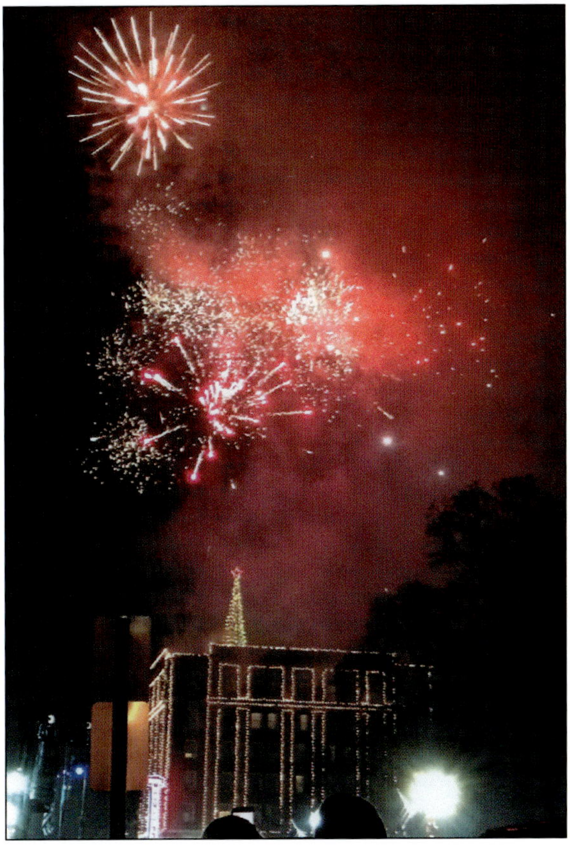

The Hotel Bothwell at Ohio Avenue and East Fourth Street is the centerpiece of Sedalia's Thanksgiving Lighting & Fireworks Extravaganza. The event on Thanksgiving evening features a fireworks display, synchronized to music, from the top of the hotel. The show culminates in the lighting of the Hotel Bothwell and the Furnell Landmark Building. (Courtesy of Melanie Messerli.)

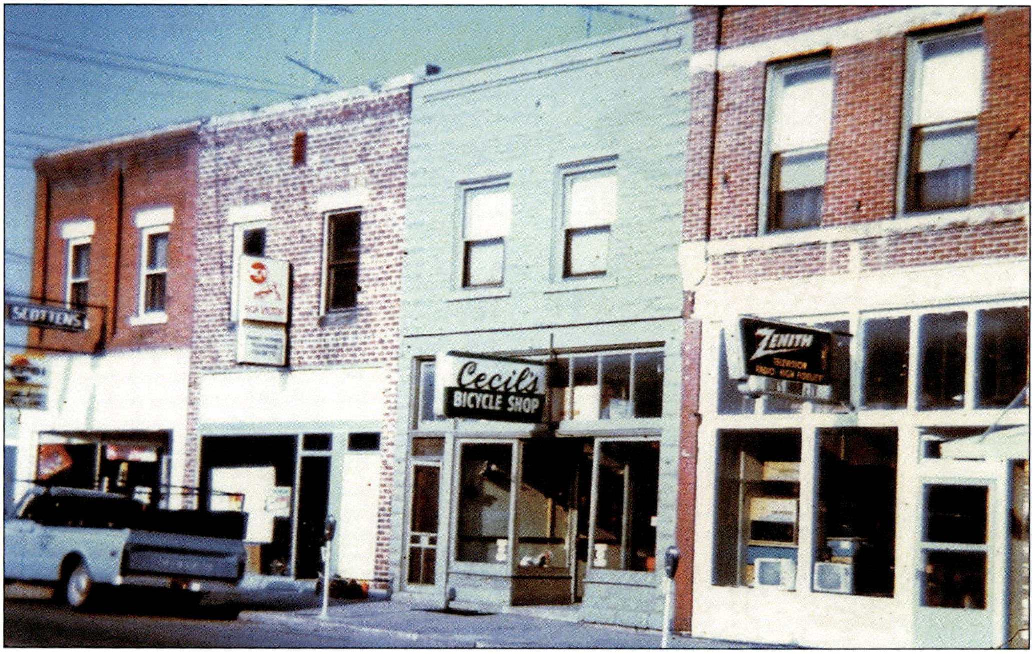

Gerald Cecil founded Cecil's Bicycle Shop in 1936. He expanded into radios and televisions, introducing Sedalia's first television set in 1949. Gerald's business eventually occupied four stores in the 700 block of South Ohio Avenue, and he was proud to provide a livelihood for those who worked for him through the years. He and his wife, Helen, passed away nine months apart in 2015 and 2016. (Courtesy of Greg Cecil.)

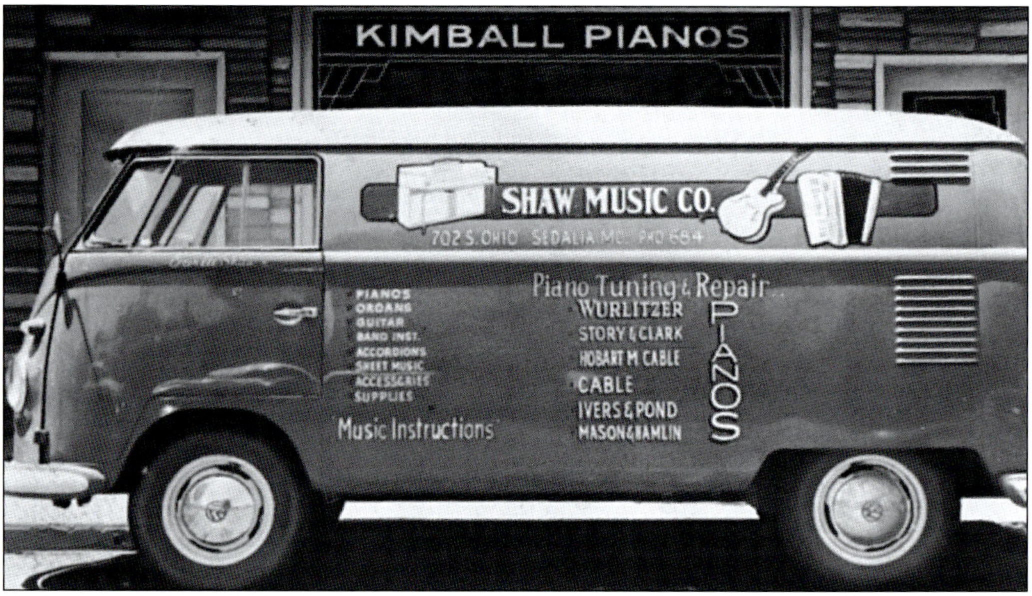

Shaw Music Company, owned by brothers Stanley and Orville Shaw, was founded in 1927. As the company expanded, Stanley moved to Jefferson City to open an additional location. Orville remained in Sedalia and operated the store until his death in 1961. The company provided instruments for churches, schools, and the Missouri State Fair. Shaw Music was located at 702 South Ohio Avenue from 1932 until closing in 1988.

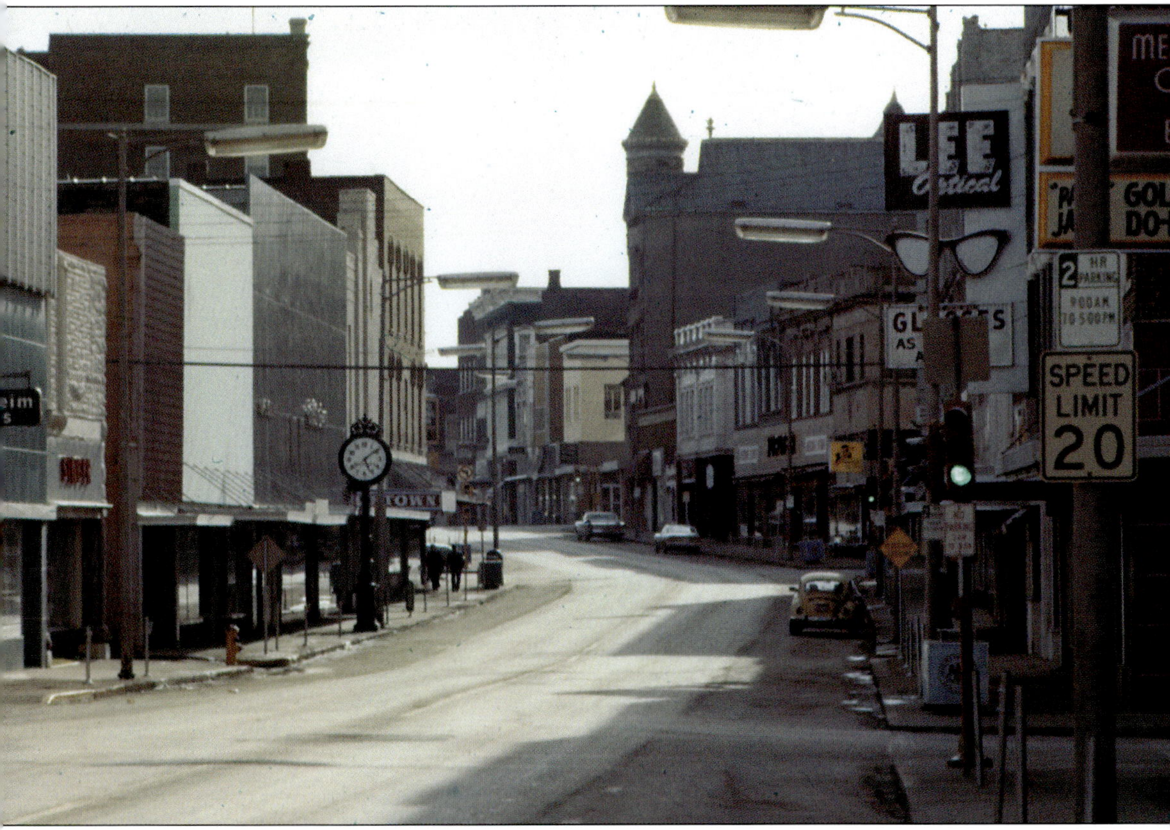

This image provides a view of Ohio Avenue looking south from near Second Street in 1981. Businesses on the left side of the street include, from left to right, Priddy's Shoe Store, Singer Sewing Store, optometrist Dr. Russell Drenon, Bichsel Jewelry (with its signature post clock), the C.W. Flower Company, Hudson Jewelry, and the Uptown Theatre. On the right side are, from front to back, Merle Norman Cosmetics, Papa Jake's Donut Shop, Lee Optical, Russell Brothers Clothing, Goodheart's Jewelry, Zip Discount Drugs, Jupiter Discount Store, Harvey's Card Shop, Burton's Dress Shop, and Felton Appraisal. By the 1980s, downtown Sedalia had fallen into a decline consistent with nationwide trends. Efforts to reverse the downhill trek included removing parking meters, as evidenced by the short metal poles in this photograph, and covering historic facades with multicolored metal panels. Now, a new generation of visionaries is reviving culture and commerce in the historic district. (Courtesy of Tom C. Taylor.)

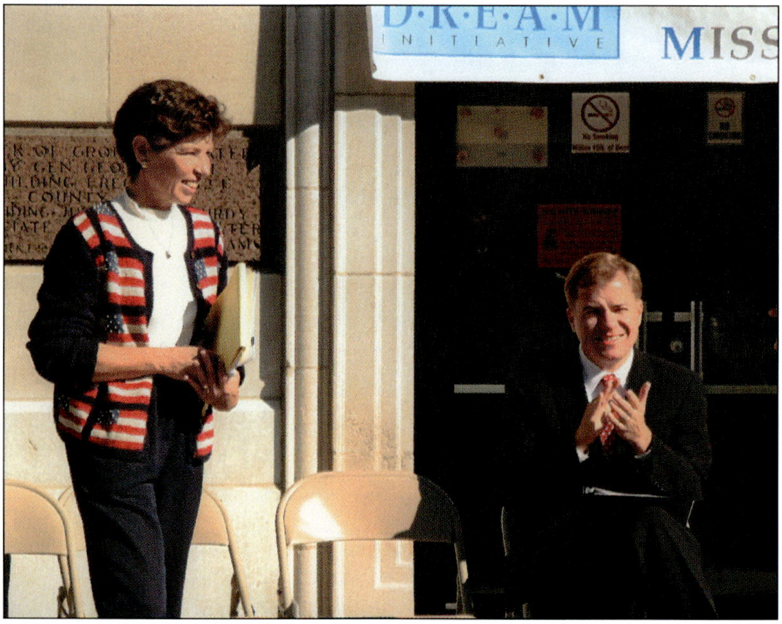

In 2006, Sedalia was among the first 10 Missouri cities to be selected for the DREAM initiative. DREAM is an acronym for Downtown Revitalization and Economic Assistance for Missouri. Sedalia was the first DREAM city visited by Gov. Matt Blunt, pictured with Meg Liston, director of Sedalia Downtown Development, Inc. (Courtesy of Randy Kirby.)

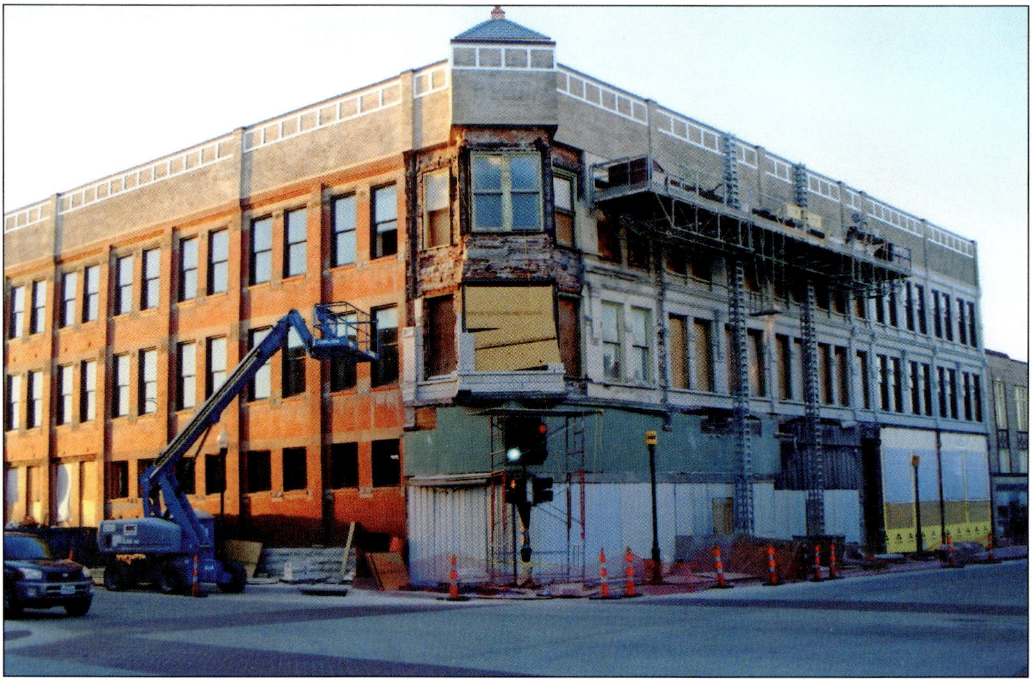

Shortly after downtown Sedalia received the DREAM designation, the Fulton Housing Group of Kansas City purchased the Commerce/Ilgenfritz building at 232 South Ohio Avenue. Erected in 1885, the building had survived a major fire, arson, and bomb attempts before falling into disrepair. Fulton Housing invested $6 million to convert the structure into the Commerce Building Lofts, 25 single- and double-bedroom apartments.

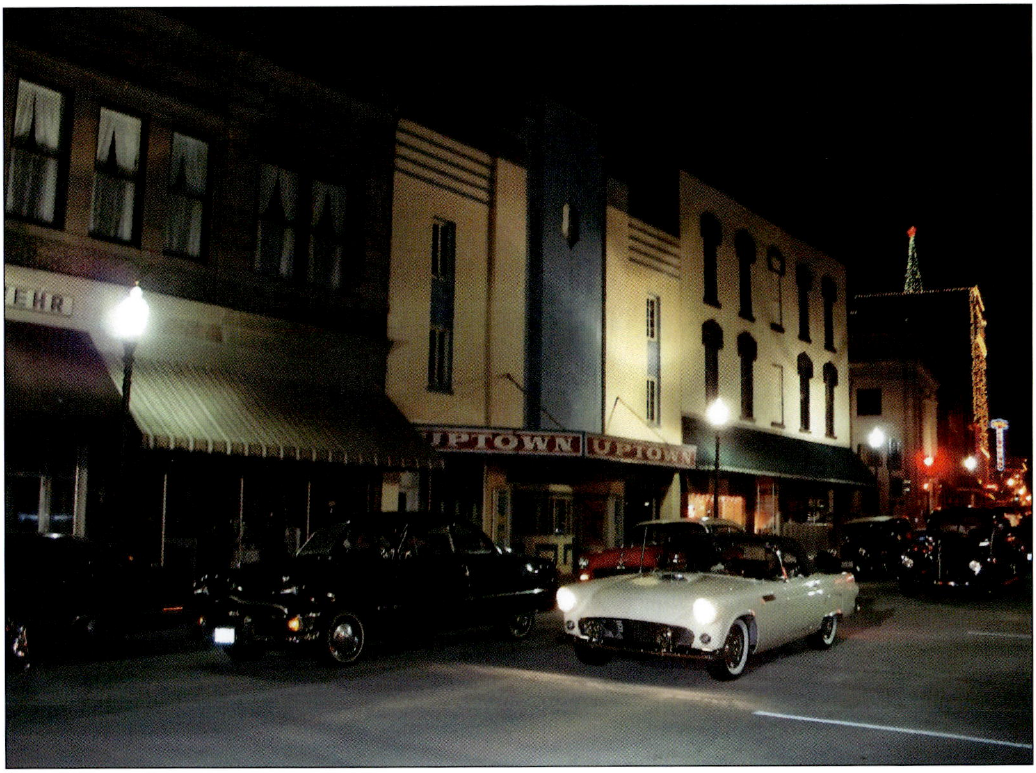

Phase I of downtown Sedalia's streetscape was dedicated in 2009 with a procession of vintage automobiles. Longtime downtown business owners Gerald and Helen Cecil, known for their "moonlight drives" along Ohio Avenue, rode in the lead car. Streetscape enhancements included new paving for streets and sidewalks, new curbs, brick crossings, and streetlights.

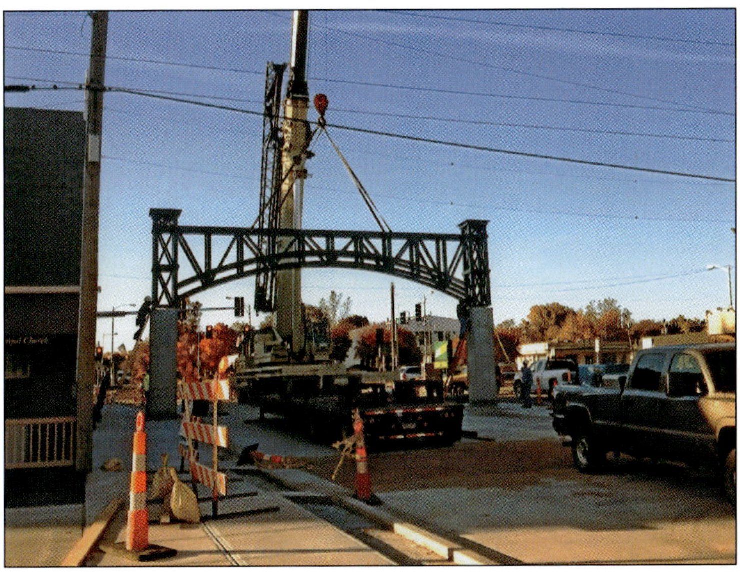

Phase IIIa of the streetscape provided a new entrance to downtown Sedalia at Missouri Highway 50 (Broadway Boulevard) and Ohio Avenue. The 47-by-27-foot gateway resembles a railroad trestle, honoring Sedalia's railroad heritage. The arch is pictured during installation in 2015. Lettering that reads "Sedalia Historic District" was added, along with LED lighting with changeable colors.

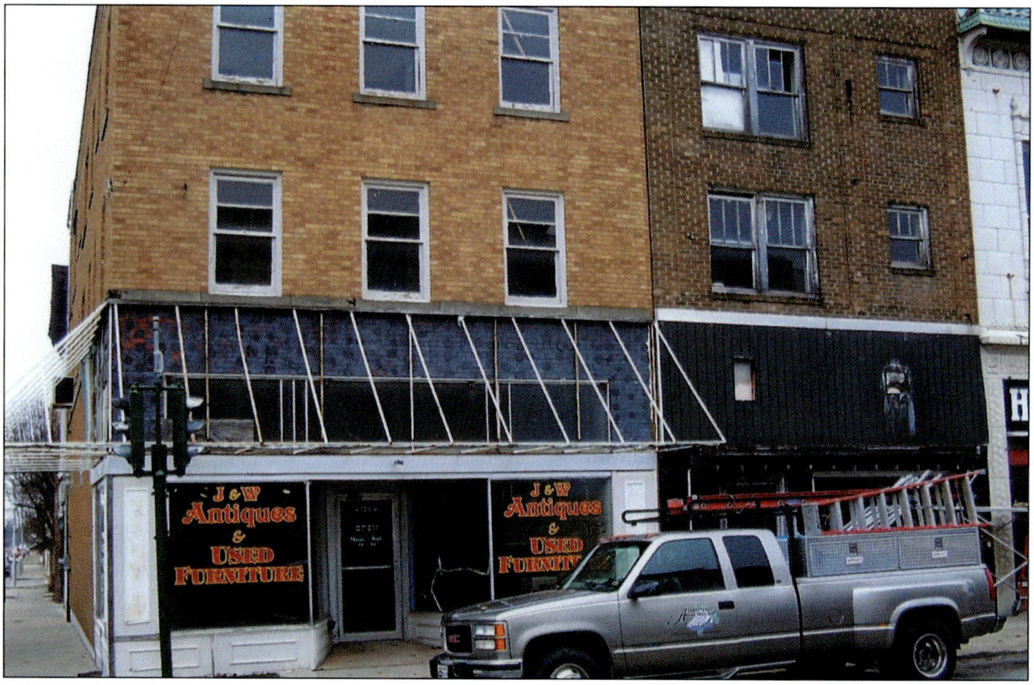

John and Michelle Swords are committed to providing family-owned, hometown service in the heart of historic downtown Sedalia. They own Swords' Family Pharmacy, located at 300 South Ohio Avenue in the former Sedalia National Bank building. The Swords also own and manage eight historic downtown properties, including retail spaces and loft apartments. Pictured are before and after renovation photographs of 122 and 124 South Ohio Avenue, which the Swords purchased in 2005. The corner building, the longtime home of the Lockett's Ladies' Shop, was restored according to a 1940s photograph. Papa Jake's Donut Shop, another landmark Sedalia business, was located in the adjacent building. Michelle serves as president of Sedalia Downtown Development, Inc., and is a member of several organizations dedicated to civic improvement and historic preservation. (Both, courtesy of John and Michelle Swords.)

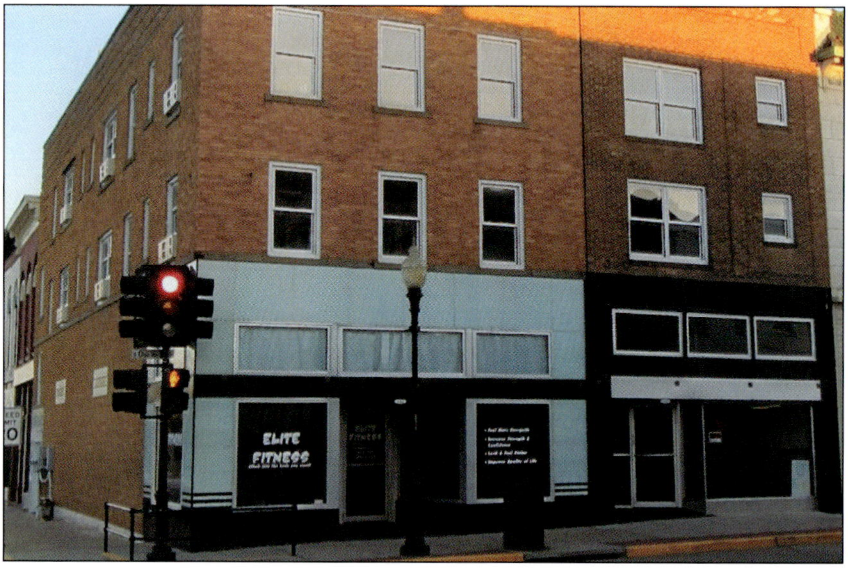

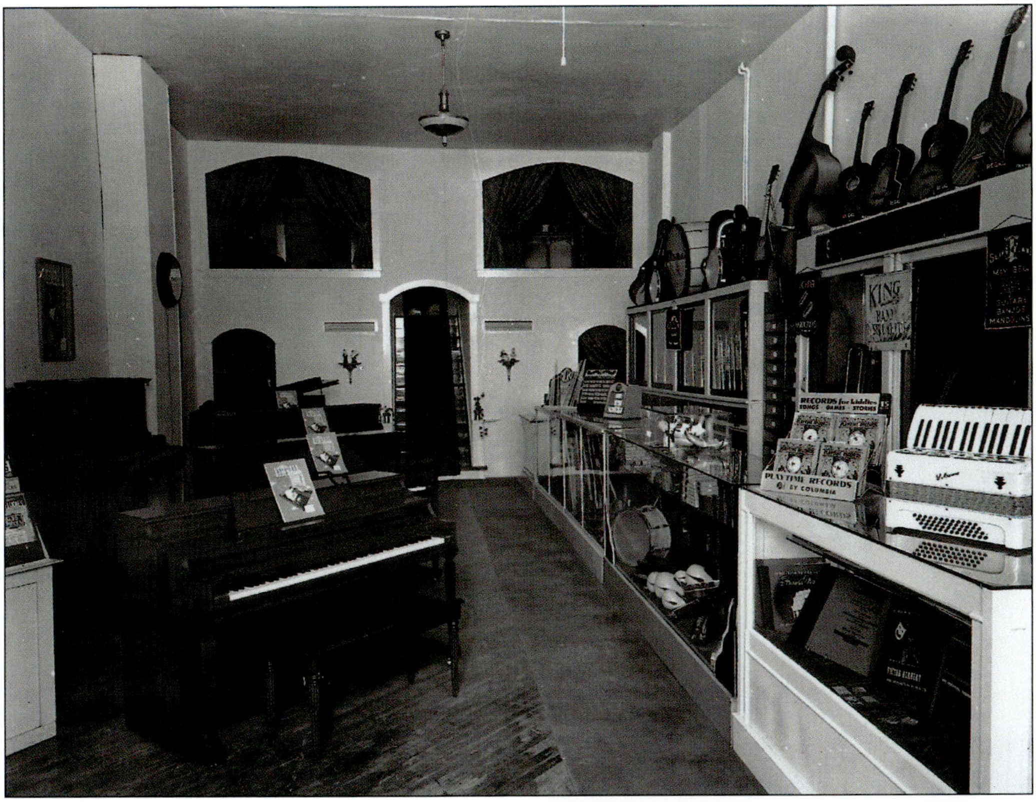

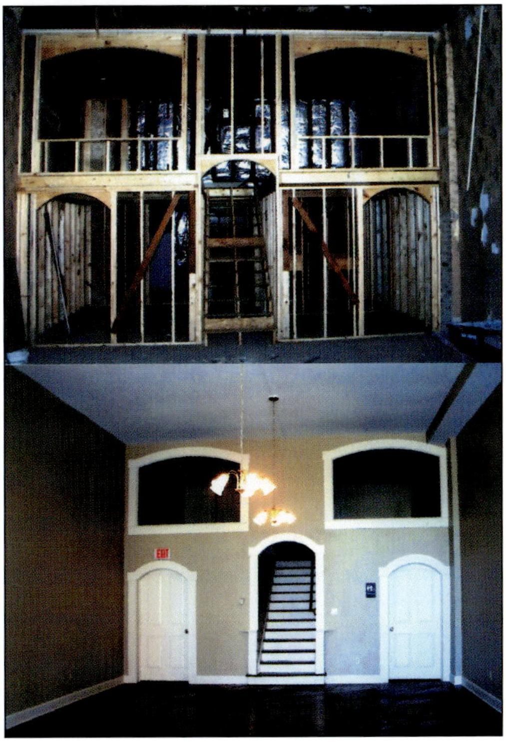

Like many downtown businesses, the Shaw Music Company at 702 South Ohio Avenue modernized its store interior during the 1960s. Cosmetic changes included installing wood paneling over plaster walls and lowering the ceiling. More significant changes were made to the balcony, as discovered when the above photograph was found in the building during restoration in 2008. The balcony stairway had been moved from the center to the north side of the building, and square windows had replaced the original arched openings. Restoration involved removing the 1960s "improvements" and re-creating the building's balcony (right) according to national historic standards and current building codes. The building was returned to retail use in 2009 after being vacant for 21 years.

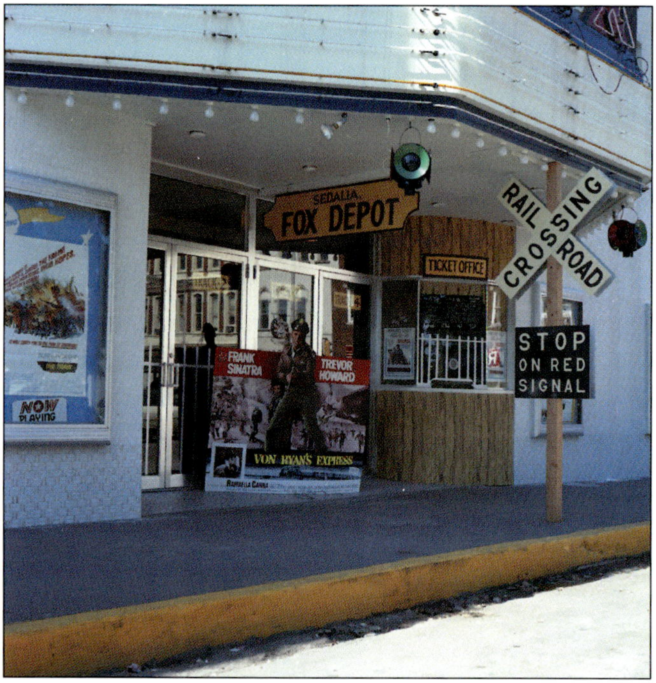

The Fox Theatre opened in 1940 and played a vital role in the community. Besides showing motion pictures, it hosted war bond drives, fashion shows, Christmas parties, contests, school functions, fundraisers, and concerts. The front of the theater is pictured in 1965 when it was converted to a "depot" for the movie *Von Ryan's Express* starring Frank Sinatra.

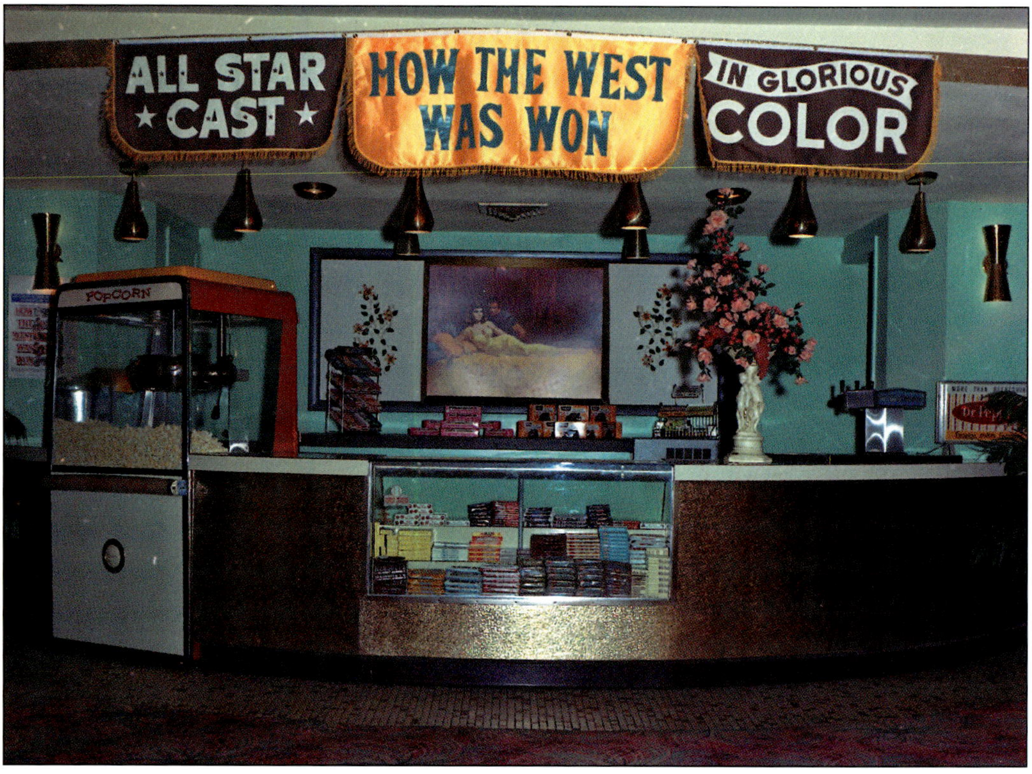

Even the Fox Theatre snack bar promoted the latest movies, such as *How the West Was Won*, a $15 million Western released in 1963. By the time the movie reached the Fox, it had garnered three Academy Awards. Tickets for the show cost $1.25 for adults and 50¢ for children.

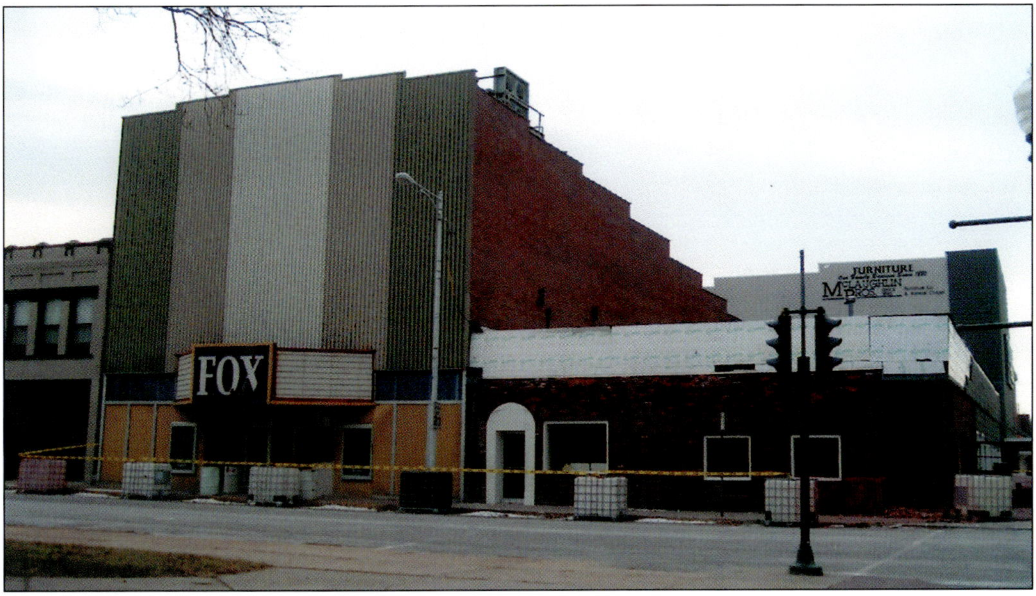

The Fox Theatre was remodeled in 1972, the same year the Jerry Lewis Twin Cinemas opened in the State Fair Shopping Center. The Fox closed in 1987 and remained vacant until the Furnell Companies purchased the theater and the adjoining single-story building at the corner of South Ohio Avenue and East Fifth Street. The corner building is pictured in preparation for demolition, prior to construction of the Furnell Landmark Building.

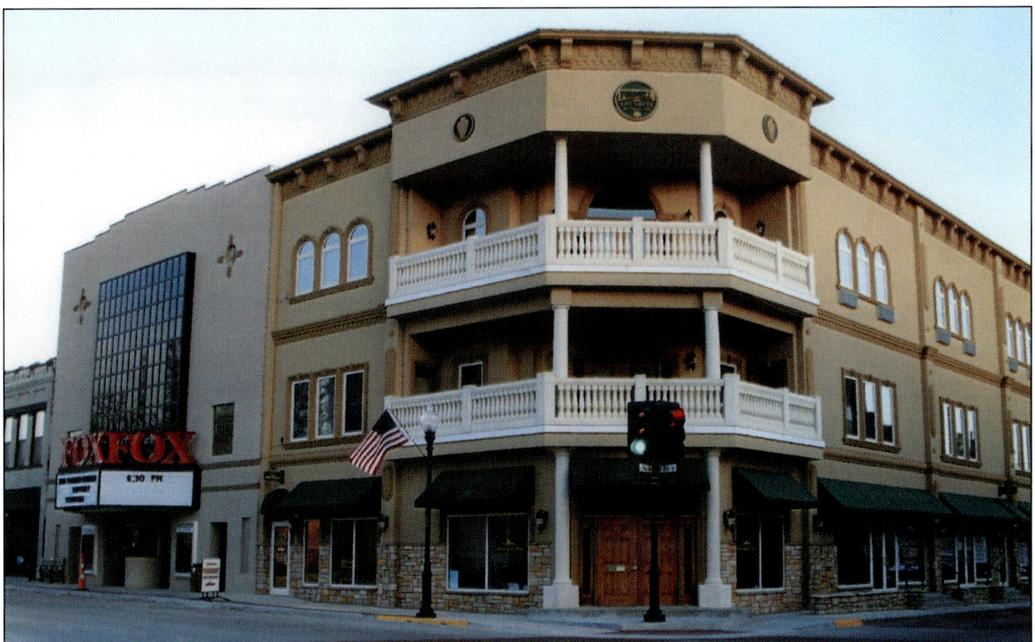

The Fox Theatre Event Center and Furnell Landmark Building opened in 2009. The project involved restoration of the theater facade and construction of a unique venue designed to accommodate a variety of business functions and private events. The adjacent Furnell Landmark Building encompasses more than 30,000 square feet of retail, office, and senior housing space.

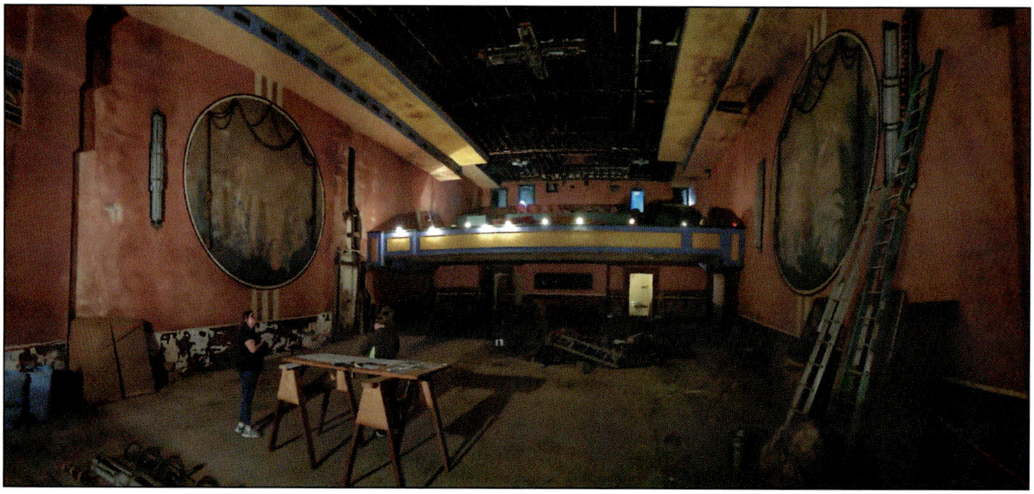

J.T. and Mercedes Ghosen opened the $50,000 Uptown Theater at 227 South Ohio Avenue in 1936. The Uptown represented a longtime dream for Ghosen, who previously managed storefront theaters, or store buildings converted to theaters. Designed by the Kansas City architectural firm of Boller Brothers, the Uptown seated 800 people on two floors. The Uptown closed in 1974, and the Ghosens' daughter, Margie Wagenknecht, donated it to Sedalia Downtown Development, Inc., in honor of her parents in 2006. Restoration is under way to convert the theater to a live-event center. Marty Lange is pictured below holding a sign discovered in the building during its restoration, lauding the Uptown's status as Sedalia's first air-conditioned theater. (Above, courtesy of Bob Walters; below, courtesy of Marty Lange.)

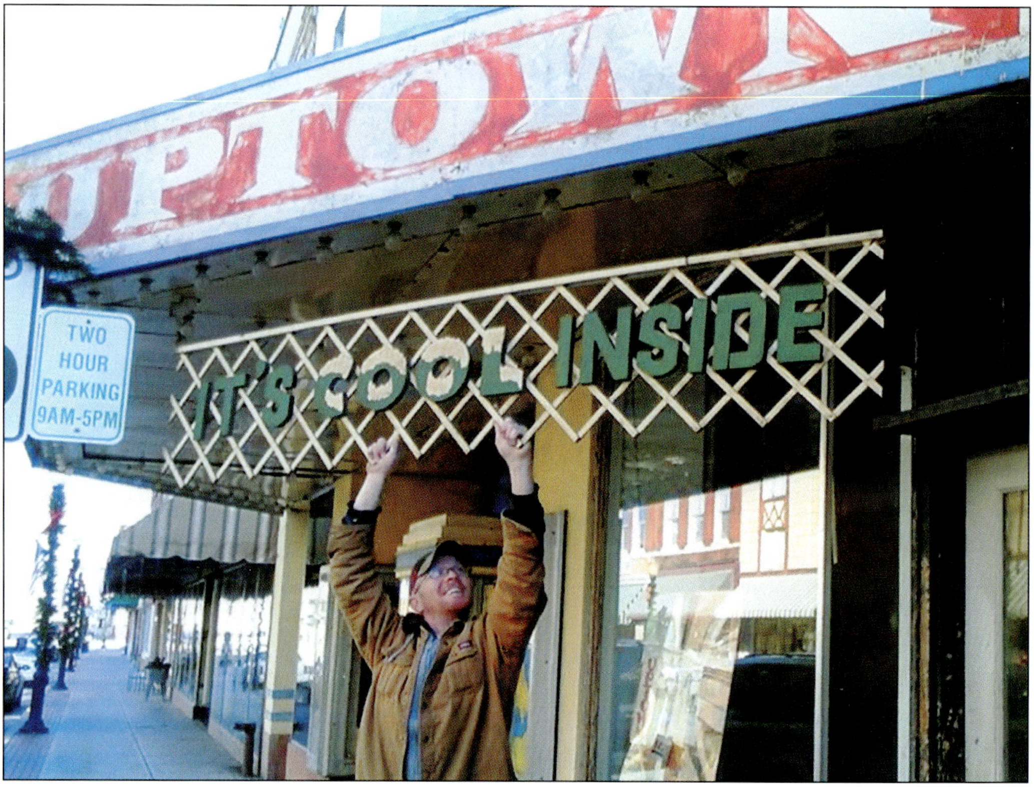

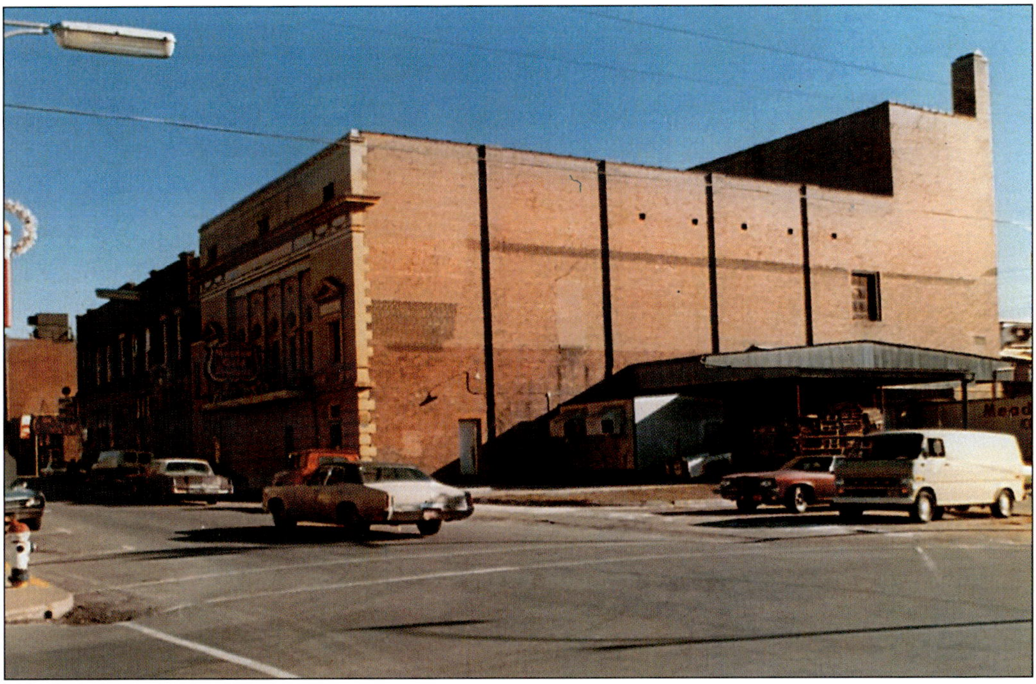

The New Lona Theater, later the Liberty Theatre, opened in 1920 on the site of a former stable at 111 West Fifth Street. Vice presidential candidate Franklin Roosevelt campaigned at the theater shortly after it opened. Roosevelt lost the vice presidential bid, and the 1,500-seat theater lost revenue through the following decades. In 1957, Beatrice Foods purchased the building and converted it to a warehouse for storing cottage cheese and ice cream until donating it to the Sedalia Community Theatre. Converting a cold-storage warehouse to a theater was a major production, with leading roles played by Ginger Swearingen, Neal Reyburn, and Jim Giokaris. In 2013, Joe Fischer helped launch the Next Stage Capital Campaign to renovate the Liberty Theatre and add an arts center to the west side of the existing facility. The 90-foot addition housing three art galleries was completed in 2016. (Above, courtesy of the City of Sedalia Archives; below, courtesy of the Liberty Center Association for the Arts.)

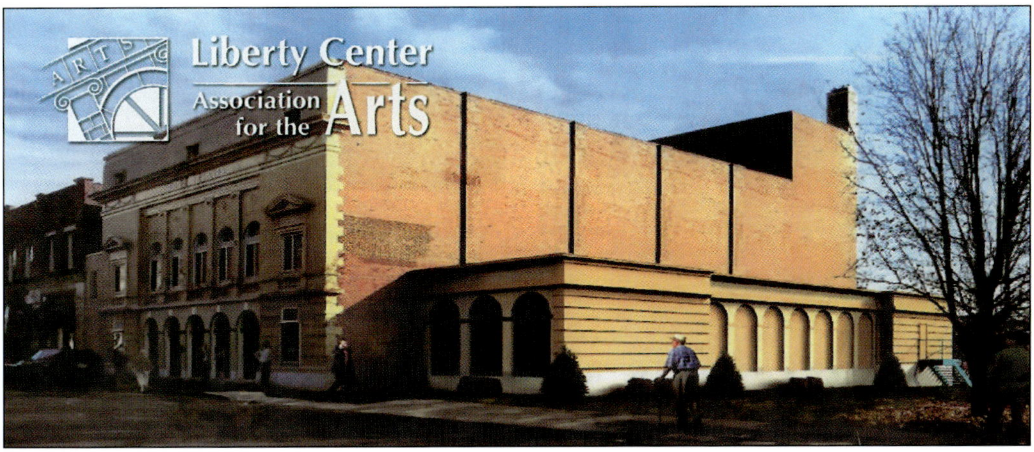

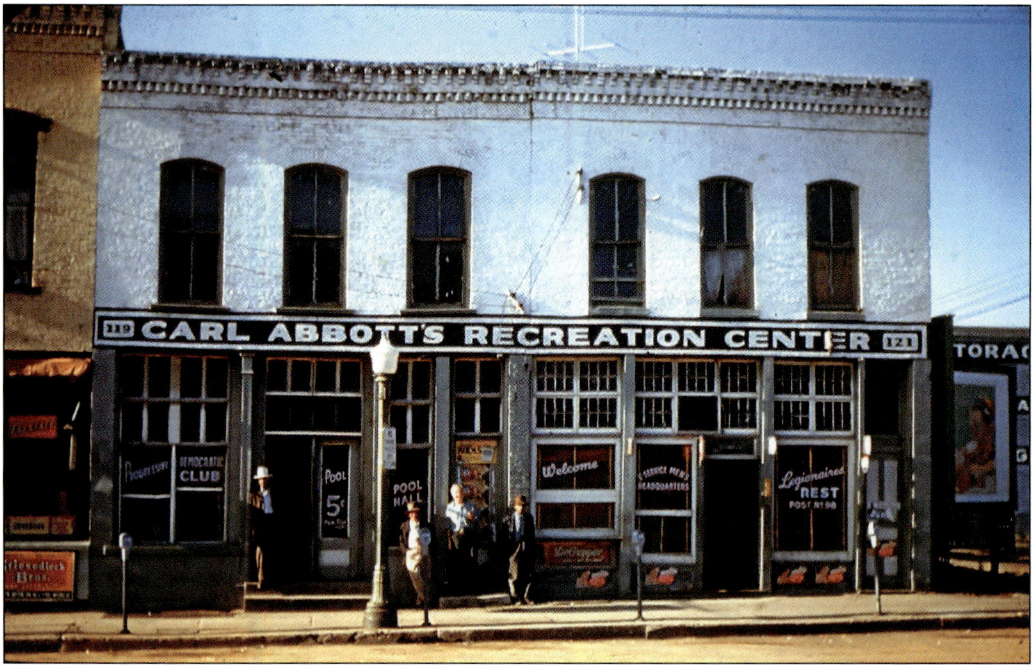

Carl Abbot's Recreation Center at 119–121 East Main Street (above) was more than a pool hall. The first floor was headquarters for the Progressive Democratic Club, X-Service Men, and Legionnaire's Post. The second floor had housed the Maple Leaf Club, where Scott Joplin played piano in the 1890s. The building was razed in 1959 for a parking lot. Ironically, the same year, Sedalia's first Scott Joplin Memorial Concerts recognized Joplin's contribution to American music. In 1974, the Jaycees re-created the facade of the Maple Leaf Club (below) on its former site for the first Scott Joplin Ragtime Festival, when High Spirits, led by Carl Reque, performed. The festival has been held annually since 1983, featuring concerts, contests, symposia, and historical exhibits. The Maple Leaf Club site returned to its ragtime roots when the Maple Leaf Park was dedicated in 1999. (Above, courtesy of Jane Harris Yount; below, courtesy of the Sedalia Ragtime Archive.)

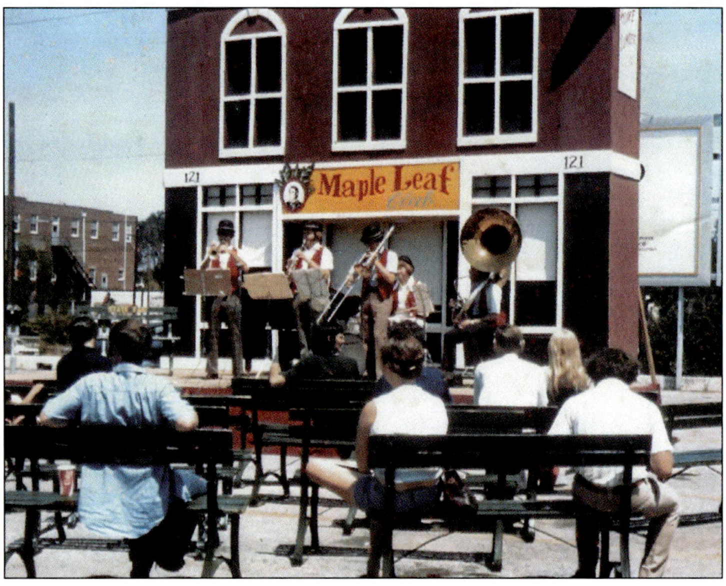

Two

Broadway and Beyond

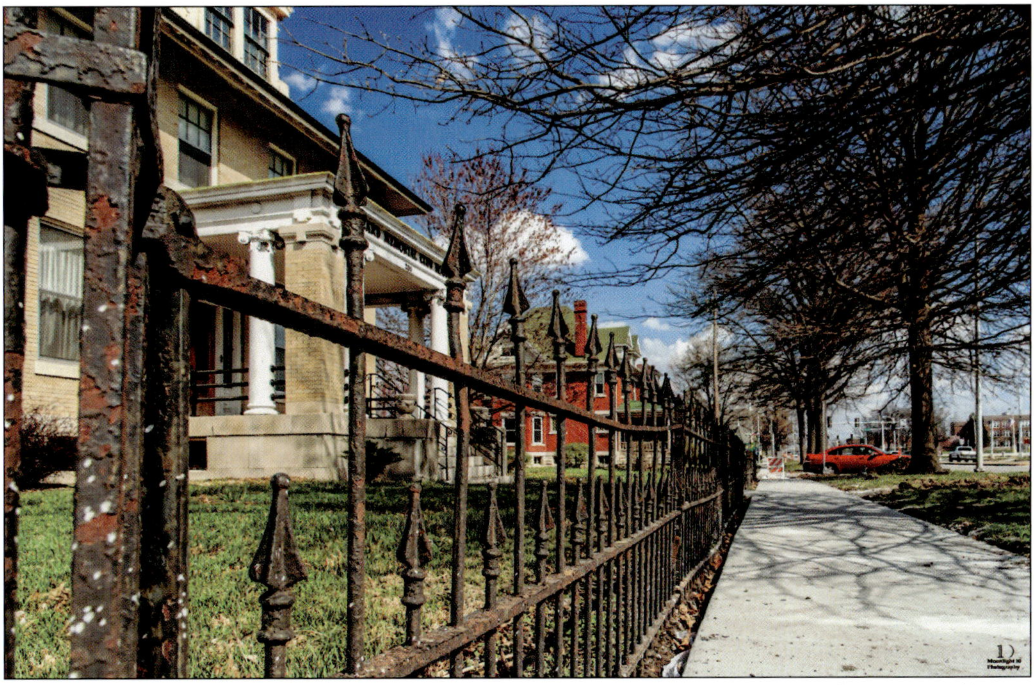

Now bordered by fast-food restaurants and filling stations, the Congressman John T. Heard home (left) remains a monument to Broadway Boulevard. The first houses on the street were built in 1871 and, by written agreement, had to cost $8,000 to $10,000 each. Broadway Boulevard, now US Highway 50, is an eclectic combination of stately homes and commercial structures. (Courtesy of Mark Hammond, Moonlight 10 Photography.)

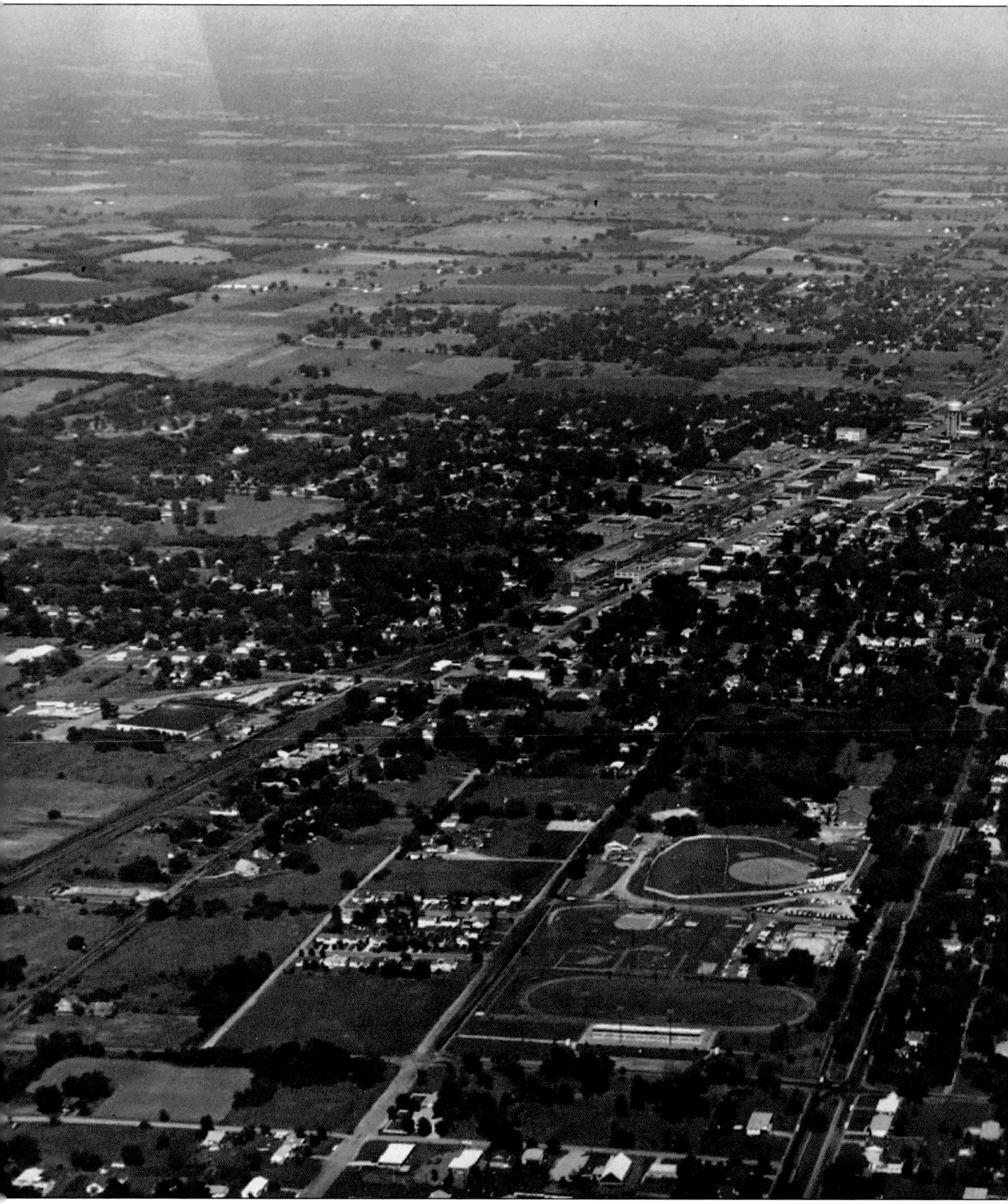

Col. A.D. Jaynes laid out a 120-foot-wide street he named Broadway in 1867. Much to the amusement of rural Pettis Countians, Jaynes arranged for 1,000 shade trees to be planted along his boulevard. "The country people called them 'posts' and came to look at the lunacy of the interlopers and innovators," the *Missouri Republican* reported. "But the posts grew and became spreading trees; the prairie was transformed into a grove." Trees continue to dominate this aerial view of Broadway,

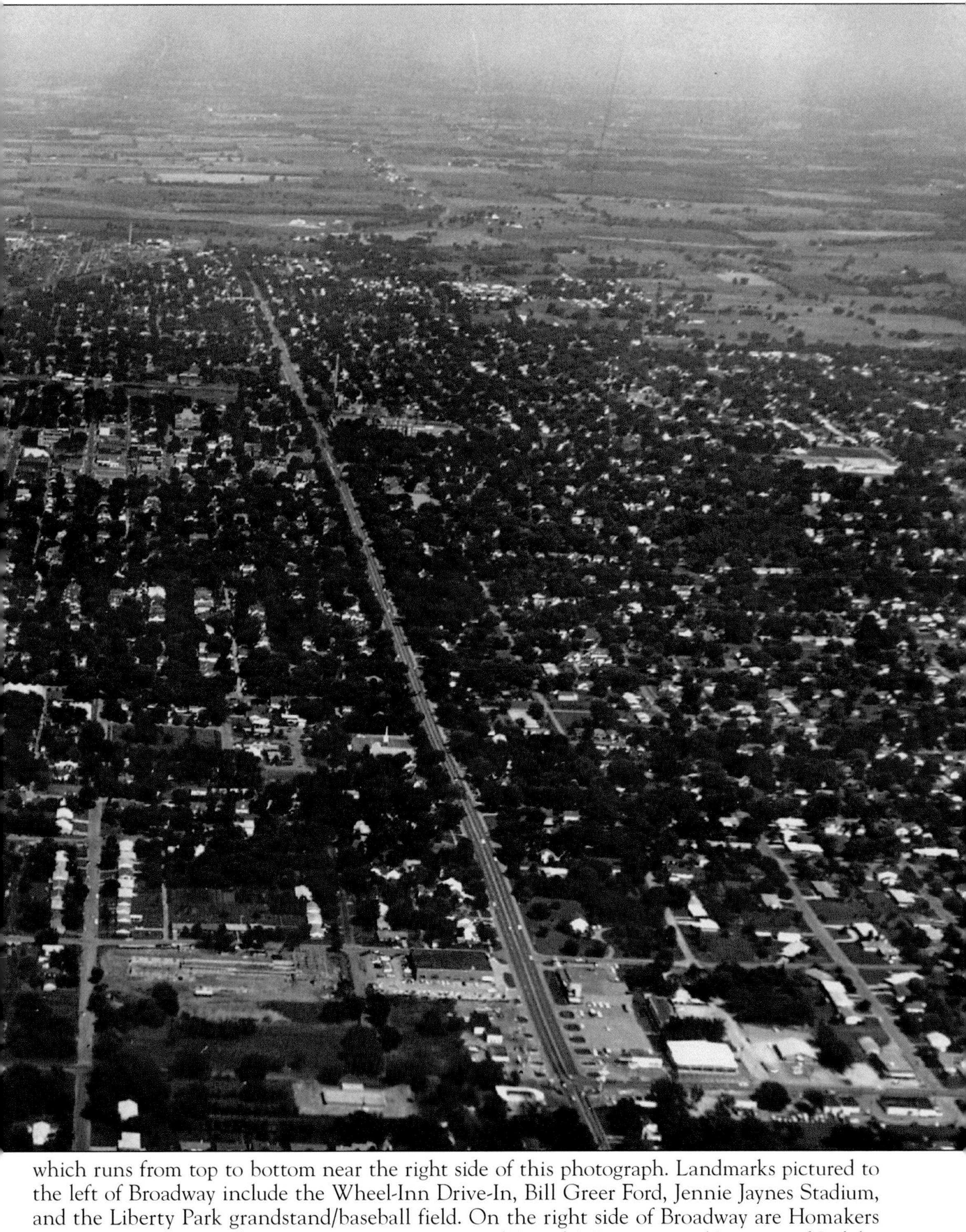

which runs from top to bottom near the right side of this photograph. Landmarks pictured to the left of Broadway include the Wheel-Inn Drive-In, Bill Greer Ford, Jennie Jaynes Stadium, and the Liberty Park grandstand/baseball field. On the right side of Broadway are Homakers Furniture, LeRoy's Steak House, Kroger's grocery, and Beverly's Restaurant. (Courtesy of Sedalia Public Library.)

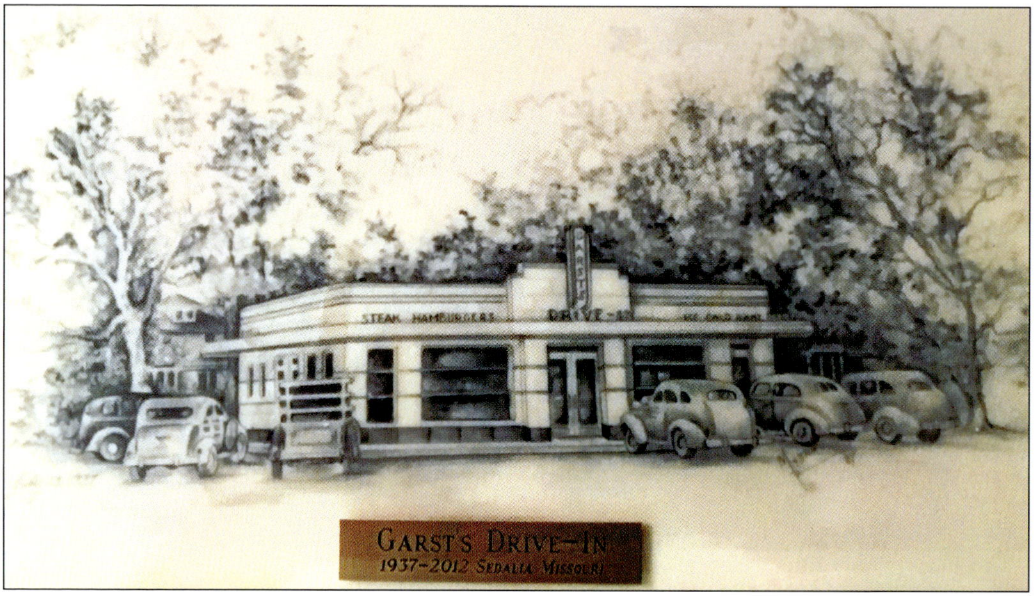

Garst's, the first drive-in west of the Mississippi River, opened in 1937. A service station later known as Craig DX was erected on the block the same year. The site originally was home to A.D. Jaynes, who built a mansion called the Maples in 1871. The Maples was converted into Maywood Hospital in 1905 and became St. Mary's Infirmary in 1915. After the Maples was razed in 1932, the area became Maywood Park. Garst's, later renamed Eddie's for Eddie Boysel, closed in 2012. Before the building was demolished in 2016, its exterior tiles were removed, and each is being etched with a drawing of Garst's (above) by Myrna Ragar. Eddie's Drive-In is pictured below with the Sedalia Armory, dedicated in 1944 and named in honor of Maj. Gen. John C. "Jack" McLaughlin III in 1992. An urgent-care center was built on the Garst's/Eddie's site in 2016. (Above, courtesy of Myrna Ragar.)

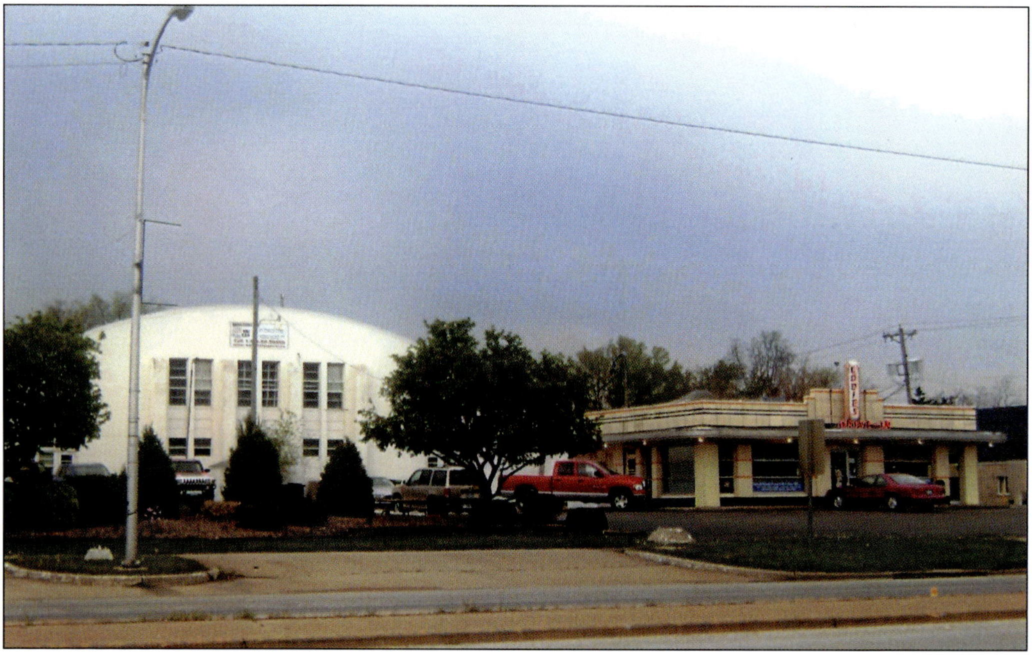

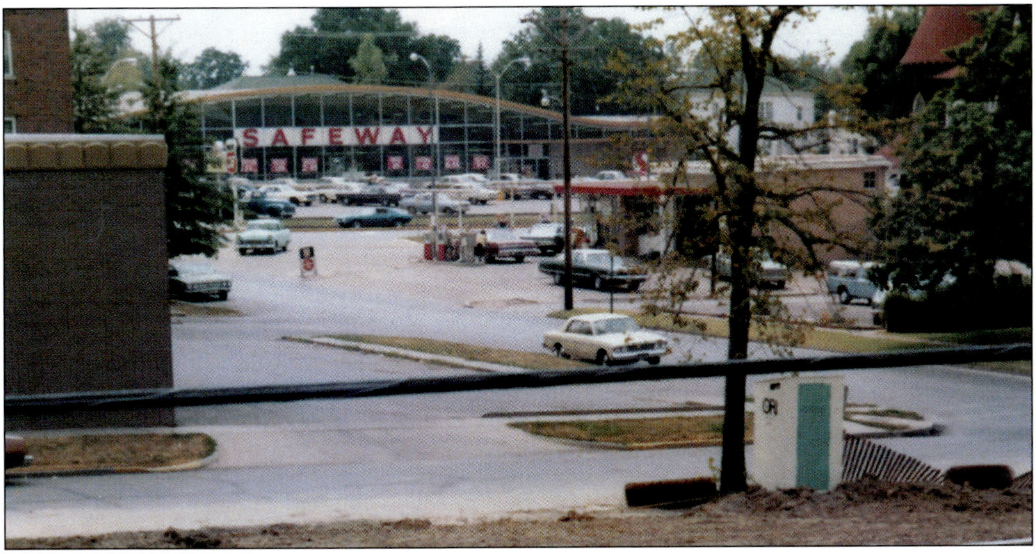

A new Safeway store opened on the former site of the Cyrus Newkirk mansion in 1965. Newkirk, president of First National Bank, moved to the corner of Broadway Boulevard and Ohio Avenue in 1871. His home featured marble mantels, hot and cold water, gas heat, and servants' bells. In 1911, a row of Craftsman-style houses replaced the Newkirk mansion. These houses were removed in 1964 for construction of the Safeway. (Courtesy of First Baptist Church.)

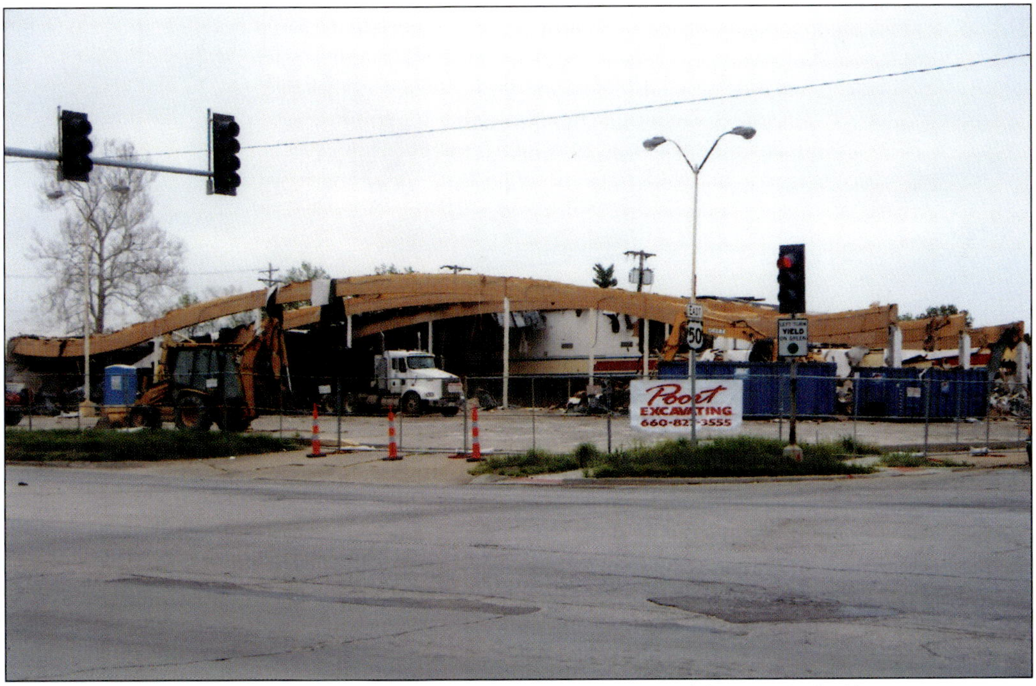

The distinctive architecture of the Safeway building remained for nearly half a century, even after Safeway closed. The grocery store became Woods Supermarket and remained until 2013, when Woods moved to 701 East Broadway Boulevard. The Safeway store building was razed in 2013 for construction of a CVS Pharmacy.

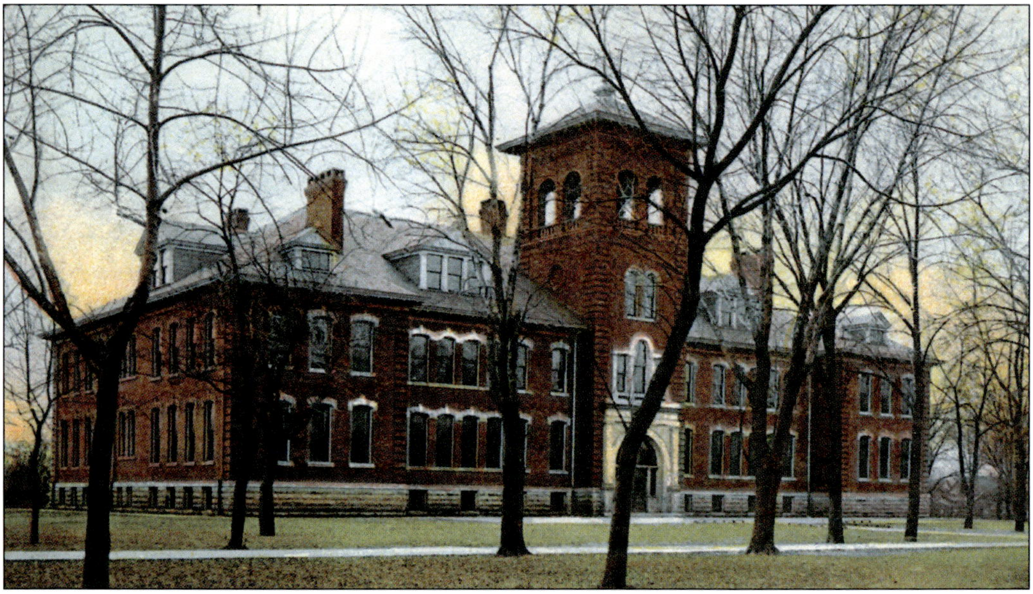

Broadway School at 301 West Broadway Boulevard was completed in February 1868 at a cost of more than $20,600. The Broadway School most Sedalians remember (pictured) was built in 1904, replacing the 1868 structure. Broadway School operated until 1962. The school building was torn down in 1968.

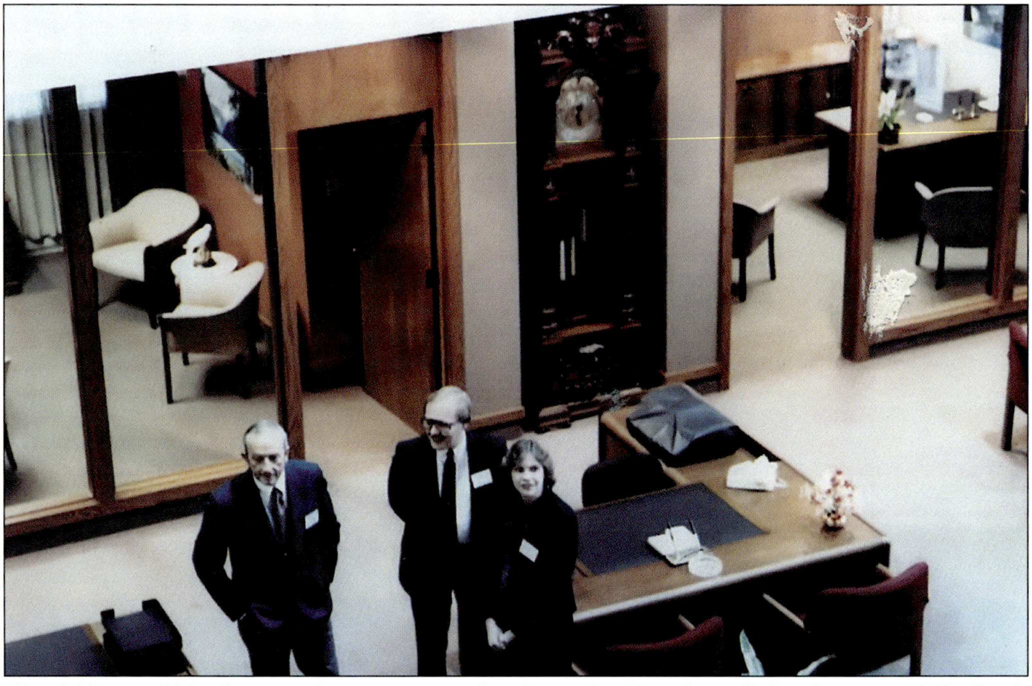

Third National Bank erected its new main bank on the Broadway School site in 1980. Bank president H.W. Harris is pictured at left during the bank's grand opening. In the background is a grandfather clock Harris's grandfather Henry Wilson Harris purchased for his wife, Leona Boggs Harris, in 1906. The $550 timepiece graced their home at 705 West Sixth Street before it was moved to Third National Bank. (Courtesy of Jane Harris Yount.)

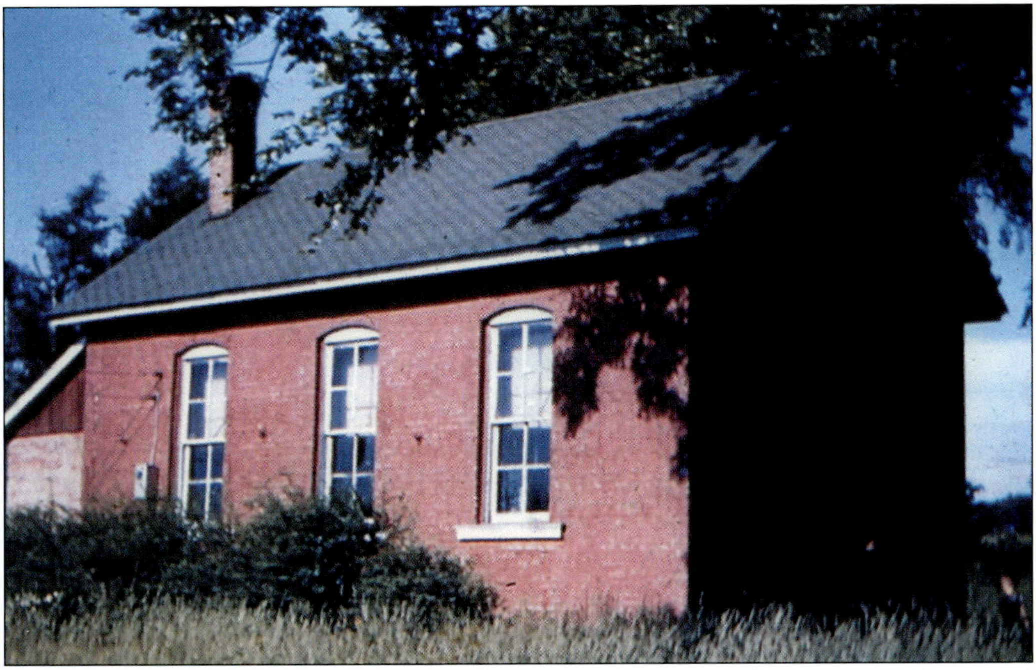

McVey School, a one-room schoolhouse at Sedalia's east city limits, was built in 1886 and remained in service until 1956. In 1966, the Pettis County Historical Society leased the school from the Sedalia Board of Education for $1 a year and worked to restore the structure's interior and exterior. The school officially opened as a historical landmark in 1971 when Rep. William Randall (below) raised a flag over the school that had flown over the Capitol. Randall is pictured with a plaque bearing the seal of the City of Sedalia, presented to him by Sedalia mayor Jerry Jones. (Both, courtesy of Jane Harris Yount.)

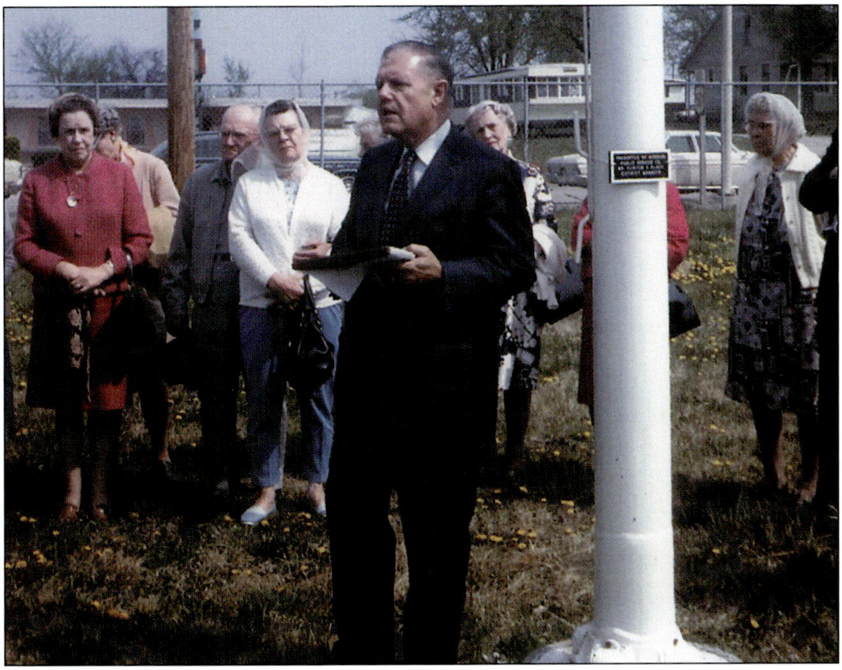

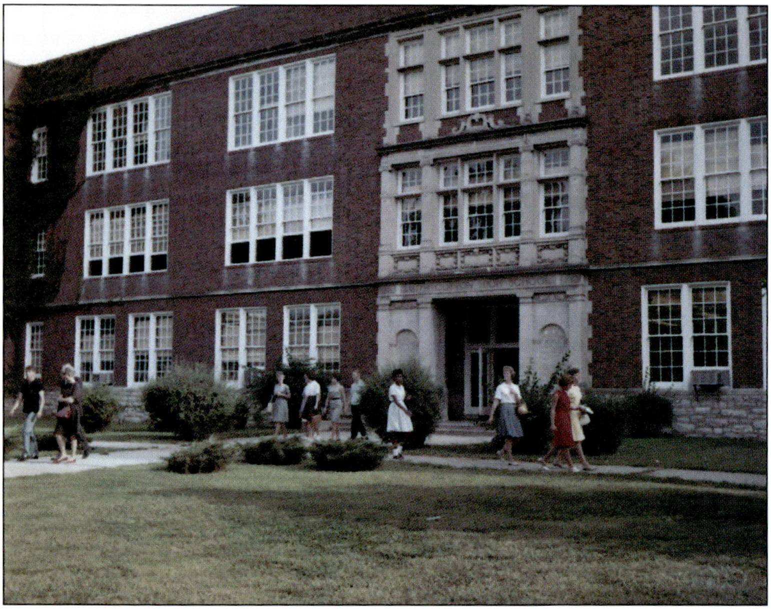

Smith-Cotton High School opened in 1925 on land donated by Sarah Smith-Cotton, the daughter of Sedalia's founder, George R. Smith. The $400,000 school was built directly behind the Smith mansion at 312 East Broadway Boulevard. When a new Smith-Cotton High School opened south of Sedalia in 2010, this school became Smith-Cotton Junior High.

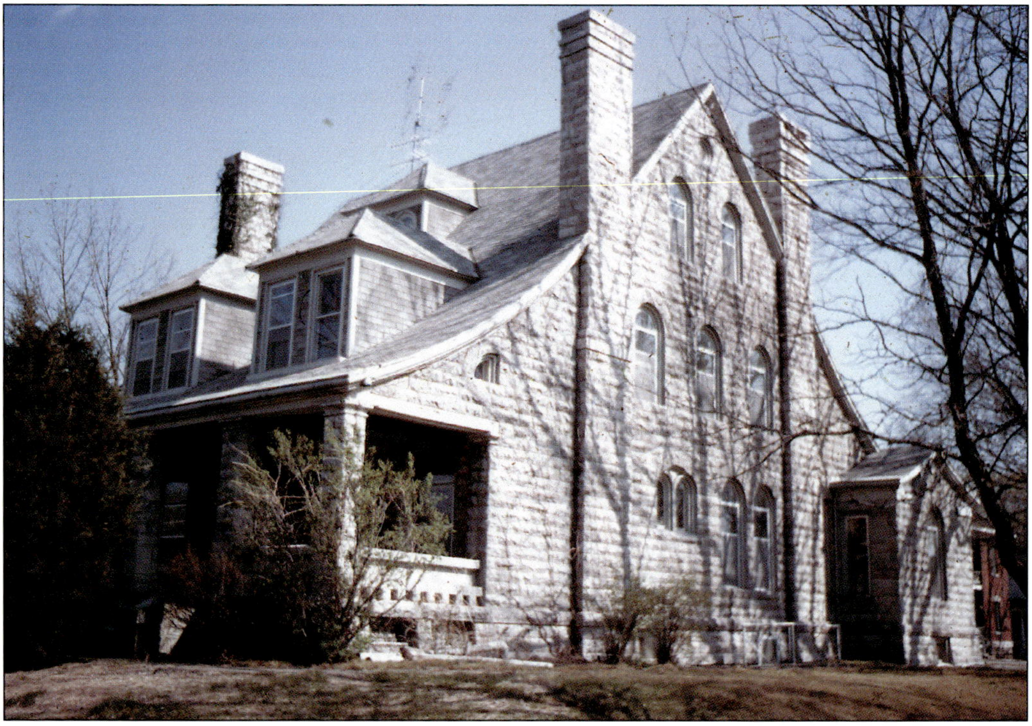

The J.C. Quigley home was located immediately west of Smith-Cotton High School, on the corner of Broadway Boulevard and Massachusetts Avenue. Stately in its own right, the $10,000 house was erected in 1900 on the site of Albert Parker's 1871 mansion. Parker was the first president of Third National Bank. The Quigley home was razed in 1969 to provide a practice field for the high school. (Courtesy of Jane Harris Yount.)

W.H. Powell, president of Citizens Bank, purchased this home at 209 East Broadway Boulevard around 1905. On November 1, 1931, he shot himself amid concern about the impending Depression. He died three days later, and Citizens Bank closed permanently. Powell's home and a neighboring house were torn down in 1964. Griff's Burger Bar was erected in their place.

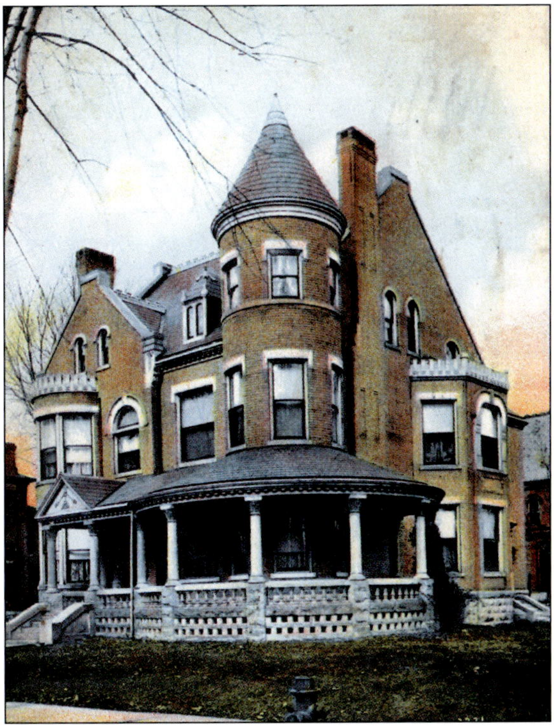

Griff's Burger Bar offered 15¢ hamburgers when it opened in 1965. Harry Naugel, Abe Silverman, and W.D. Whitaker owned the Sedalia franchise. *Sedalia Democrat* columnist Travis McMullen noted that "the Griff's grief was thick" when the burger bar closed in 2011, as demonstrated by the fact that the restaurant ran out of food before its last day of scheduled operation.

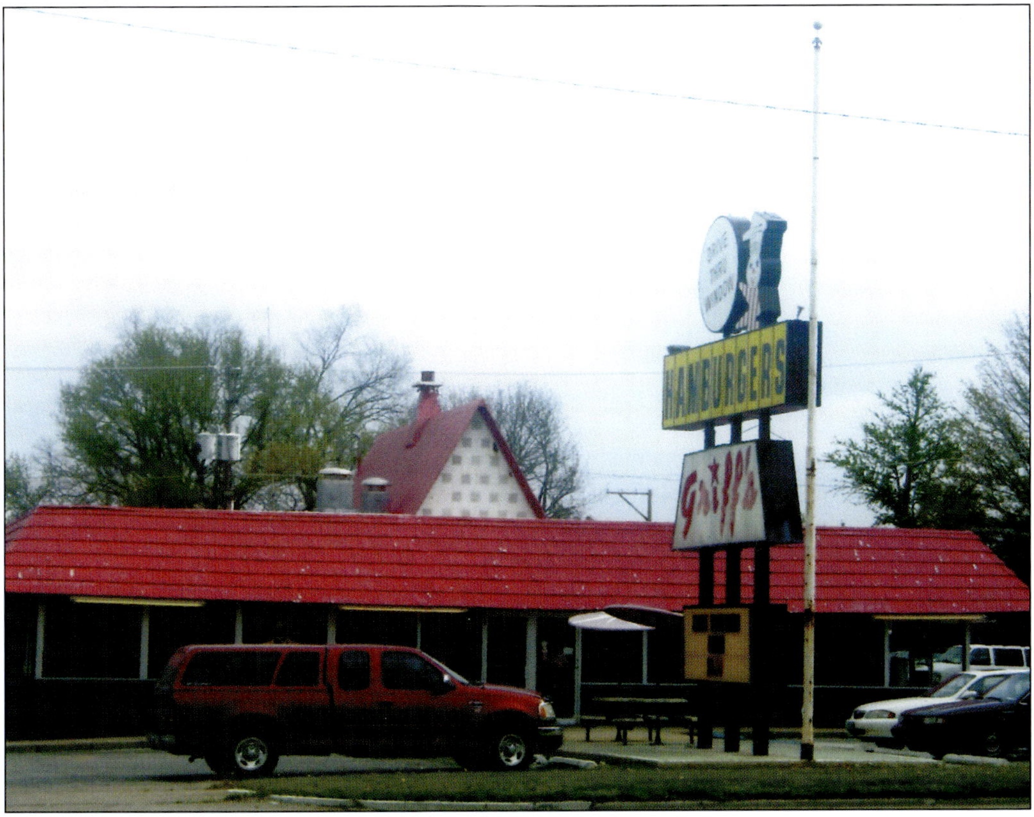

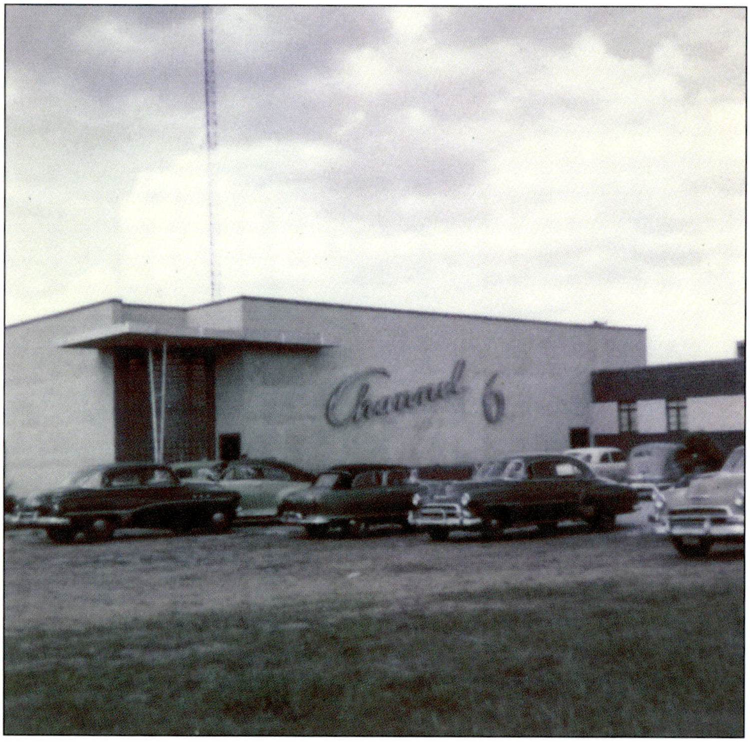

In 1939, Albert and Robert Drohlich received a permit to operate Sedalia's first radio station, KDRO. Its first broadcast occurred on September 15, 1939, from the Liberty Theater. The Drohlichs erected a building at Broadway and State Fair Boulevards for the radio station. An adjoining studio for KDRO's television station, KMOS-TV Channel 6, was completed in 1954. The television studio was the largest between Hollywood and Chicago. (Courtesy of KDRO Radio.)

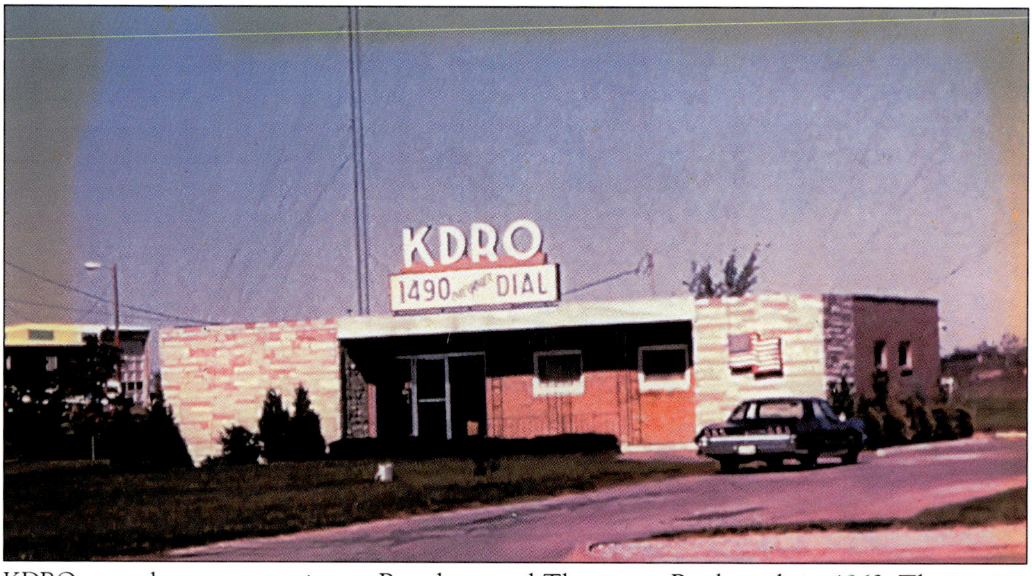

KDRO moved to a new station at Broadway and Thompson Boulevards in 1963. The station featured 1,700 square feet on the ground floor, including a control room, studio, transmitter room, newsroom, three offices, and full basement. The station planned to increase reception by boosting power to 1,000 watts during daylight hours and 250 watts at night. (Courtesy of the Sedalia Public Library.)

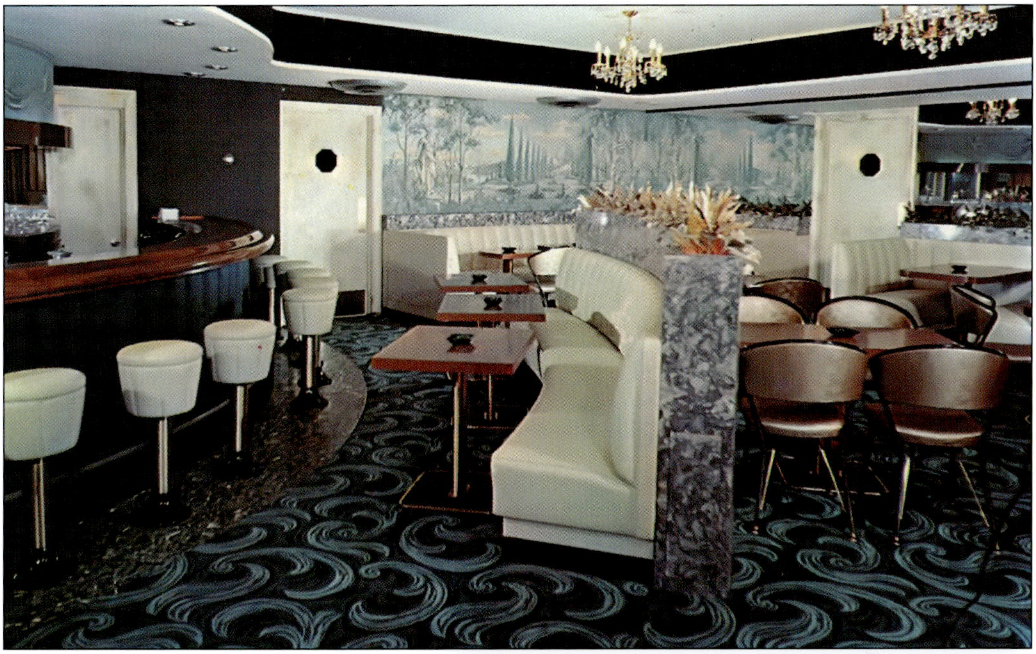

Charles Thompson and Jim Carter opened Broadway Lanes at 2119 West Broadway Boulevard in 1957. Built at a cost of more than $300,000, the bowling alley featured 16 lanes and seating for 100 spectators. This image highlights the Empress Room, part of a 1963 remodel that the *Sedalia Democrat* described as a "picturesque French setting." Broadway Lanes became known as Shooters Lanes in 2009 and as Strikerz-Sedalia in 2015.

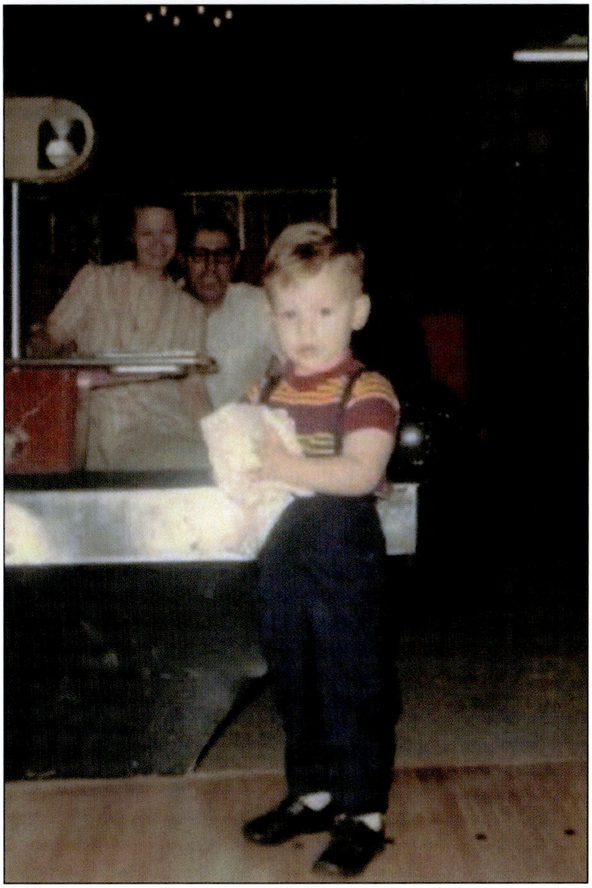

Betty Rose Thompson, wife of Charles Thompson, snapped this photograph of Kevin Walker on Lane 11 at Broadway Lanes around 1967. Kevin's parents, Mary and Carl Walker, are seen in the background. Kevin bowled in the Bantams, a children's league, and later brought home a trophy from a state tournament in the junior/senior leagues. (Courtesy of Kevin Walker.)

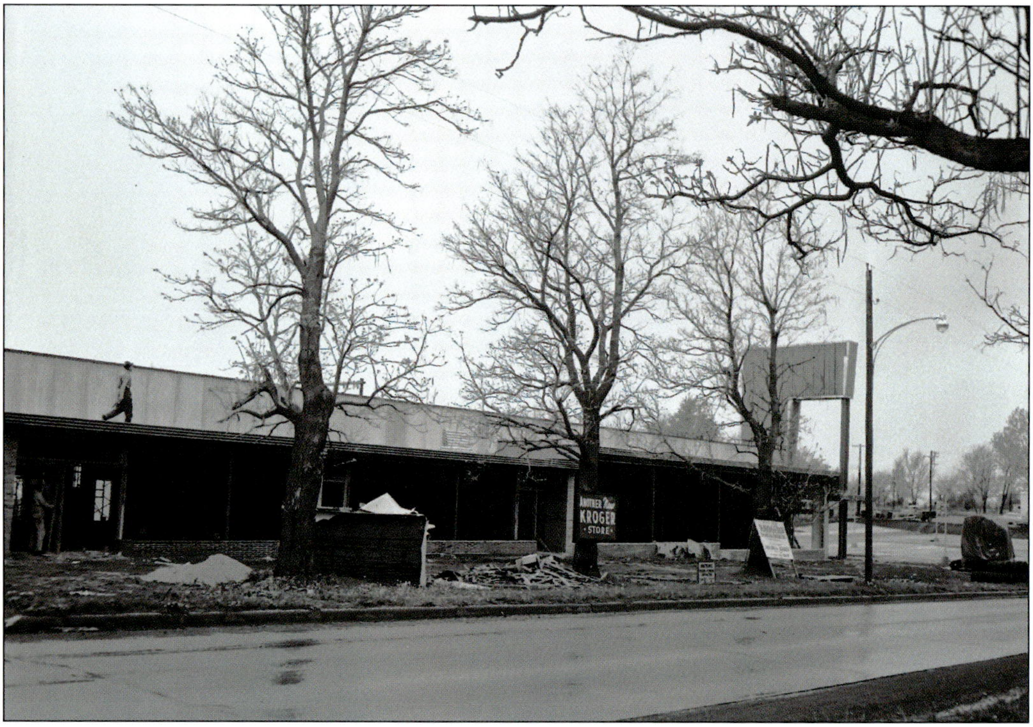

When businesses began moving from downtown in the early 1950s, the Kroger grocery store was among the first to make the exodus. The supermarket relocated from its longtime home at 602 South Ohio Avenue to a new shopping center called Broadway Plaza at Broadway Boulevard and South Warren Avenue. The new 12,000-square-foot store featured a 90-car parking area.

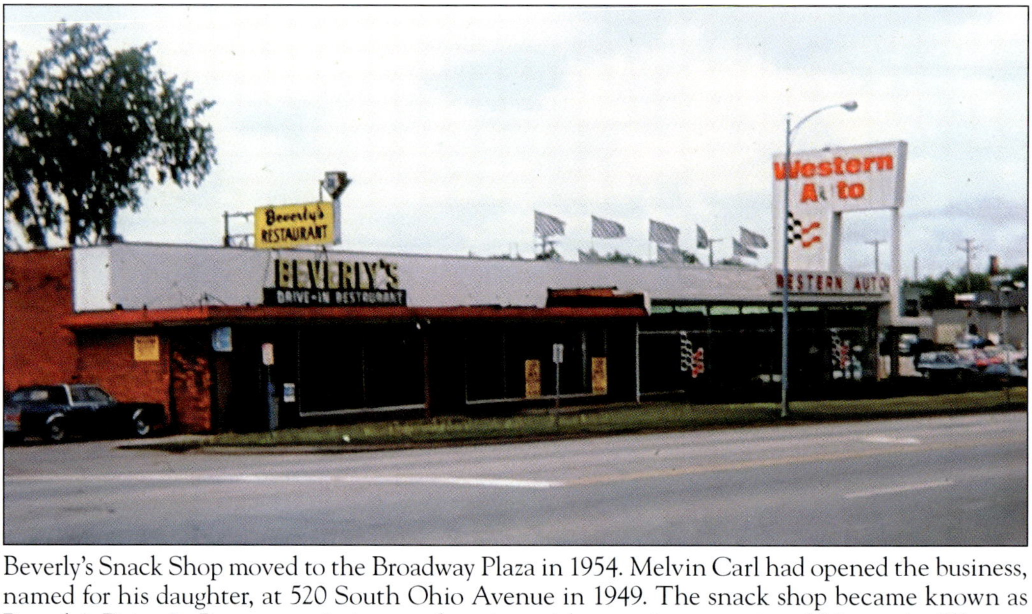

Beverly's Snack Shop moved to the Broadway Plaza in 1954. Melvin Carl had opened the business, named for his daughter, at 520 South Ohio Avenue in 1949. The snack shop became known as Beverly's Drive-In Restaurant in its new location with a seating capacity of 90 people. Western Auto had moved to the Kroger building by the time this photograph was taken. (Courtesy of the Sedalia Public Library.)

E.W. Thompson broke ground for the Thompson Hills Shopping Center in January 1964. The $4 million venture was located on Broadway Boulevard, west of Sedalia on Thompson's cattle ranch. Pictured are, from left to right, Consumer's Market, Tempo, Lee's Shoes, Julie Ann Fabrics, and TG&Y. (Courtesy of the Sedalia Public Library.)

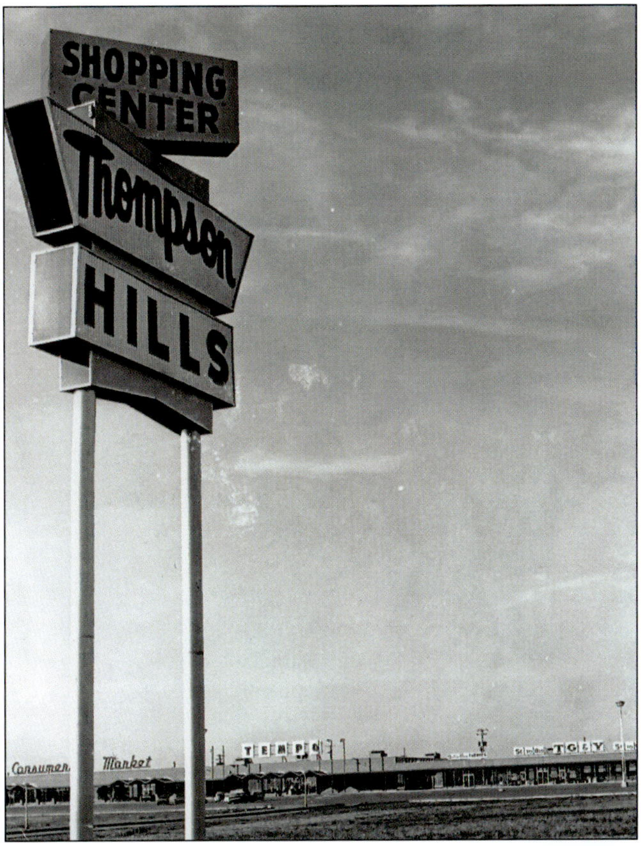

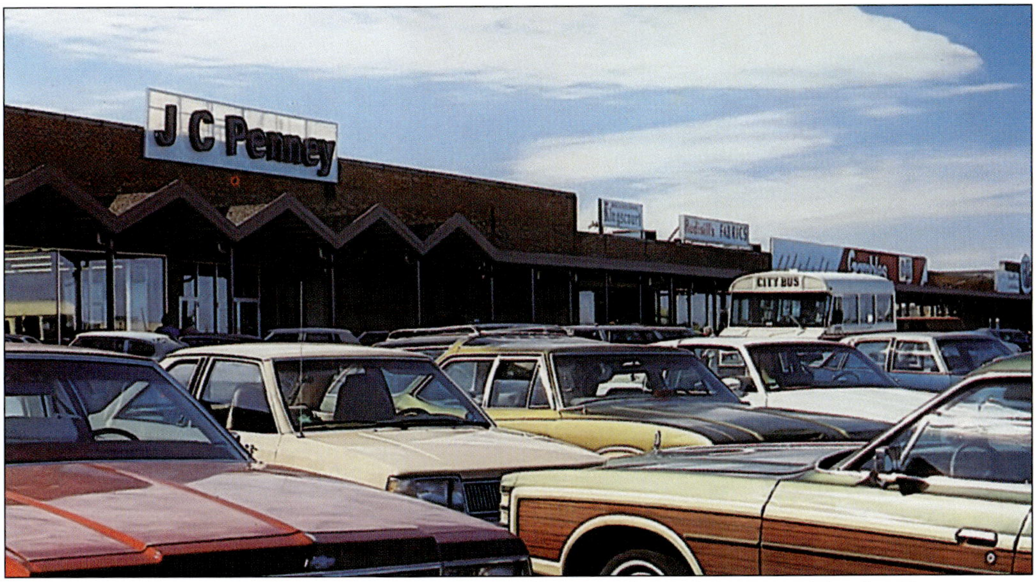

In 1975, J.C. Penney moved to the Thompson Hills space formerly occupied by the Tempo store. Penney's had been located at 232 South Ohio Avenue in downtown Sedalia for nearly half a century. Also shown in this 1980s photograph are, from left to right, Kingscourt Factory Outlet, Rudisill's Fabrics, and Gambles. (Courtesy of the Sedalia Area Chamber of Commerce.)

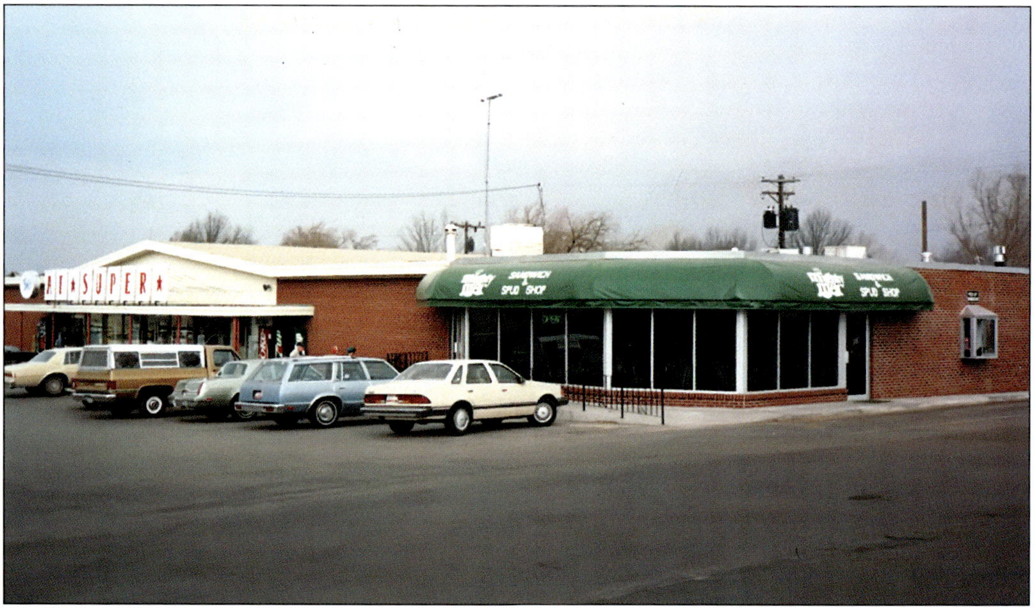

In 1988, Bob Wasson fulfilled his dream of owning a grocery store when he purchased the local IGA from McNuff, Inc., and opened Bob's AF Super (above) at 2402 West Broadway Boulevard. Bob began his career with Safeway in San Diego, where he met his wife, Elle. In 1974, Bob and his family moved to his native Sedalia, where he was a store manager for Consumers Market. Elle opened a Mighty Melt Sandwich and Spud Shop in 1984, which moved to a new building next to Bob's AF Super in 1989. Bob and Elle Wasson are pictured below with their son-in-law Rick Vaughan in Bob's AF Super in 1995. The Wassons sold Mighty Melt to Dale and Ginny Arnett in 1990 and closed the grocery store in 1999. Wasson was serving his second term as mayor of Sedalia at the time of his death in 2009. (Both, courtesy of Elle Wasson Duggan.)

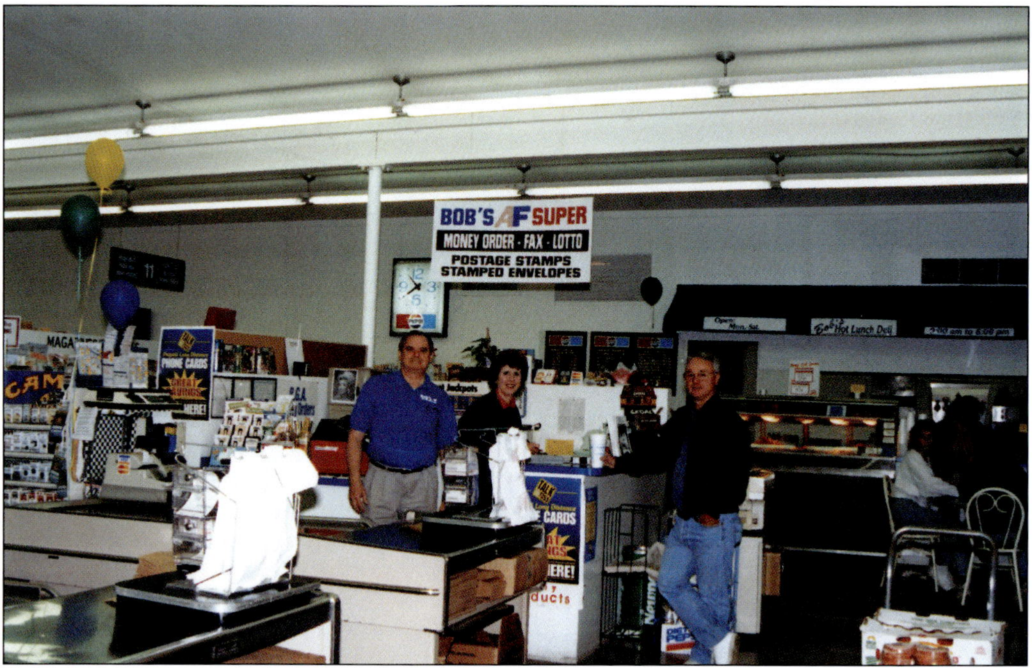

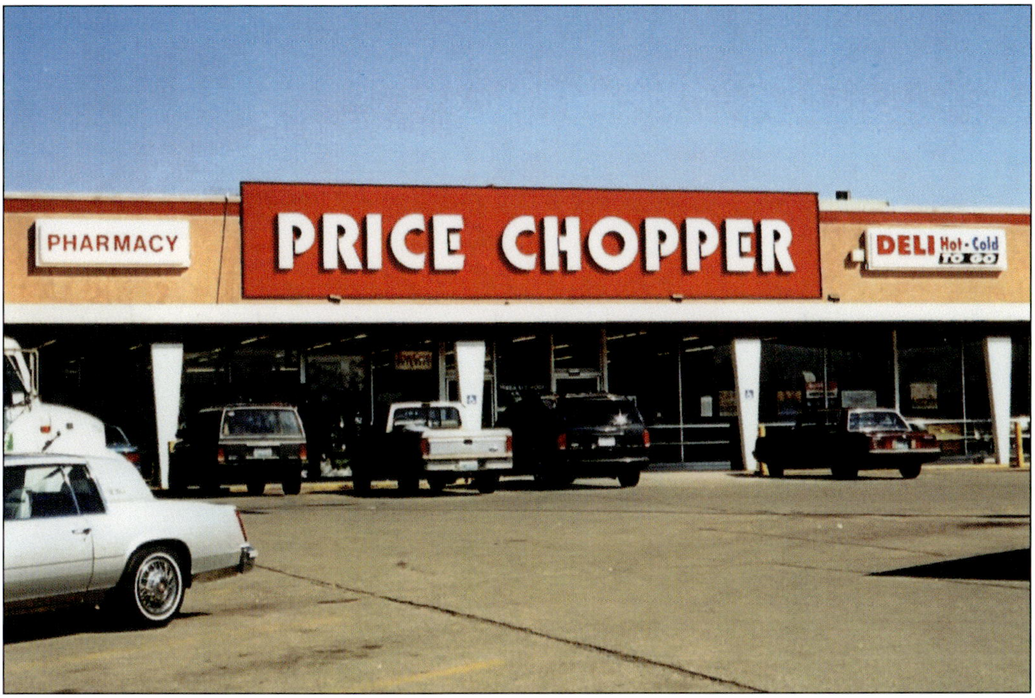

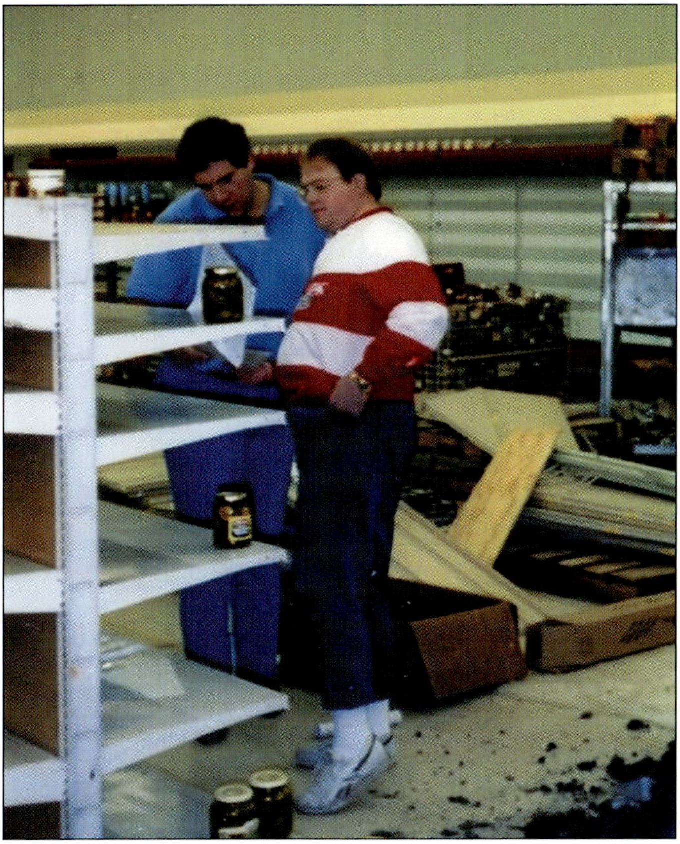

Price Chopper was located on the former site of the Missouri-Kansas-Texas railroad hospital, which was razed in 1931; the location became Washington Park. In 1968, construction began on a Kroger Family Center at the site. Kroger's at 711 East Broadway Boulevard devoted one-third of its 50,000 square feet to groceries and food items. The other two-thirds offered general merchandise, such as men's and women's clothing, records, toys, gifts, hardware, and sporting goods. The family center also included a pharmacy, snack bar, and two-bay automobile service area. East Consumer's and Woods supermarkets later moved to the site. Mike Bolin (left) and Jim Bremer are pictured at right in Price Chopper. (Both, courtesy of Tom Munson, WEB & Sons.)

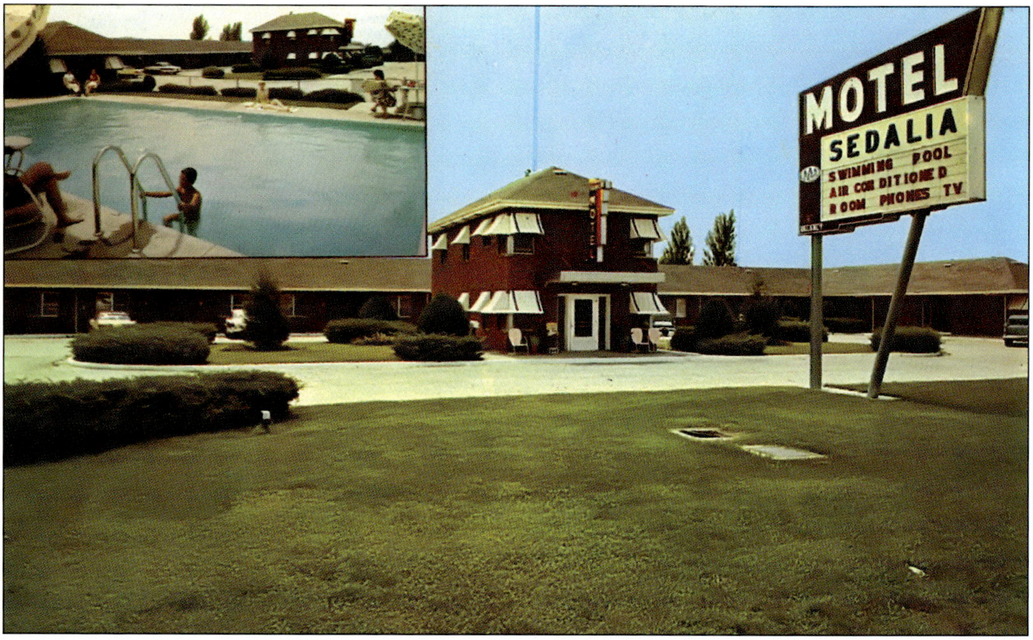

Sedalia's first three motels, or "tourist courts," were constructed in 1950, including the Sedalia Motel. It was located at 2601 West Broadway Boulevard, then a quarter mile west of the Sedalia city limits. Owned by Lloyd and Dorothy Phillips, the 20-unit motel was built with living quarters in the center of the structure. An automotive store is now located at the site.

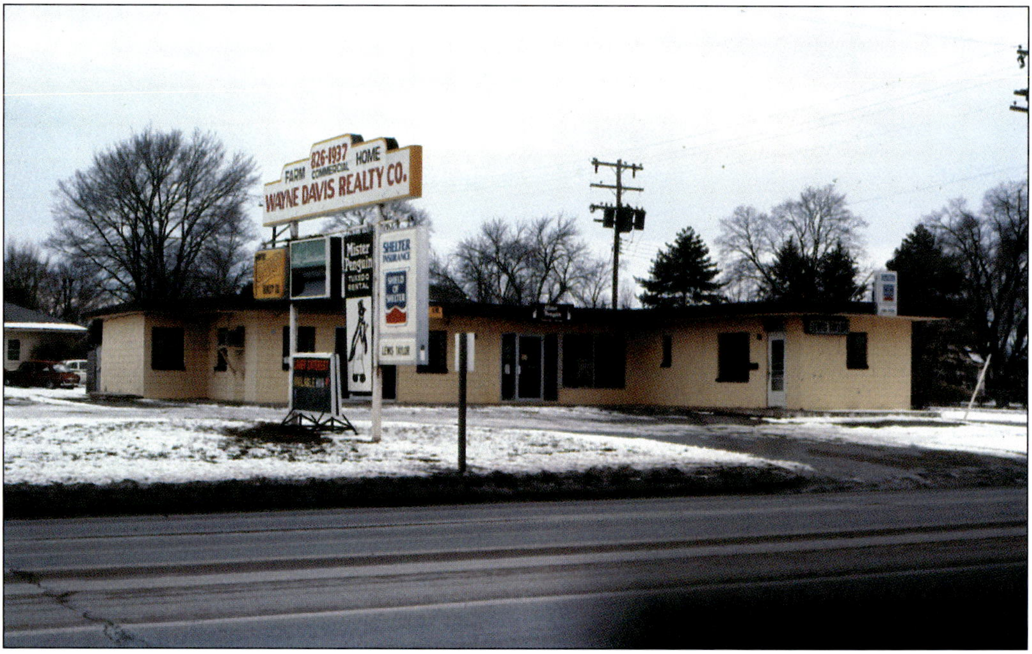

The Boots Hotel Court, owned by Loyd and Dorothea Boots, was built in 1950. Located at State Fair and Broadway Boulevards, the $50,000 motel featured 10 units. By 1960, each room had been equipped with a television and radio. The property was later converted to offices, as shown in this 1982 photograph. (Courtesy of Tom C. Taylor.)

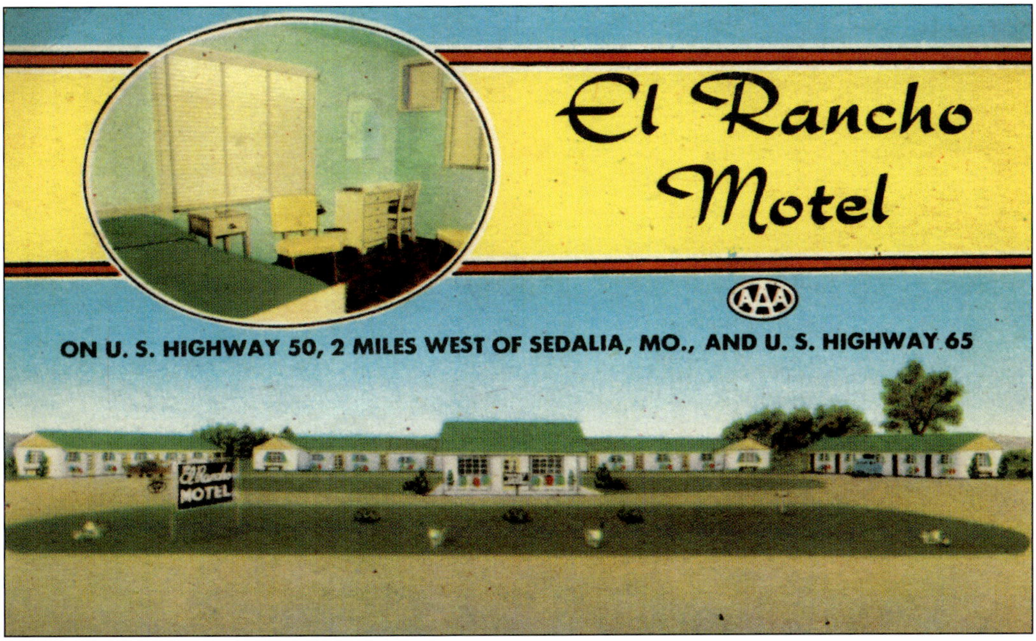

Wes and Lillian Morris built the El Rancho Motel on 22 acres two miles west of Sedalia in 1950. Described in an early postcard as "new and modern in every respect," the ranch-style motel offered 18 single and four double units. Because of its distance from Sedalia, the motel had its own central heating plant and drilled well.

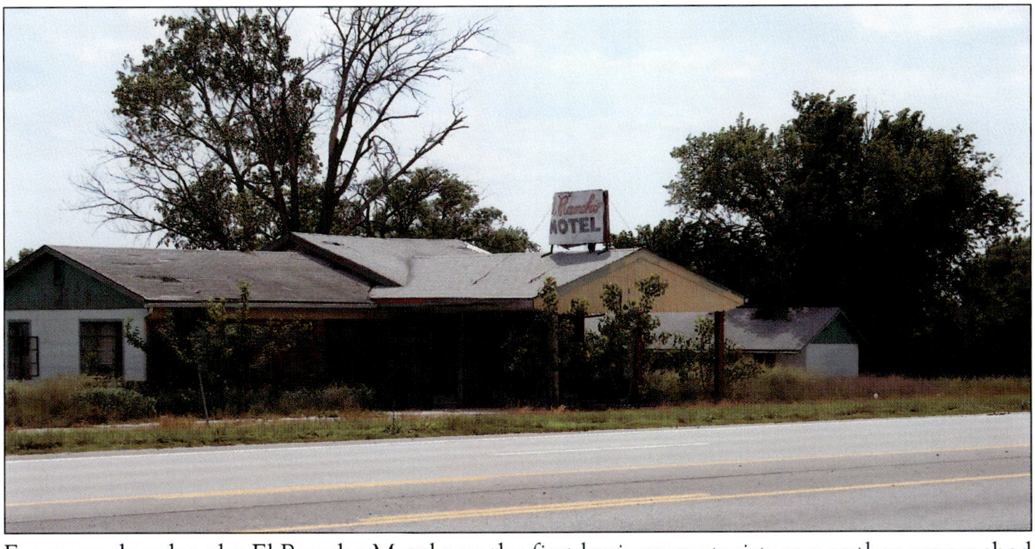

For many decades, the El Rancho Motel was the first business motorists saw as they approached Sedalia from the west. It became an eyesore after it was abandoned in 2004. By this point, Sedalia's development had moved westward, and new businesses had opened near the dilapidated structure. The motel was demolished in 2012.

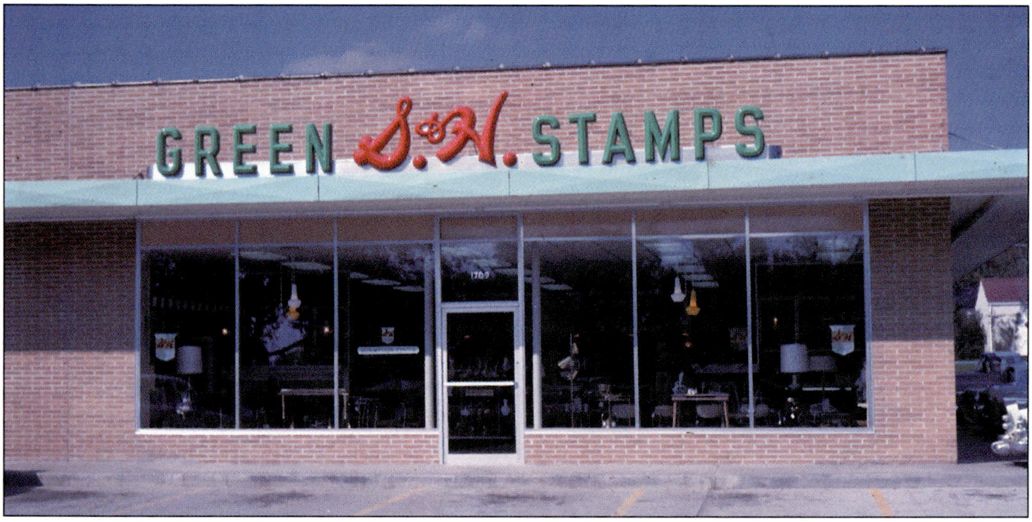

S&H Green Stamps opened a new redemption center at 1709 East Broadway Boulevard in 1962. Pictured shortly after its August 1 ribbon cutting, the business offered a choice of more than 1,500 "famous brand name products." Sedalians could earn trading stamps by buying groceries or dry goods, as well as practicing the piano or test-driving a new car.

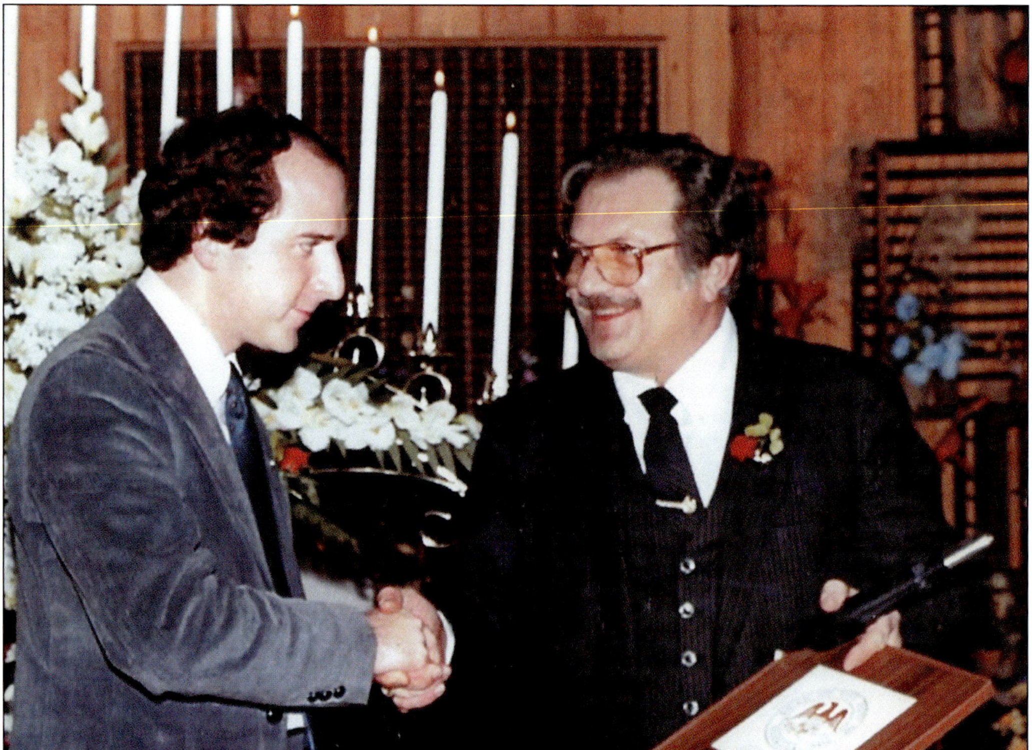

In the early 1980s, Greg Cecil (left), executive vice president of the Sedalia Chamber of Commerce, presented Bill Cline with a plaque from the Sedalia mayor recognizing Kim Originals' outstanding contribution to Sedalia's economic development. Kim Originals erected a new building at 2500 East Broadway in 1967 for its permanent floral and decor business. (Courtesy of Greg Cecil.)

Three

UNLIMITED LIMIT

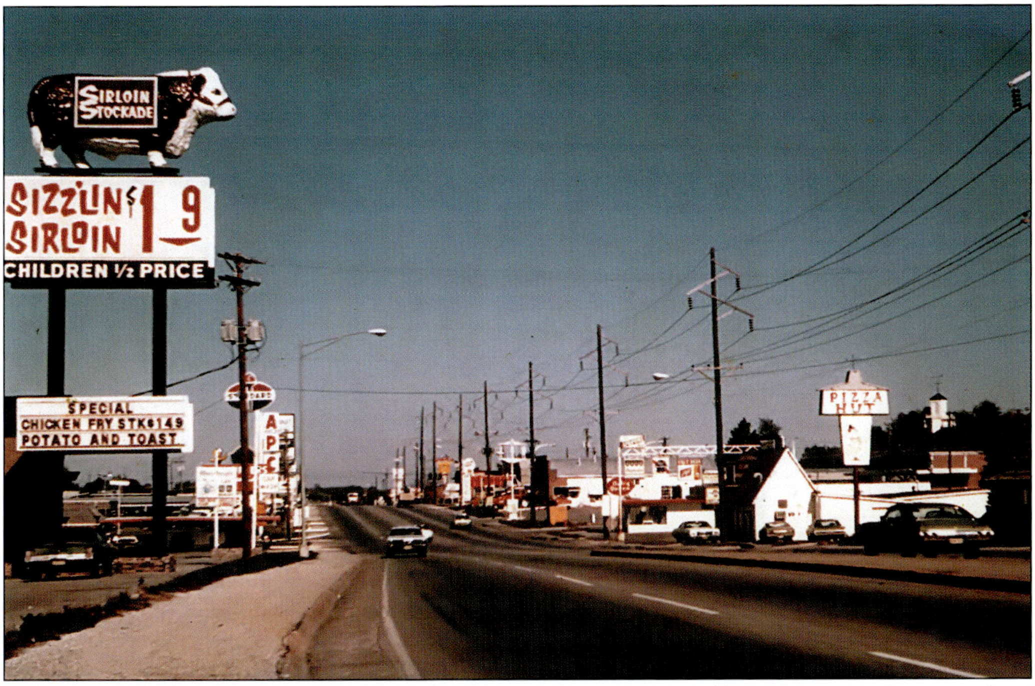

Sirloin Stockade's "Big Cow" attracted motorists to a variety of businesses in this stretch of South Limit Avenue. The steak house opened at 1500 South Limit Avenue, near the State Fair Shopping Center, in 1973. The $60,000 building seated 180 people and offered free ice cream with each meal. Healthy Habits, a health food store, is now located in the building. (Courtesy of the Sedalia Public Library.)

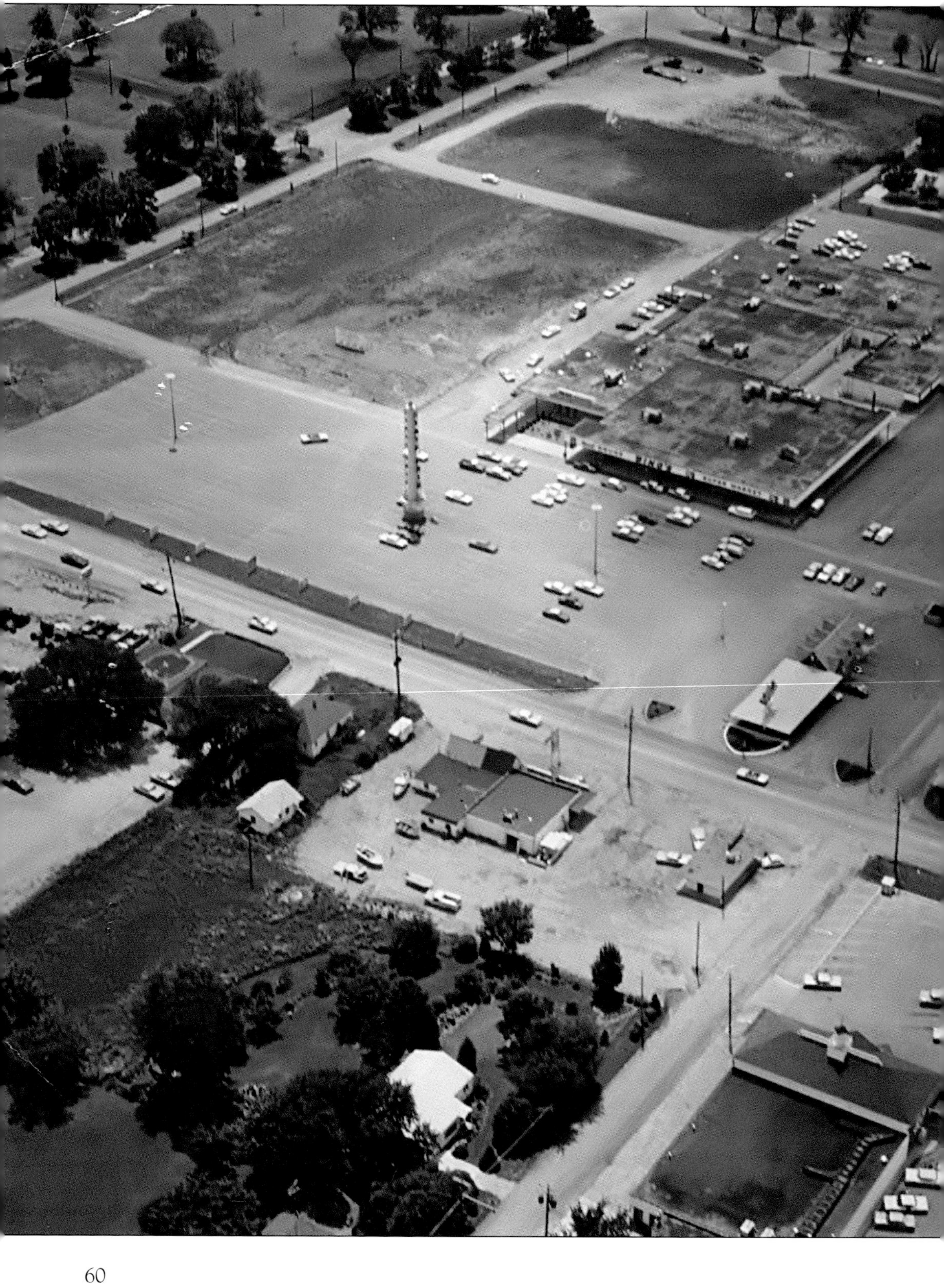

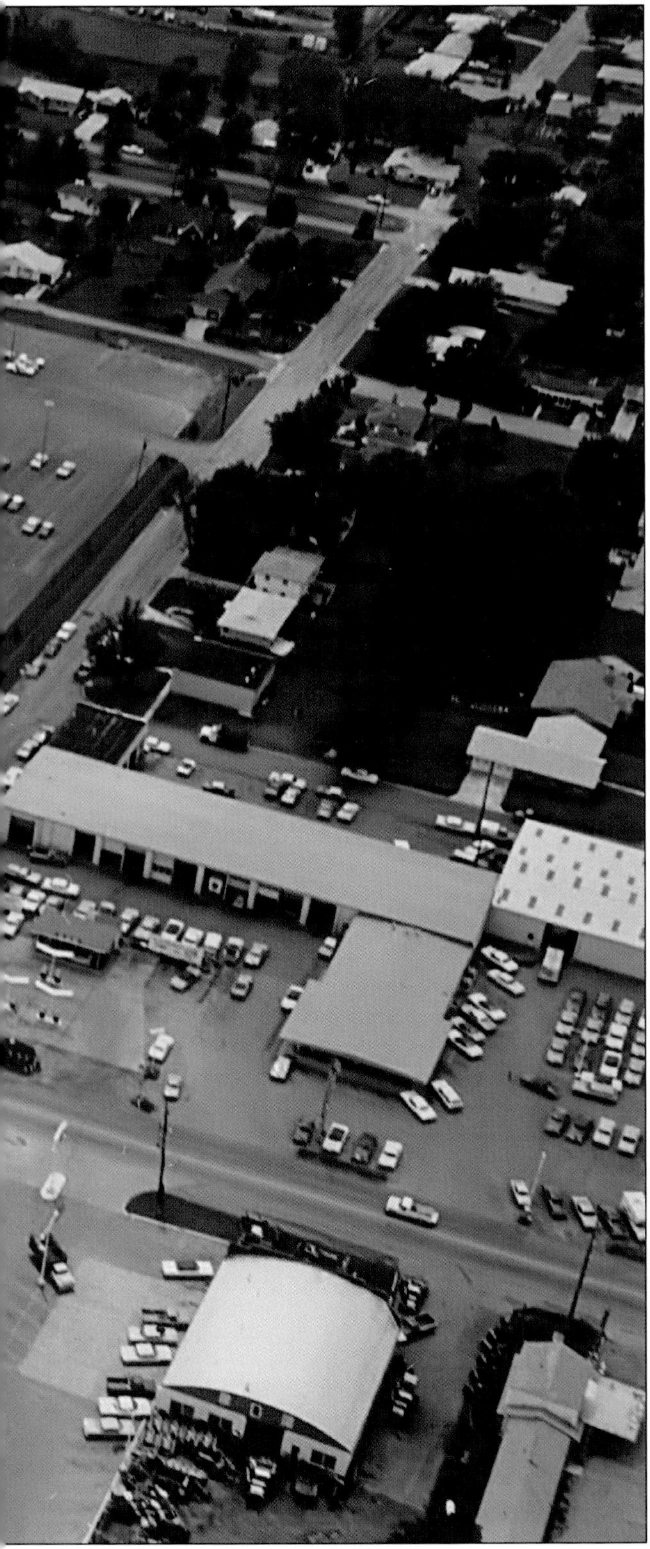

This aerial view of South Limit Avenue was taken between construction of the State Fair Shopping Center in 1965 and construction of the W.T. Grant department store (now Kmart) in 1969. State Fair Shopping Center appears near the center of the image. Sixteenth Street is at the upper left, separating the Missouri State Fairgrounds from the shopping center. Businesses in the photograph include, from left to right, (upper) State Fair Shopping Center, Ku Ku Burger Bar, John's Apco, and Mike O'Connor Chevrolet-Buick-GMC; (lower) White's Cleaners, State Fair Marine, Dairy Queen, A&P Foods, Gibson Implement, and the Show-Me-Kort Motel. (Courtesy of the Sedalia Public Library.)

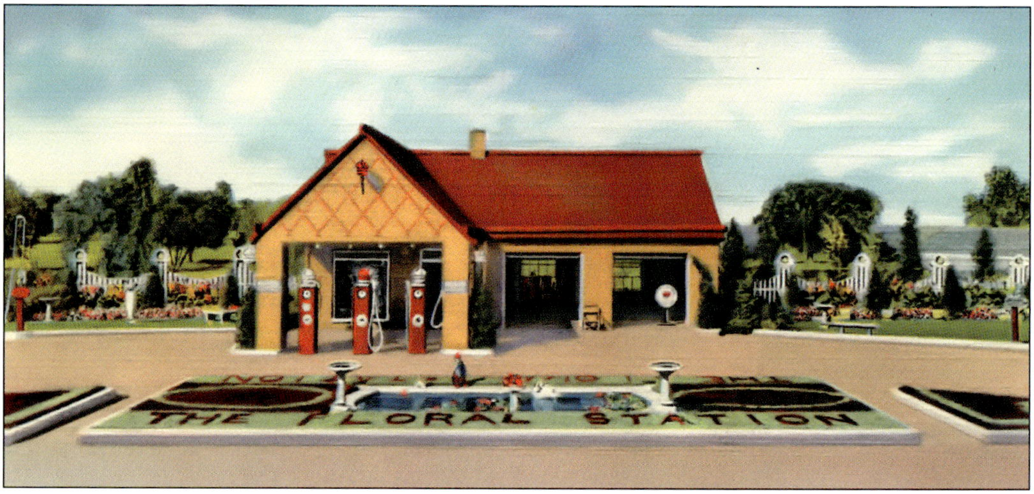

Dr. Julian Cannaday's Floral Station at Sixteenth Street and South Limit Avenue featured a goldfish pond and playhouse for children. The lavish landscaping is not surprising, as Cannaday owned the State Fair Floral Company. His greenhouses were located behind the station. Dr. Cannaday, a nationally recognized physician for treating skin diseases, died in 1956.

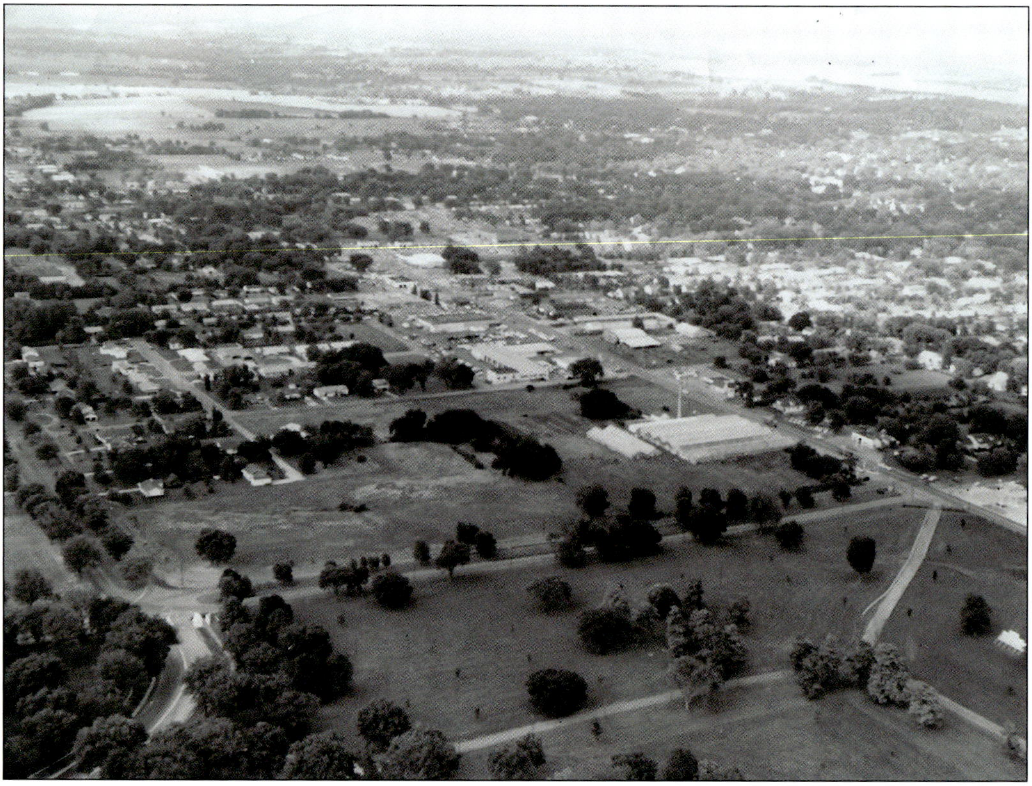

The State Fair Floral Company's greenhouses appear in this aerial view of South Limit looking northeast from the Missouri State Fairgrounds. The Floral Station was located to the east of the greenhouses, facing South Limit Avenue. When the State Fair Shopping Center was built on the site, the smokestack from the greenhouses became the shopping center's distinctive sign. (Courtesy of the Sedalia Public Library.)

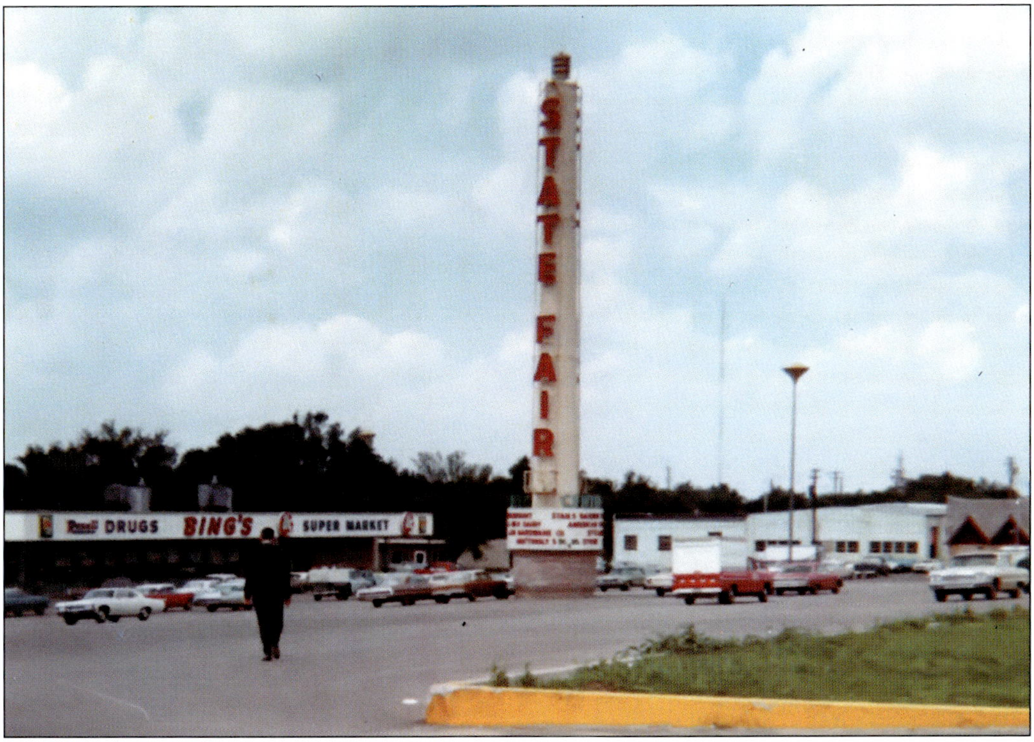

W.E. Bingaman built State Fair Shopping Center on 14 acres at the corner of South Limit Avenue and West Sixteenth Street. Its first phase, including Bing's Supermarket, opened in 1965. Bingaman founded Bing's at South Limit Avenue and Eleventh Street in 1952. Operating as WEB & Sons, Bingaman's descendants now manage the vast real estate holdings that branched out from a single supermarket. (Courtesy of Tom Munson, WEB & Sons.)

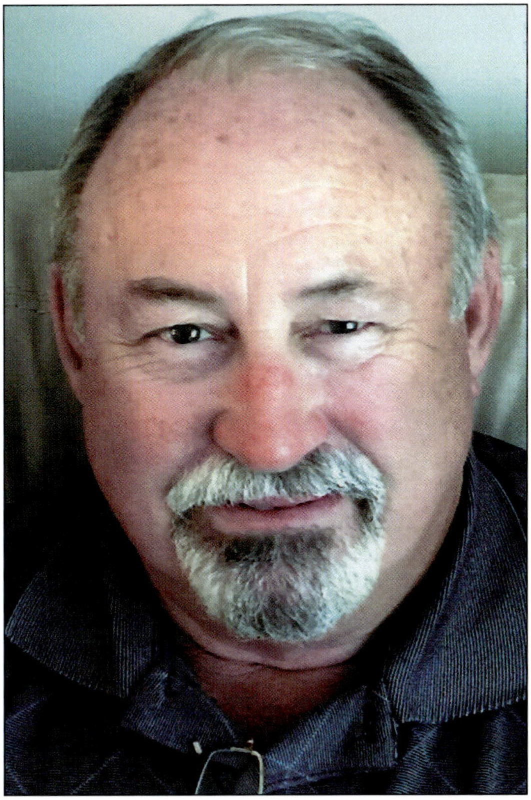

Tom Munson began his career with WEB & Sons as a building, maintenance, and construction supervisor in 1975. He previously worked in the carpenter shop for the US Army Corps of Engineers. He currently is president of WEB & Sons and provided photographs for this book dating from the time he started working for the corporation. (Courtesy of Tom Munson, WEB & Sons.)

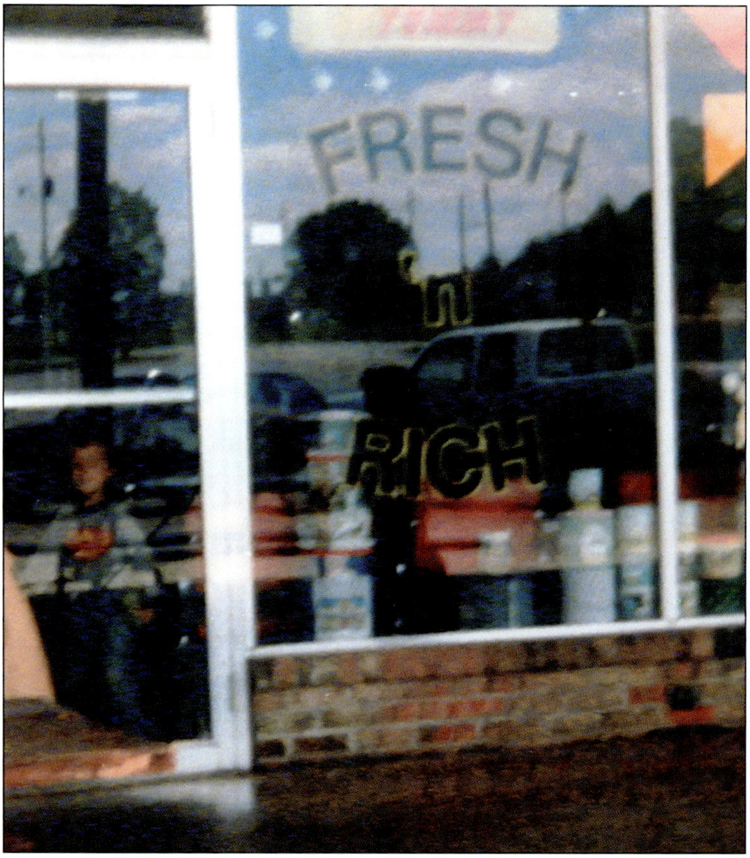

The Fresh 'n Rich Ice Cream Shop was a favorite destination for sweet treats. One of the original stores when the State Fair Shopping Center opened, it offered assorted flavors of ice cream, sundaes, malts, and other frozen items. The ice-cream shop was operated by the Tullis Hall Dairy, which owned a similar business at 541 East Fifth Street. (Courtesy of Duane and Brenda Edwards.)

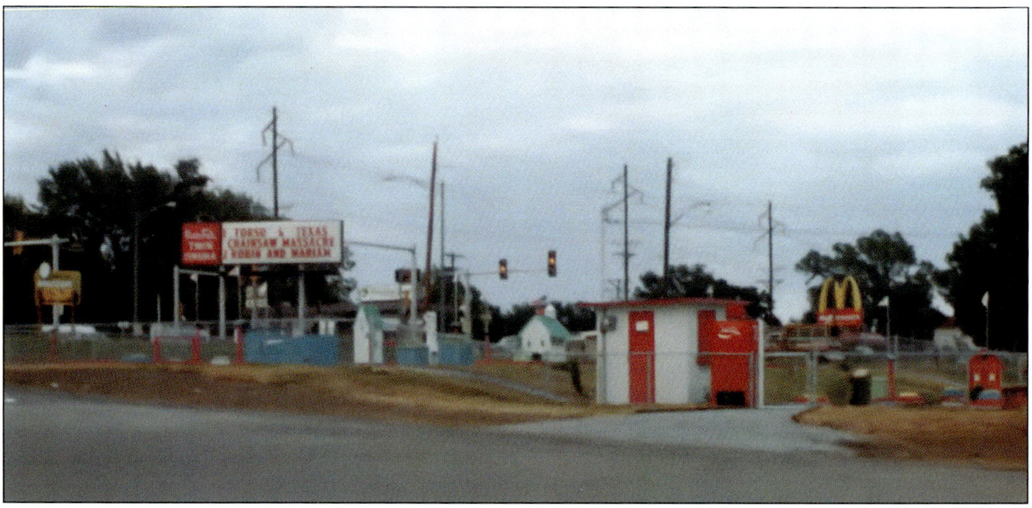

What was better than a hole in one at the State Fair Miniature Golf Course? Winning a free pizza from nearby Ken's Pizza—an incentive offered to hole-in-one golfers on Tuesday nights. The miniature golf course opened at the corner of South Limit Avenue and West Sixteenth Street in 1976. Also pictured are McDonald's and the marquee for the State Fair Twin Cinema (originally Jerry Lewis Twin Cinemas), both of which opened in 1972. (Courtesy of Tom Munson, WEB & Sons.)

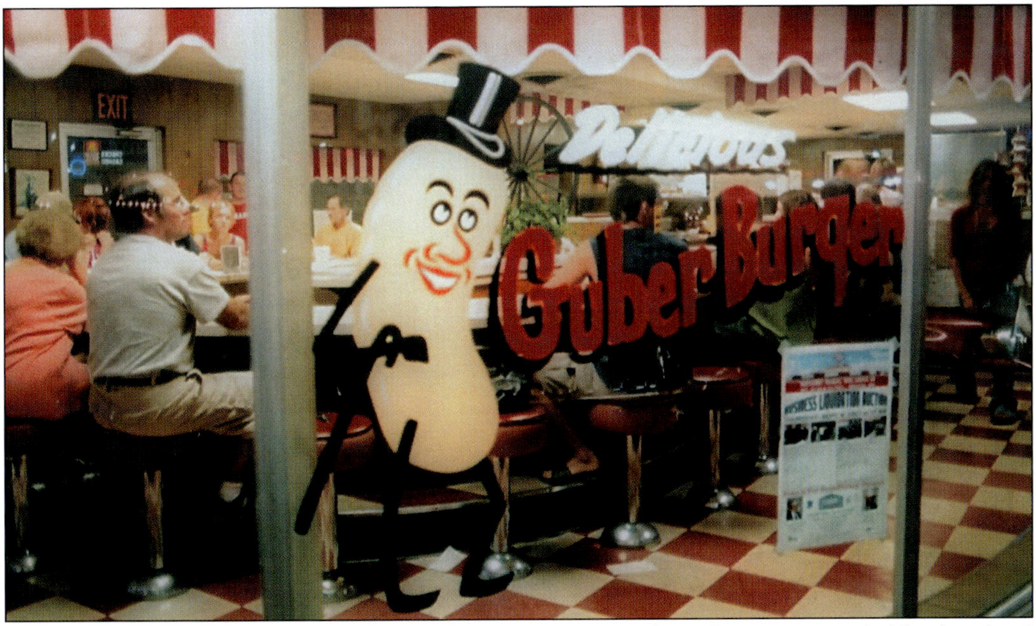

The Wheel-Inn at South Limit Avenue and Broadway Boulevard was surrounded by farmland when opened by Lyman and Ruth Keuper in 1947. The drive-in grew to national prominence while Sedalia's growth and highway construction ate away its surrounding land. In 2007, intersection expansion made it necessary to close the drive-in—but patrons will long savor memories of its famous "Guber Burger." (Courtesy of Tom C. Taylor.)

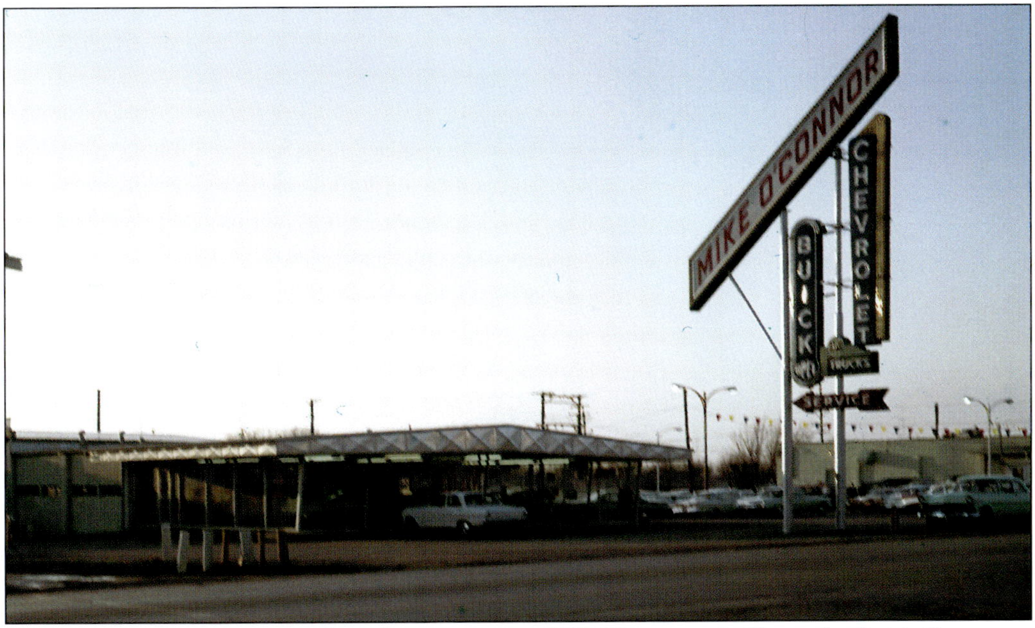

In 1951, Mike O'Connor purchased an interest in E.W. Thompson's Chevrolet-Buick Company. The newly named Thompson-O'Connor Chevrolet-Buick Company was located at West Fourth Street and Osage Avenue. O'Connor became sole owner of the dealership in 1953 and changed the name to Mike O'Connor Chevrolet-Buick Company. The dealership moved to 1300 South Limit Avenue (pictured) in 1960. (Courtesy of the Sedalia Area Chamber of Commerce.)

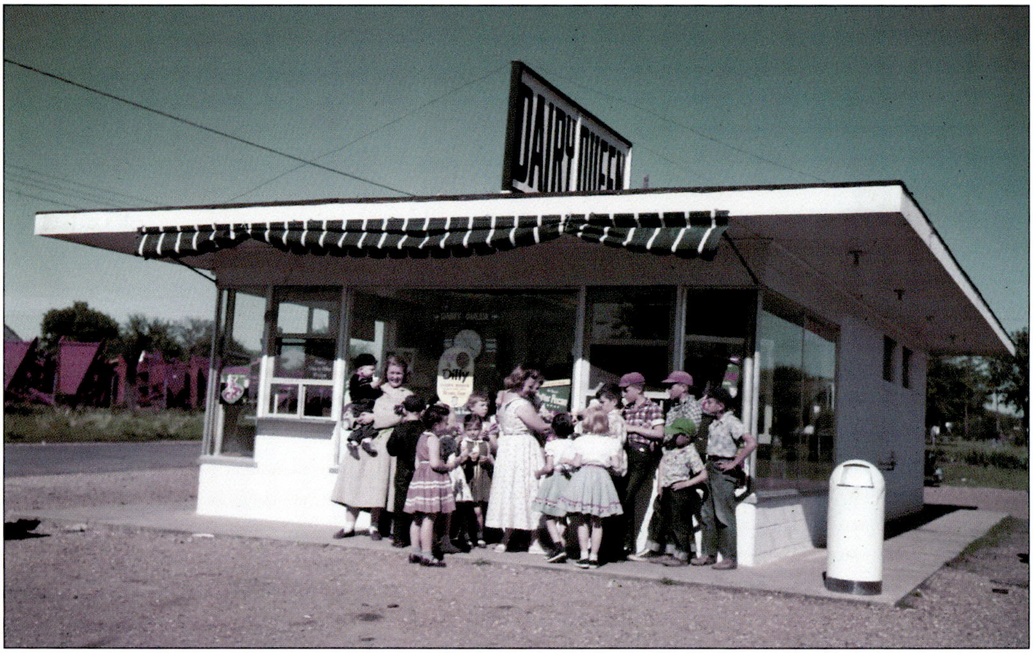

When Frank Wich and Richard Johnson opened a Dairy Queen at 1401 South Limit Avenue in 1947, it was one of only 100 such stores in the world. Sedalia's Dairy Queen remained a walk-up location until 2012, when a new DQ Grill & Chill was built a few blocks south at 1811 South Limit Avenue.

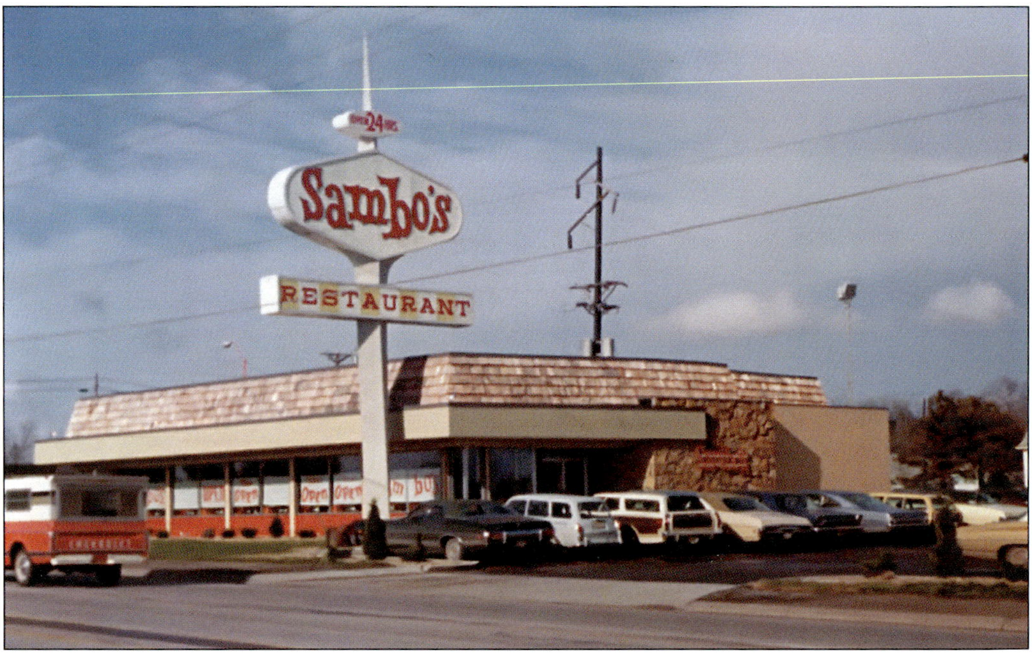

Sambo's Family Restaurant opened at 2001 South Limit Avenue in 1974. The restaurant offered seating for 160, with a banquet room for 75 people. It was the only restaurant in Sedalia open 24 hours a day, seven days a week, in the mid-1970s. County Kitchen is now at the site. (Courtesy of Tom Munson, WEB & Sons.)

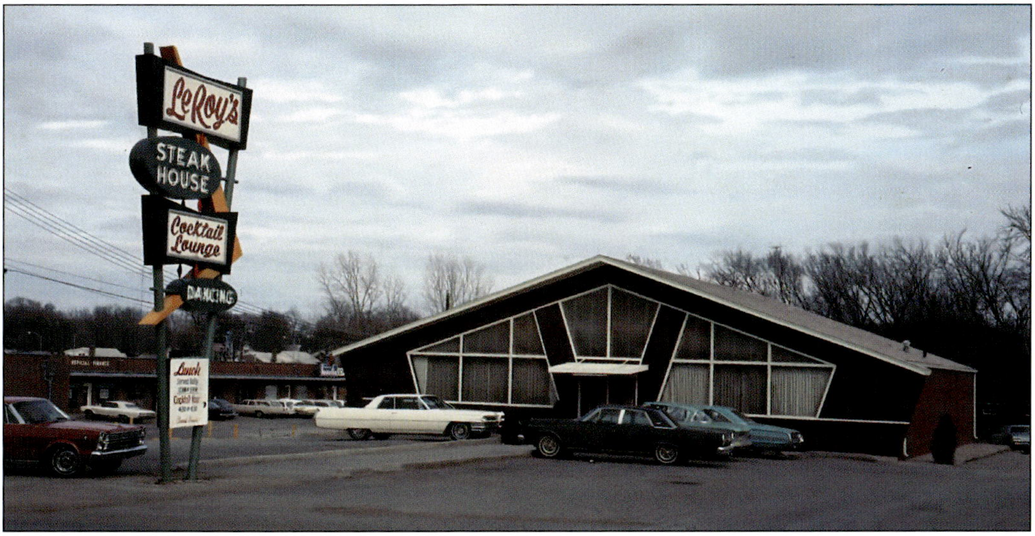

LeRoy Wells built his namesake restaurant at 905 South Limit Avenue in 1960. Wells also managed the coffee shop in the Hotel Bothwell. Jim and Doris Mathewson began operating LeRoy's in 1965, when it offered an eight-ounce boneless rib steak dinner for $1.95. The Mathewsons converted the steak house to the Carnival Pizza Pub & Eatery in 1973. The building was destroyed by a fire in 1974.

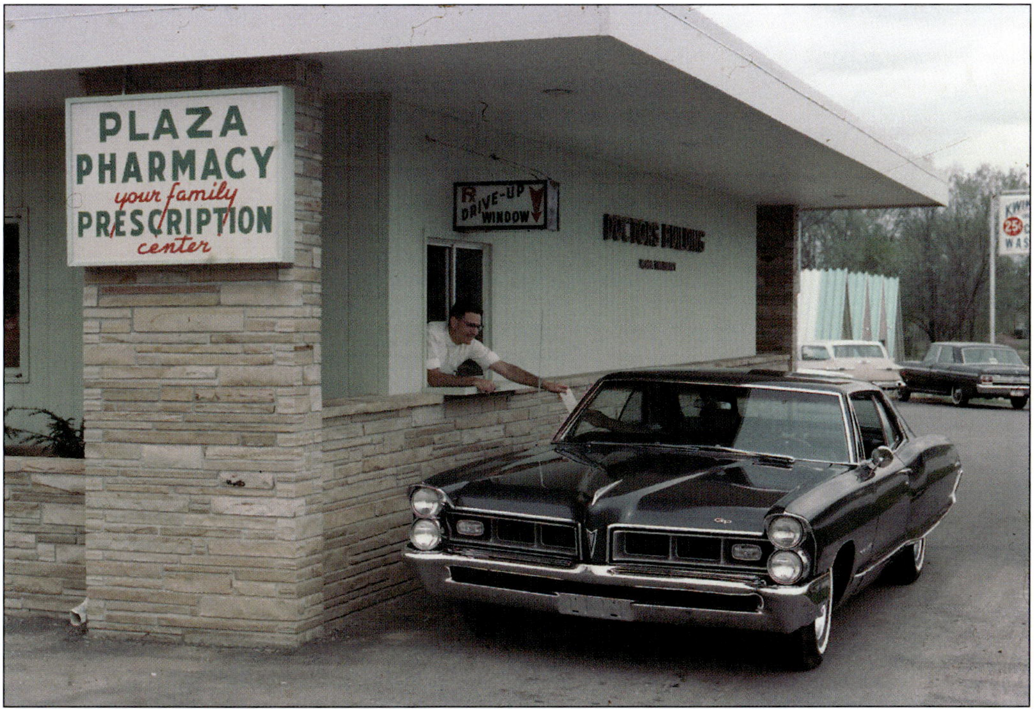

Ewing Gibson is shown serving a customer at Plaza Pharmacy in 1964, shortly after the pharmacy was expanded and remodeled. Sedalia's first drive-through pharmacy opened in the new Doctors Building at 700 South Limit Avenue in 1958. Gibson was its first registered pharmacist, followed by Bill McWhirt in 1964 and Bob Bailey in 1971. Now known as Plaza West Pharmacy, the business is located at 3330 West Tenth Street.

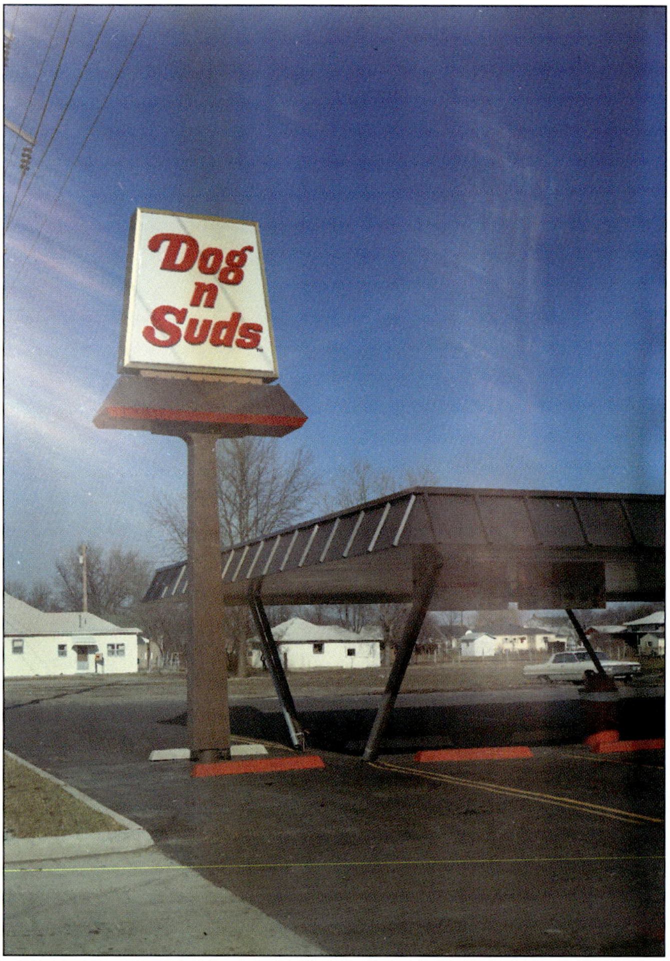

The Ed Kehde Jr. family moved from Webster Groves, Missouri, to Sedalia in 1947. In 1955, Ed opened his first drive-in restaurant, a Dog n Suds franchise, at 1120 South Limit Avenue. In 1960, he moved Dog n Suds to 1611 South Limit Avenue. After losing his lease in 1970, Kehde erected a building at 1915 South Limit Avenue in 1971 (left). In 1974, he added a restaurant at 1700 East Broadway, which closed in 1976. That same year, the Kehdes decided to go independent and started their own barbeque restaurant at their South Limit location (below). Kehde's Barbeque is now operated by second-generation John Kehde, his son Roger Kehde, and daughter Mare Kehde Schlup, with fourth-generation Lakin, Honor, and Edson Kehde becoming involved in the operations. John and Chelsea Kehde also own Chelsea's Antiques at 712 South Ohio Avenue.

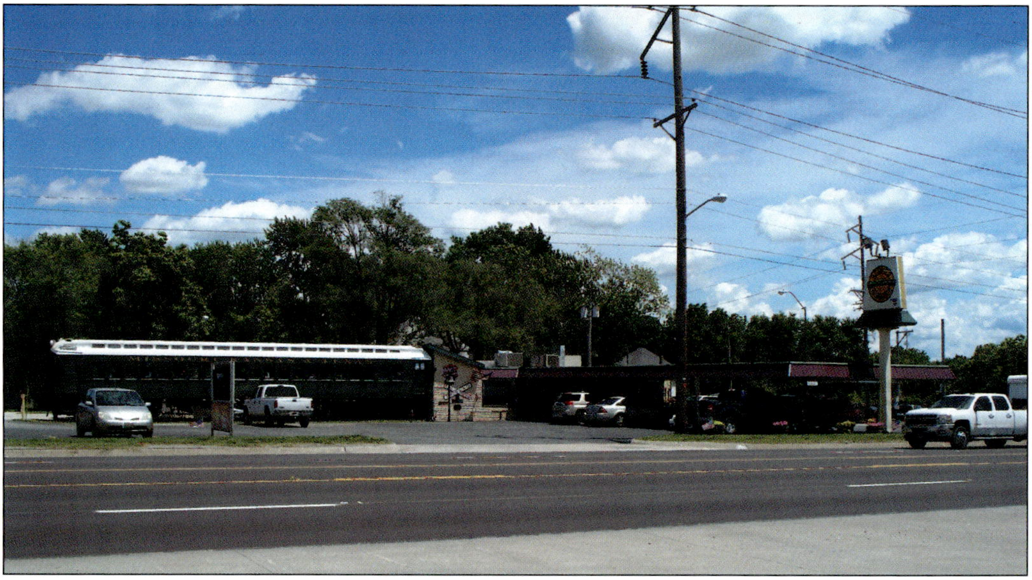

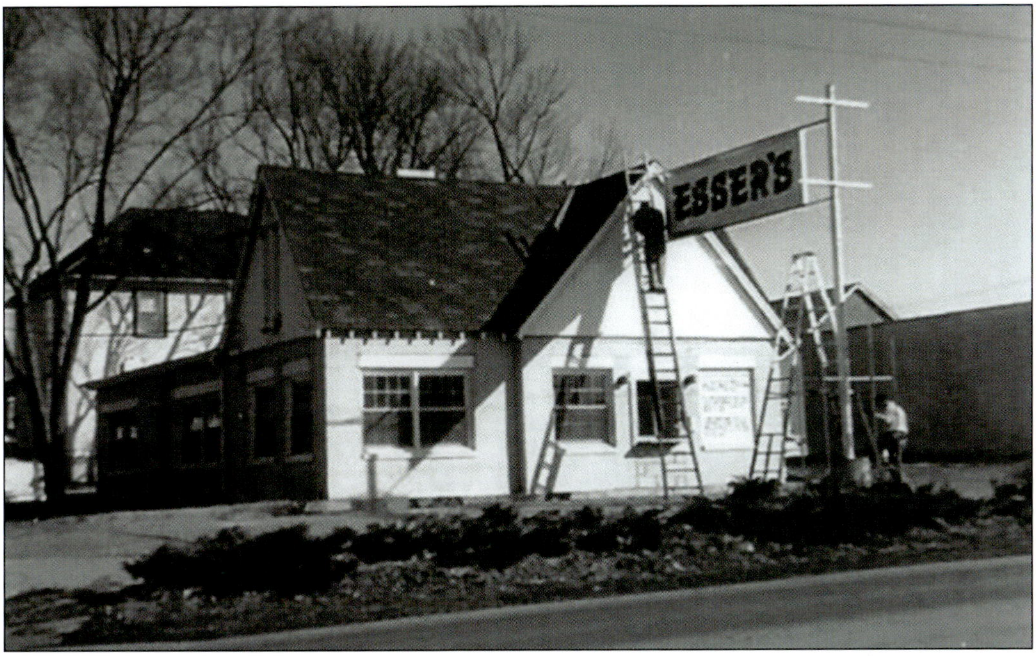

Richard Esser opened this drive-in package liquor store at 1801 South Limit Avenue in 1964. The building had previously housed a diverse array of tenants, including the Club Savoy, Paramount Club, Fairway Furniture, Jefferson Piano Company, City Laundry, and Kenny Miller Real Estate. Snappy Photo was its last business, occupying the site from 1982 to 1992. The building was razed to build a new office for Prudential Home Realty. (Courtesy of David Esser.)

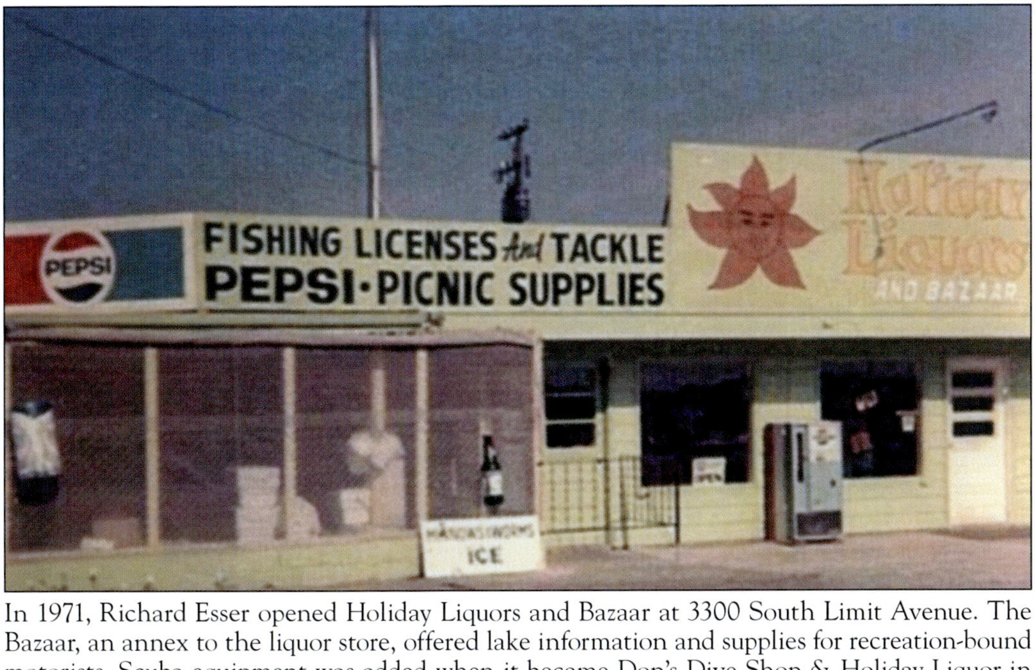

In 1971, Richard Esser opened Holiday Liquors and Bazaar at 3300 South Limit Avenue. The Bazaar, an annex to the liquor store, offered lake information and supplies for recreation-bound motorists. Scuba equipment was added when it became Don's Dive Shop & Holiday Liquor in 1974. LeMaire's Cajun Catfish & Seafood House was located at the site until moving to West Broadway Boulevard. This building was razed in 2010. (Courtesy of David Esser.)

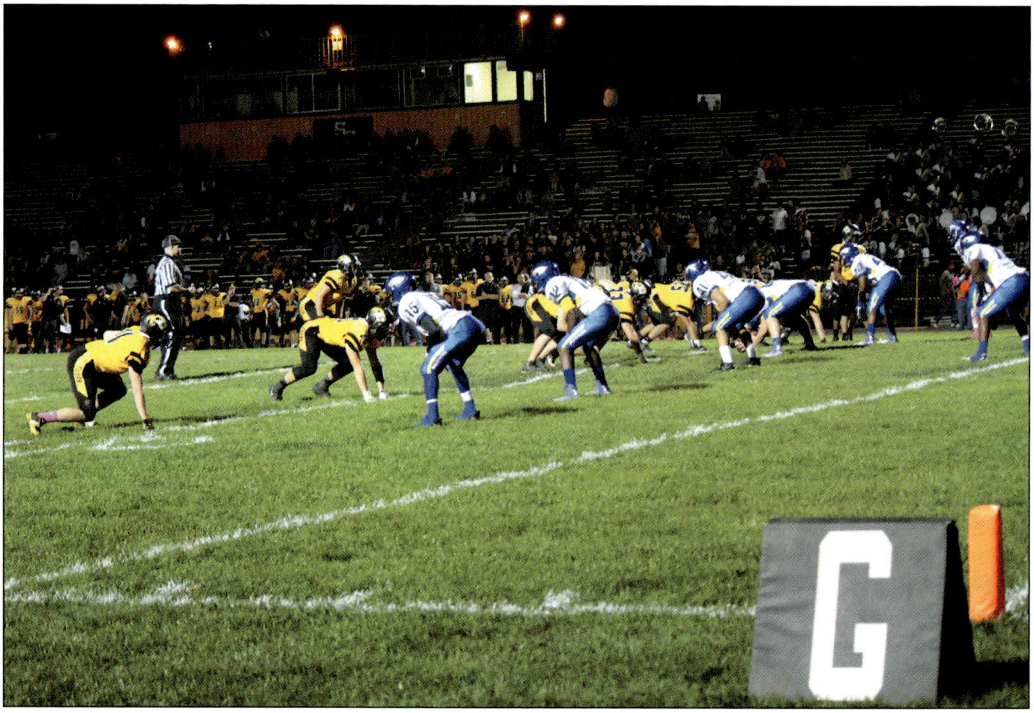

The Jennie Jaynes Stadium was named for Jennie Jaynes Lewis, a daughter of Col. A.D. Jaynes, who settled in Sedalia after the Civil War. Her will recommended that trustees use part of her estate to establish a recreational center for Sedalia. The stadium, with a capacity of 3,000, was dedicated on North Limit Avenue, near Liberty Park, in 1953. Pictured is the final game played at the stadium, a 19-12 Smith-Cotton High School district playoff win over Ruskin High School in October 2014; and below is the stadium during demolition in July 2015. (Above, courtesy of Bob Satnan.)

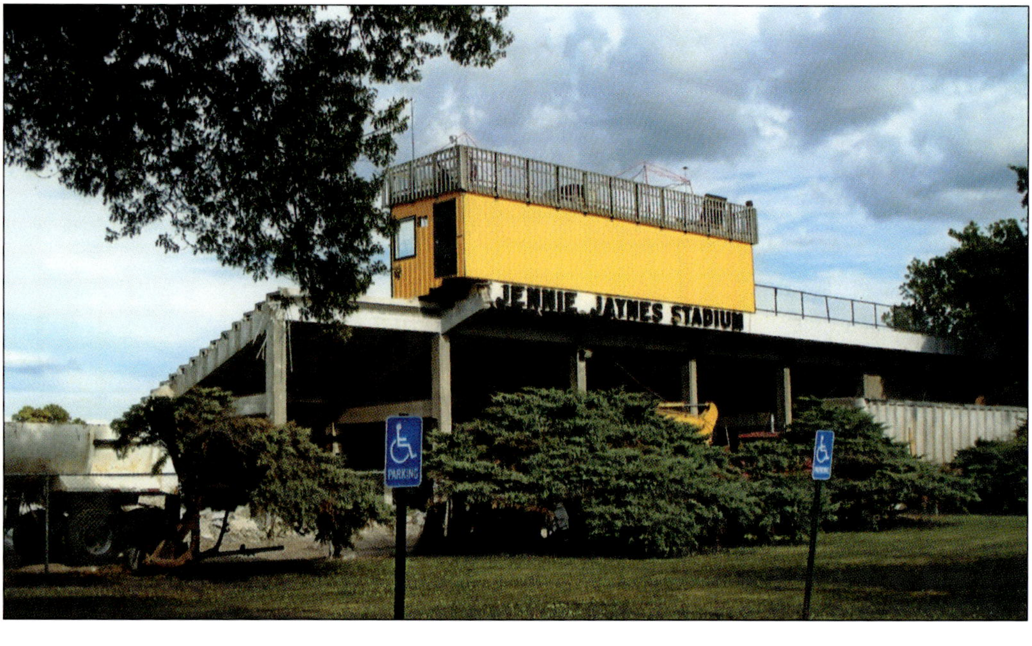

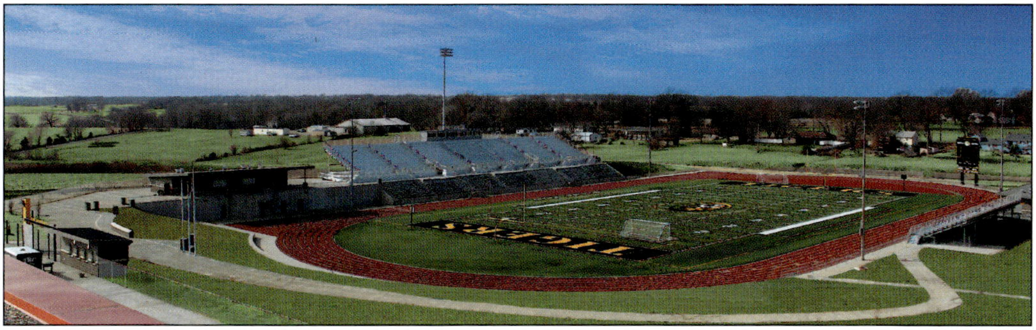

In 2013, the Sedalia City Council approved purchase of the Jennie Jaynes Stadium from the Sedalia 200 School District for $1 million in preparation for constructing a new stadium near the new Smith-Cotton High School. The new $6 million Jennie Jaynes Complex was dedicated in March 2015. This aerial view of Tiger Stadium was taken from the gymnasium roof of Smith-Cotton High School. (Courtesy of Bob Satnan.)

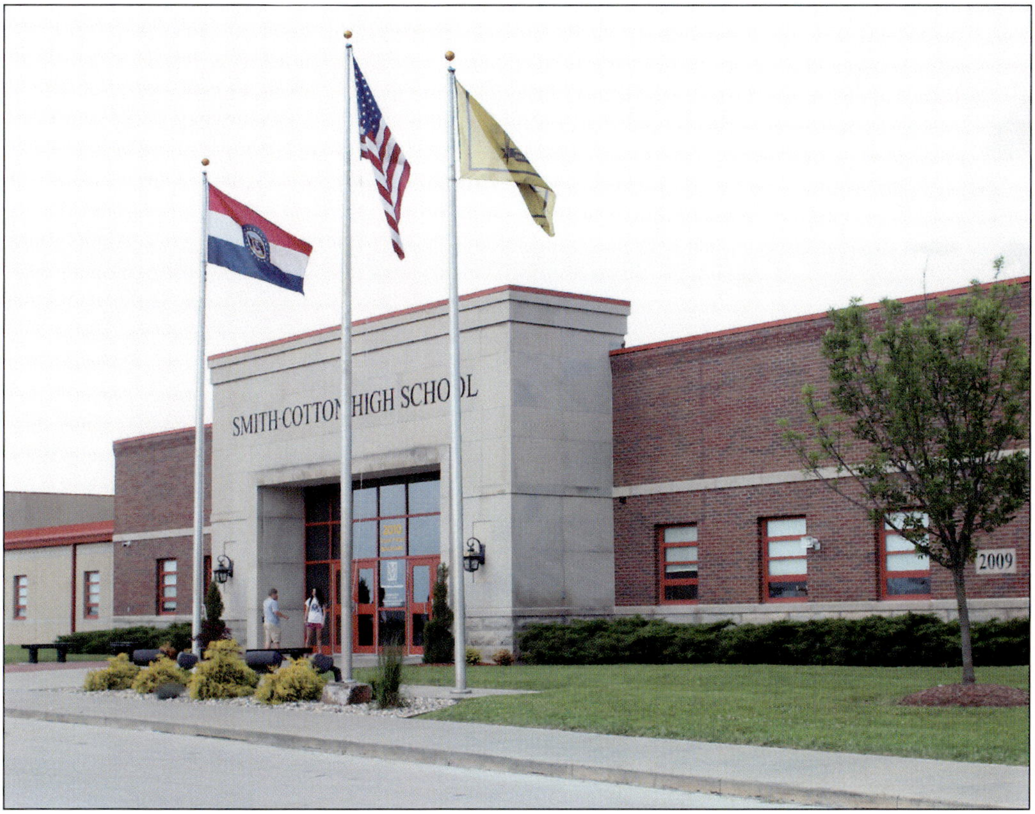

The new Smith-Cotton High School opened in 2010 at 2010 Tiger Pride Boulevard, on the south end of Sedalia. The $30 million school initially accommodated sophomores, juniors, and seniors. A freshmen addition and multipurpose classroom/gymnasium addition were completed prior to the 2016–2017 school year. The former high school became Smith-Cotton Junior High School when the new high school opened. (Courtesy of Bob Satnan.)

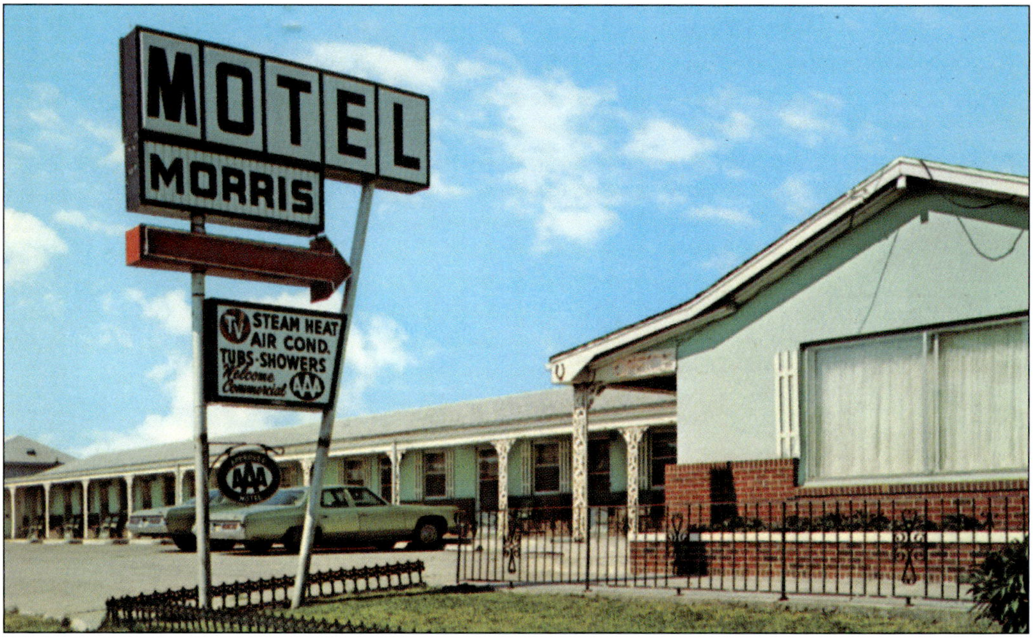

Wes and Lillian Morris opened the Morris Motel at 1000 South Limit Avenue, or two blocks south of the intersection of US Highway 50, in 1953. The area had previously been occupied by the Land-'O-Nod cabins, which were relocated to build the first units of the new motel. The Morrises also owned the El Rancho Motel, which opened west of Sedalia in 1950.

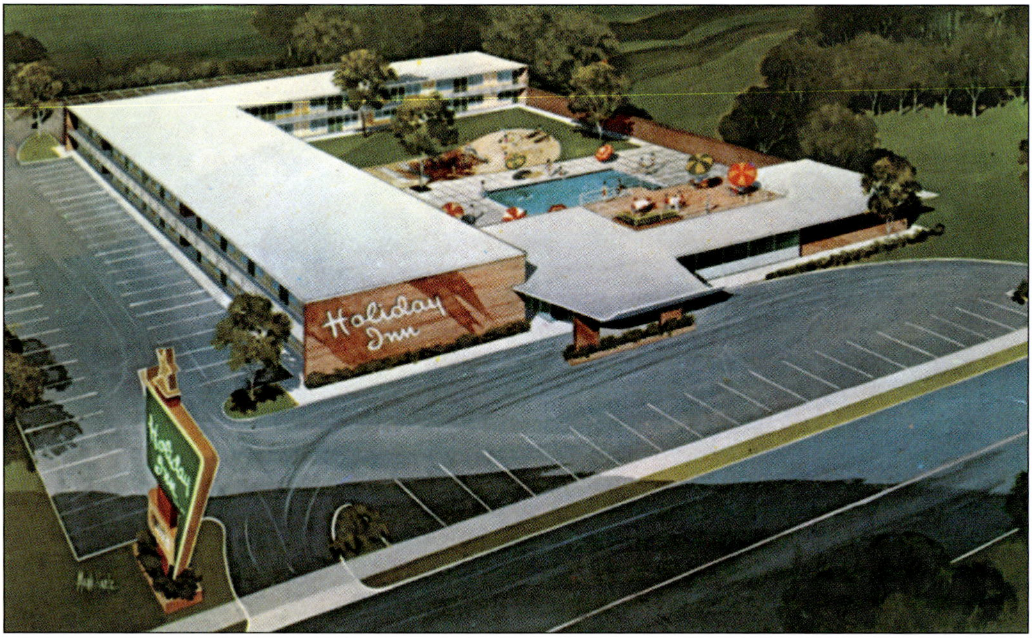

Sedalia's Holiday Inn was completed in 1963, featuring an outdoor pool, banquet room, and restaurant. Six local businessmen—William E. Bingaman, Jack Cunningham, George Dugan Jr., Morris H. Sagaloff, Abe Silverman, and W.K. Whitaker—were stockholders for the 80-unit motel located at South Limit Avenue and West Thirty-Second Street. It became the State Fair Motor Inn in 1976 and is now the Best Western State Fair Inn.

Four

Business and Industry

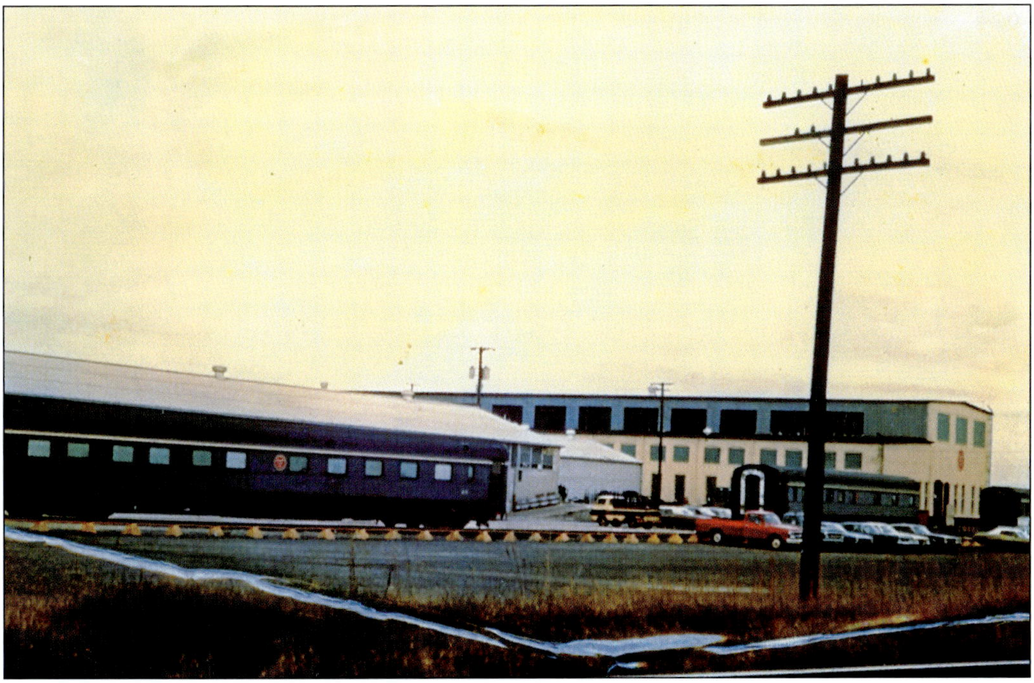

Two railroad shops, including the Missouri Pacific (pictured), sustained Sedalia's economic base for nearly a century. The Missouri Pacific shops' payroll was approximately $3 million annually when Sedalia celebrated its centennial in 1960. While the railroads were losing steam, new industry was emerging. By the time the railroad shops closed, new manufacturing plants had enabled Sedalia to sustain its population and position itself for future growth. (Courtesy of the Sedalia Public Library.)

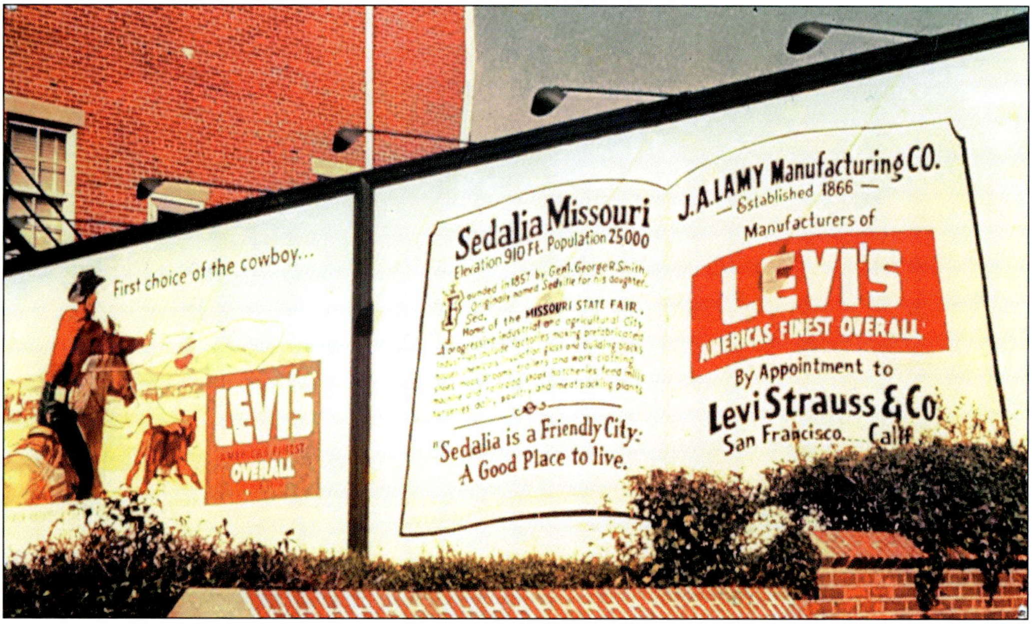

Located near the J.A. Lamy Manufacturing Company at 108 West Pacific Street, this billboard marked one of Sedalia's oldest businesses. In 1866, Ernest Lamy opened a tailoring and haberdashery business on West Main Street that became the Lamy Manufacturing Company. Elliott M. Stafford Sr. acquired the business in 1912. The company began producing Levi's in 1946, and its entire production had been devoted to Levi's by 1949. Lamy Manufacturing closed in 1998. (Courtesy of the Sedalia Public Library.)

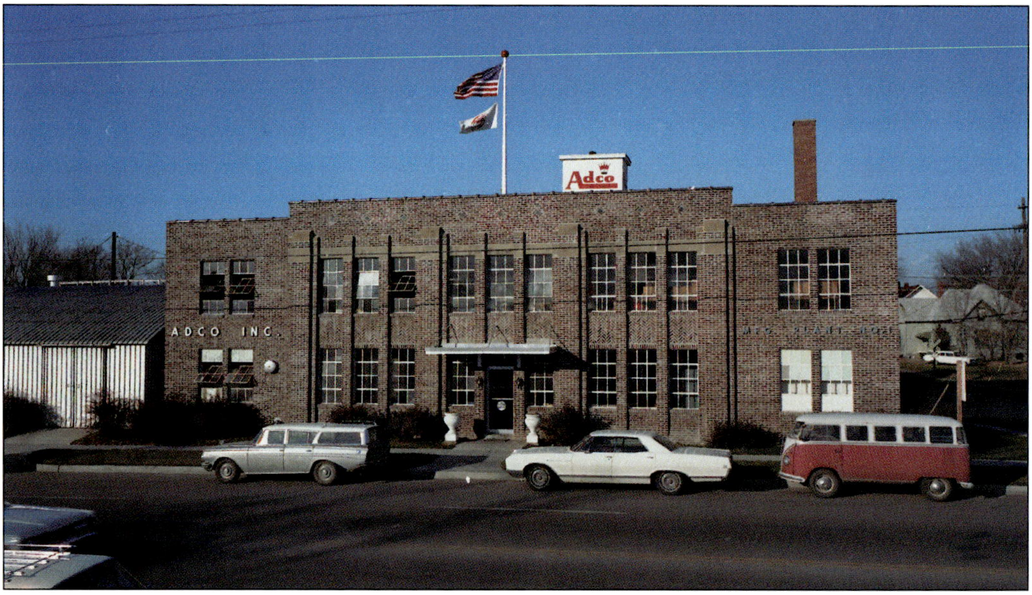

J.R. Van Dyne and his wife, Vivia D., founded the American Disinfecting Company in 1908. The company, which manufactured cleaning chemicals and products, changed its name to Adco in 1944. In 2007, the Van Dyne family sold the company to Mentor Partners of Cambridge, Massachusetts. Adco was sold again in December 2011 to Equinox Chemicals of Albany, Georgia. Adco no longer exists in Sedalia.

Some of Sedalia's manufacturing companies made lots of dough—literally. The Almquist Bakery was located at 1200 South Ohio Avenue. Described by the *Sedalia Democrat* as one of the "largest and cleanest baking institutions in the middle west," the company produced wholesale bread and cakes. After the bakery closed in the 1940s, the building was converted to apartments. It was destroyed by a fire in 2009.

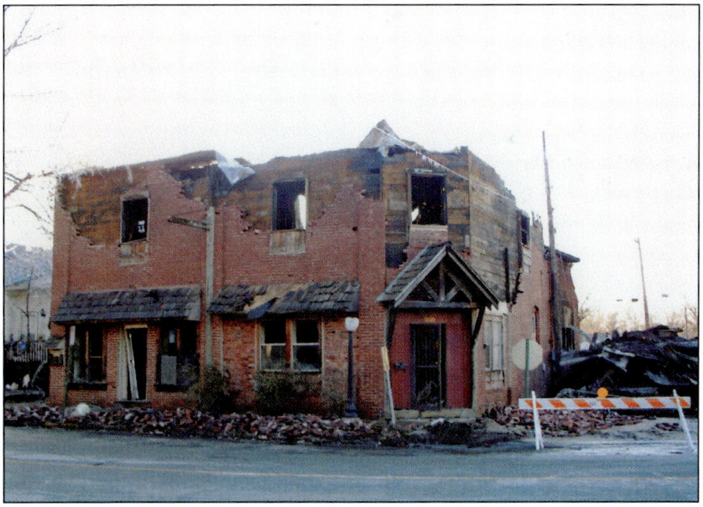

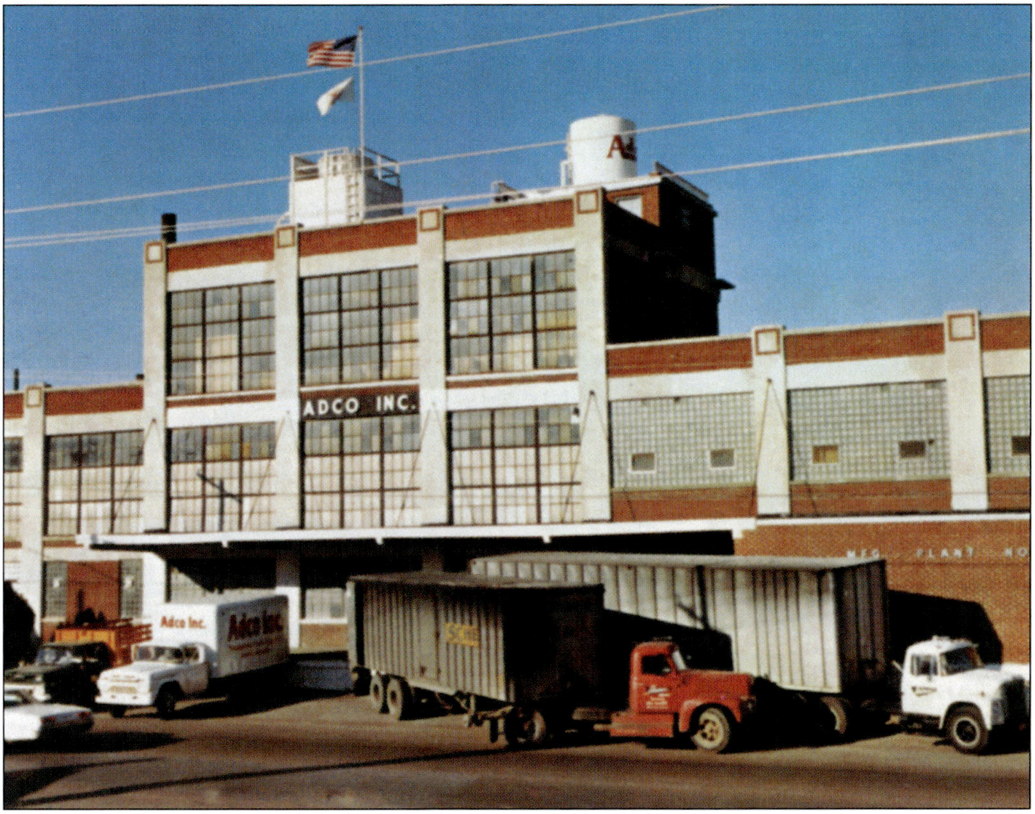

This building rose from Chris Streng's bakery, formerly located in the Streng Block at 700–704 South Ohio Avenue. Streng and his son-in-law Victor Leffler owned the Streng-Leffler Bakery. After Streng's retirement, Leffler sold the business to Nafziger Bakeries. In 1919, Nafziger constructed a new building at 726 West Main Street, which later became the Taystee Bakery. The building is pictured when owned by Adco. Bast Storage opened at the site in 2016. (Courtesy of Sedalia Area Chamber of Commerce.)

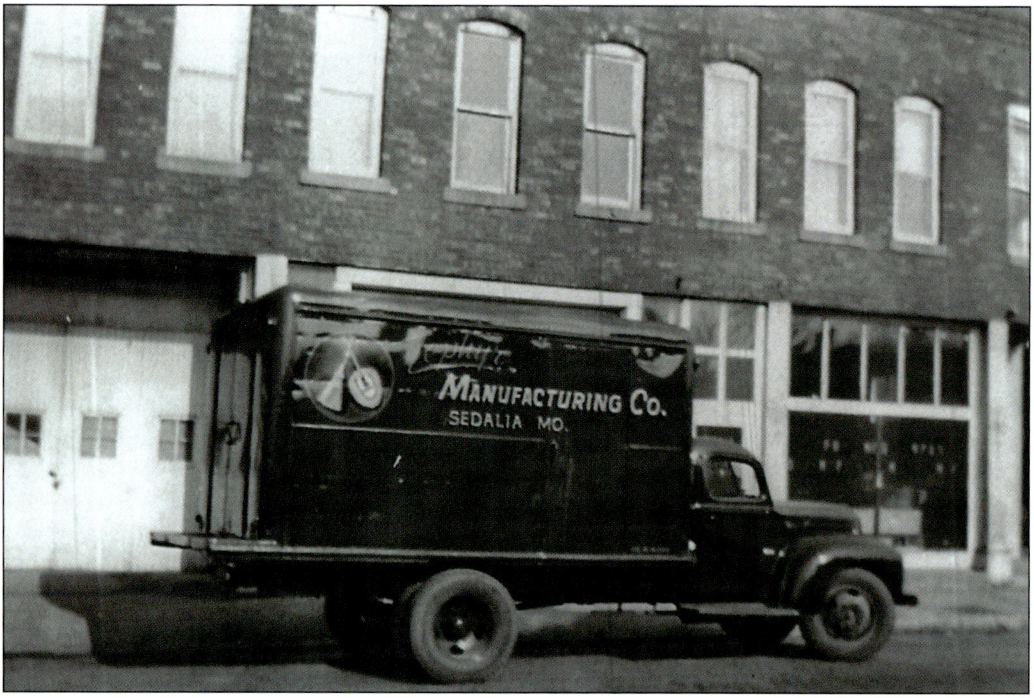

In 1927, Harry E. Lindstrom founded the Acme Broom Company in Kansas City. By 1932, the company had outgrown its building and moved to Sedalia. Acme began Sedalia operations in July 1932 with a weekly payroll of $246. Three months later, the company's payroll and output of brooms and whisks had more than doubled, and its workforce had more than tripled. Continued growth prompted a move to 400 West Second Street (above) in the 1940s. The company incorporated in 1946 and changed its name to Zephyr Manufacturing after its flagship product, the Zephyr Streamline broom. Zephyr moved to its current location (below) on Mitchell Road in 1992 and now serves North America with the most complete selection of mops, brooms, brushes, handles, and associated products available from one source. Robert (R.J.) Lindstrom became president in 2010, beginning the fourth generation of family management at Zephyr. (Both, courtesy of R.J. Lindstrom and Zephyr Manufacturing.)

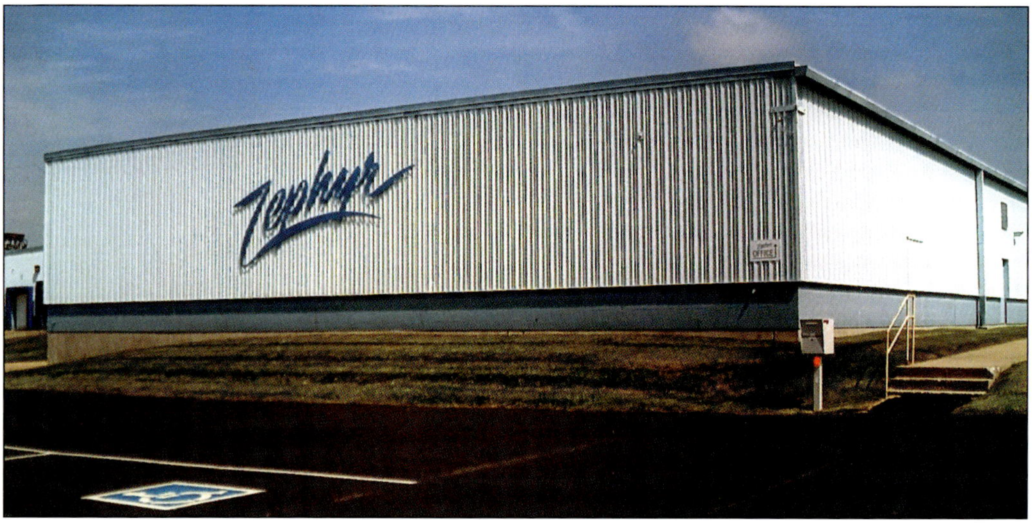

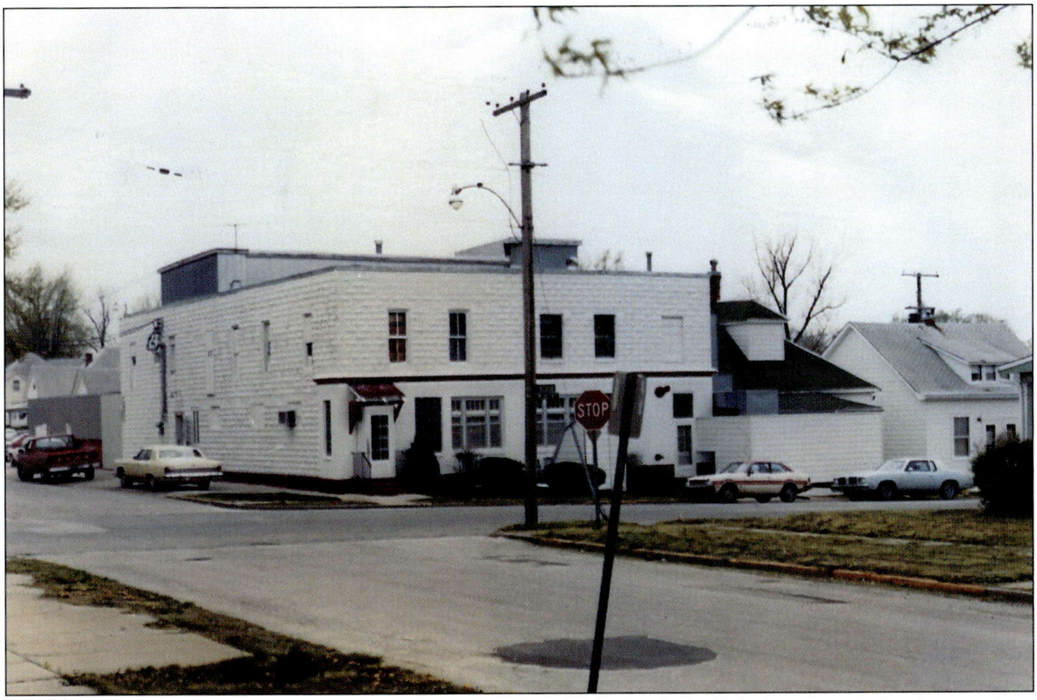

Working out of his home in downtown Sedalia, Guy Snyder founded Inter-State Studio in 1933. He named his business Inter-State because the word described his mobile photography studio, traveling the then new interstate highways to take pictures. He deliberately added the hyphen to *interstate* so educators would correct his spelling, enabling him to repeat and reinforce his company name. In 1941, Inter-State moved to a commercial building at 601 West Sixteenth Street, pictured above. As the company grew, Snyder purchased surrounding houses and erected additional buildings. Inter-State eventually occupied nearly an entire city block and parts of two others. Snyder purchased the current location on Snyder Avenue in 1984, pictured below after its 20,500-square-foot addition in 2002. Aric Snyder, Guy's son, is now chief executive officer. Inter-State Studio is America's largest family-owned school photography company, still owned by the Snyder family. (Both, courtesy of Aric Snyder and Inter-State Studio.)

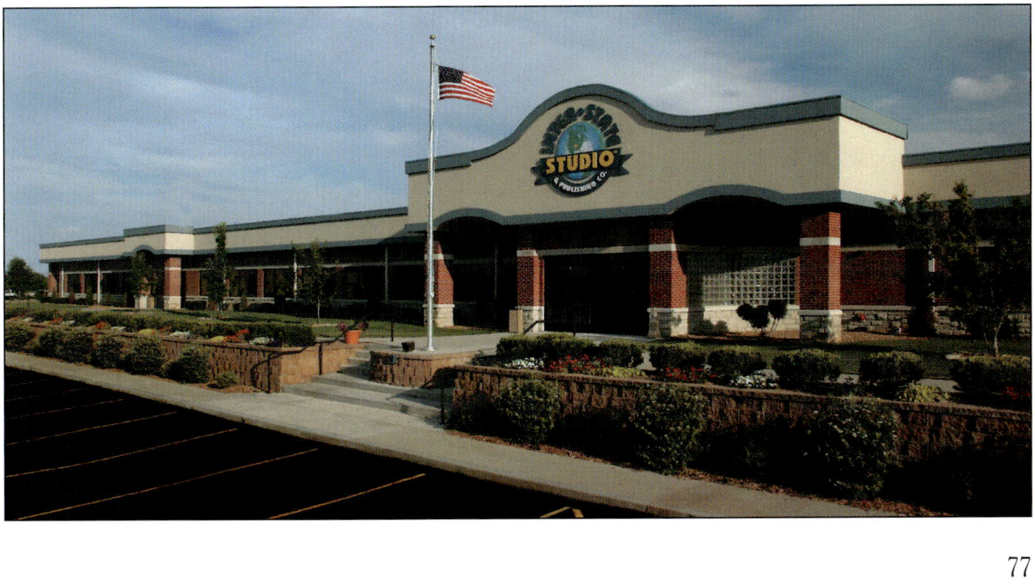

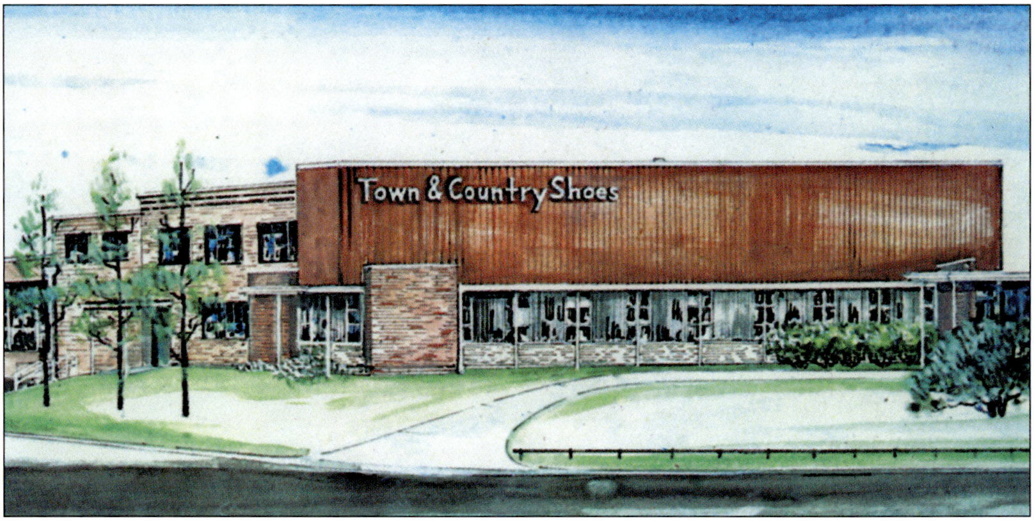

Town & Country Shoes opened in 1943 with, according to the *Sedalia Democrat*, a "handful" of employees at 210 North Missouri Avenue. In 1968, Town & Country erected this new facility west of Sedalia. At that time, the company employed 600 people and manufactured 3,500 pairs of shoes daily, which it shipped to 1,500 leading retail and department stores across the United States. The Wolverine footwear company acquired Town & Country in 1982. (Courtesy of Sedalia Area Chamber of Commerce.)

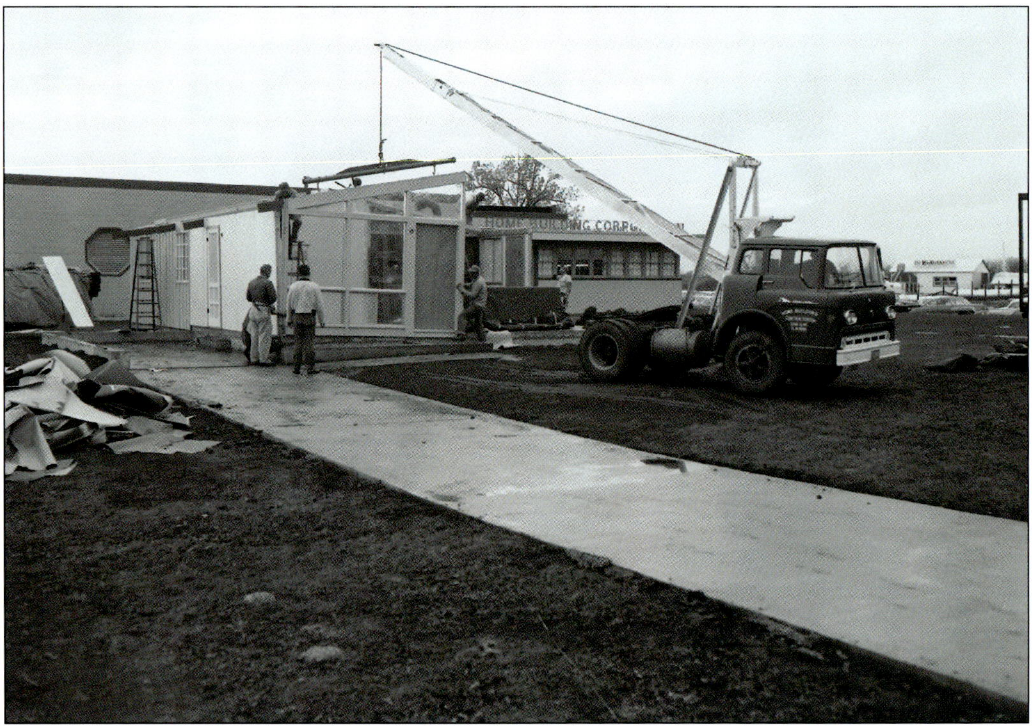

The Home Building Corporation moved to North Park Avenue in 1947, helping remedy Sedalia's severe postwar housing shortage. In 1962, *Look* magazine honored Home Building as having the most outstanding design for prefabricated homes in the United States. Neal O. Reyburn was plant architect and president of the Sedalia corporation.

In 1946, the Pittsburgh Corning Corporation selected Sedalia out of 12 cities for a $2 million plant for manufacturing glass block and insulation. Sedalia was chosen based on its central location, railroad transportation, utilities, and manpower, as well as the fact that the Home Building Corporation would make housing available for employees. (Courtesy of the Sedalia Public Library.)

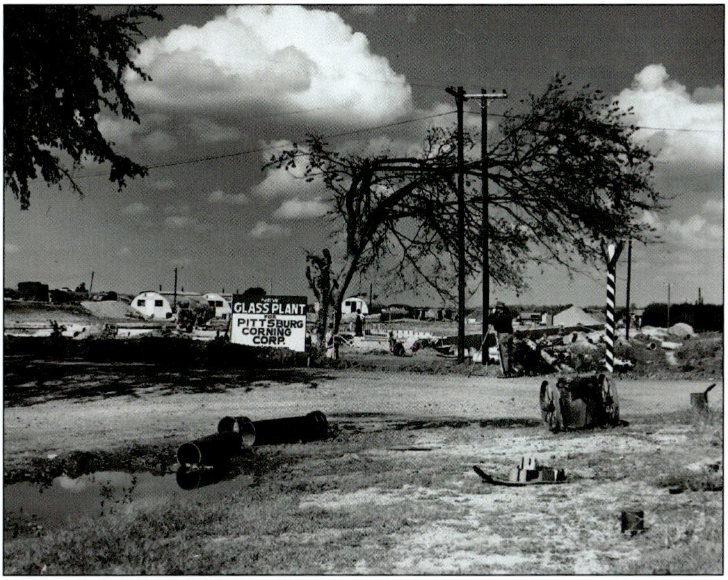

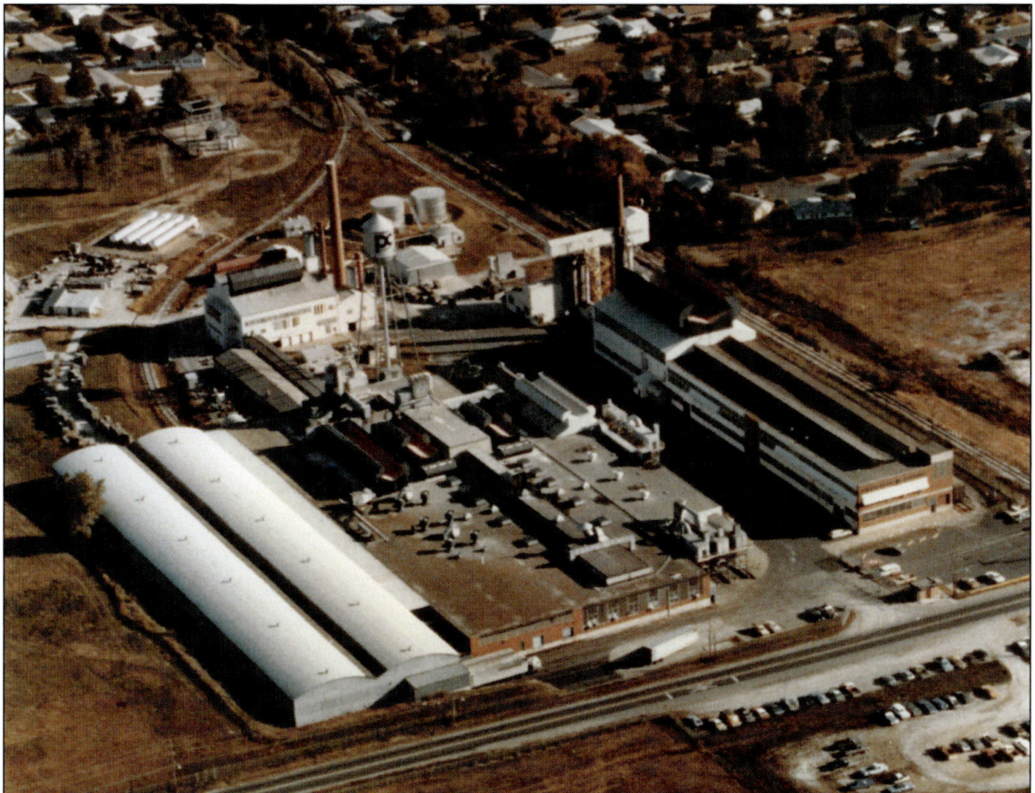

Construction for Pittsburgh Corning began in the summer of 1946 on 40 acres on West Sixteenth Street, and the company began manufacturing glass block in 1947. Its water tower became a local landmark, bearing a lighted cross each Christmas season beginning in 1952. The Sedalia plant continues to manufacture Foamglas Cellular Glass Insulation, the dominant cellular glass insulation product throughout the world. (Courtesy of the Pittsburgh Corning Corporation.)

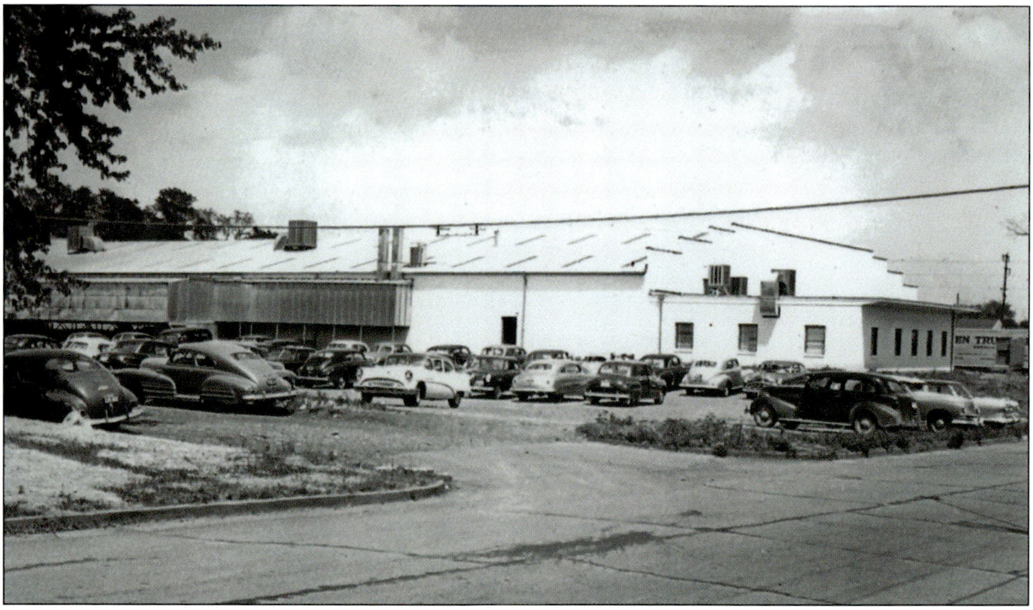

In the 1970s, nearly every Sedalian owned a Crock-Pot made by Rival Manufacturing or knew someone who worked for the company. The Rival plant on West Sixteenth Street and Lamine Avenue was built in 1953 for the National Engineering and Manufacturing Company, which made home cooling units. The "Fan Factory," as it became known, was constructed through the Sedalia Chamber of Commerce's post–World War II industrial fund. In 1959, the Steam-O-Matic Corporation purchased the facility. The subsidiary of the Rival Manufacturing Company enlarged the plant and workforce. The plant continued to grow through the years, eventually expanding to the former Klassic Trailer manufacturing facility south of Sedalia. After Rival Manufacturing ceased operations in Sedalia, its original plant stood empty until it was razed in 2015. (Above, courtesy of the Sedalia Public Library.)

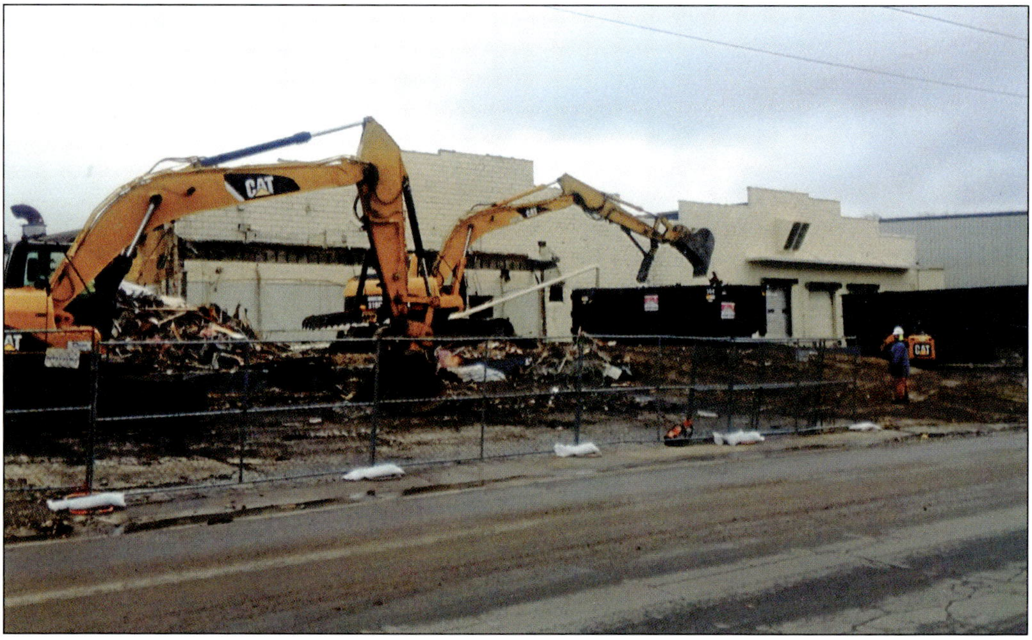

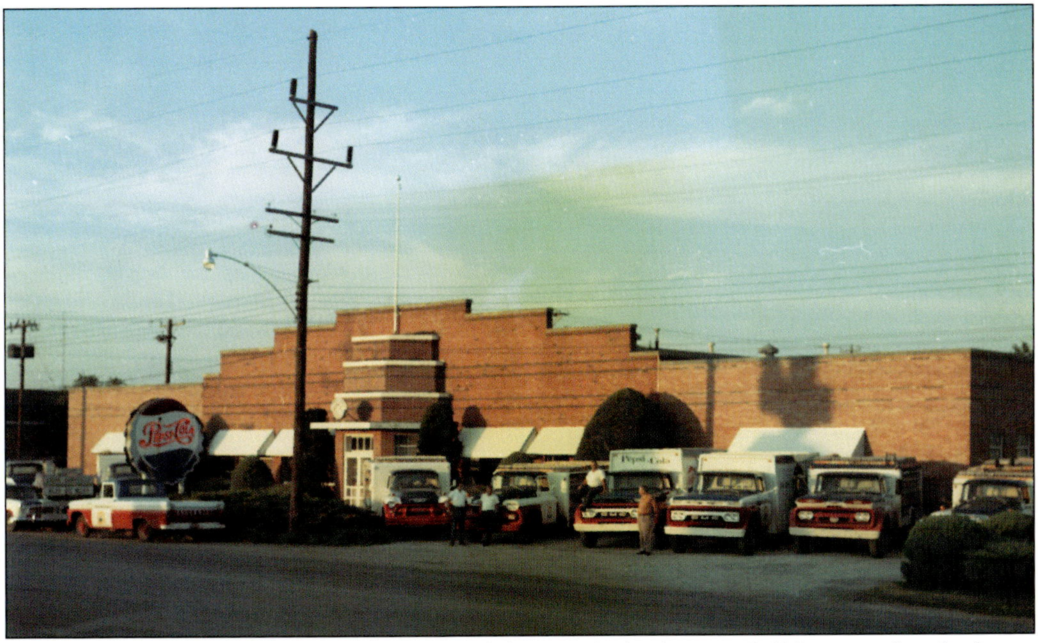

Julian Bagby, who began bottling Pepsi in Sedalia in 1939, built a new 9,600-square-foot facility at 1101 South Limit Avenue in 1942. The building was enlarged through the years, reaching 26,450 square feet by the time a January 1969 fire destroyed the building. It was said to be the largest monetary loss from a fire in Sedalia's history up to that point. Bagby built a new Pepsi plant at 2910 West Broadway Boulevard in 1969, with a production capacity of 360 bottles per minute. More than 14,000 people toured the plant during its open house in May 1970. Actress Joan Crawford, a PepsiCo board member, was on hand to sign autographs. Bagby, a three-term Sedalia mayor, died in 1990 at age 90. (Below, courtesy of the Sedalia Fire Department.)

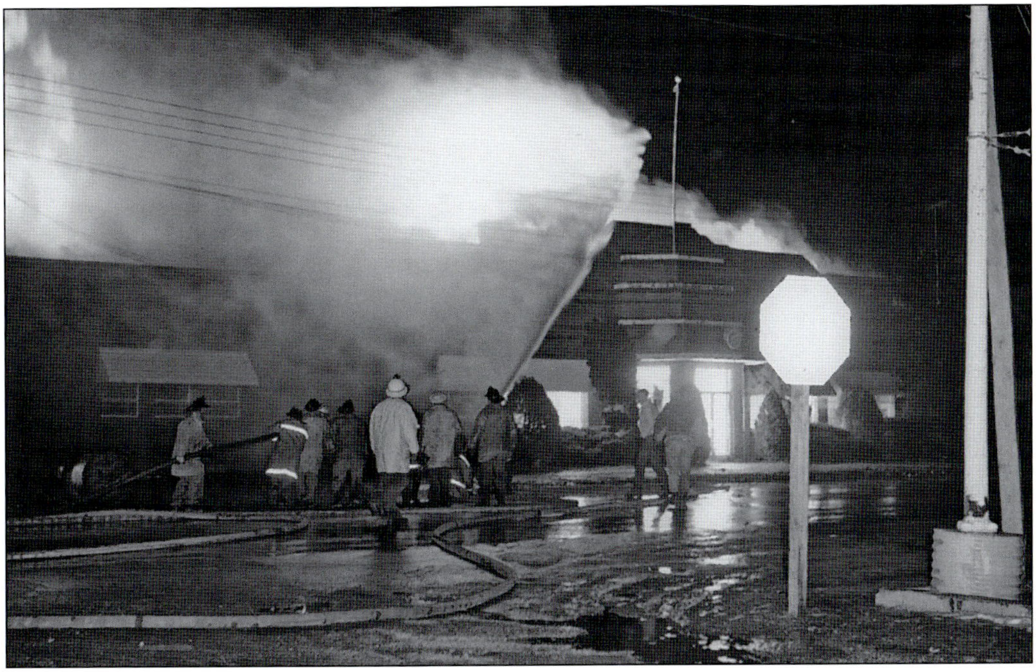

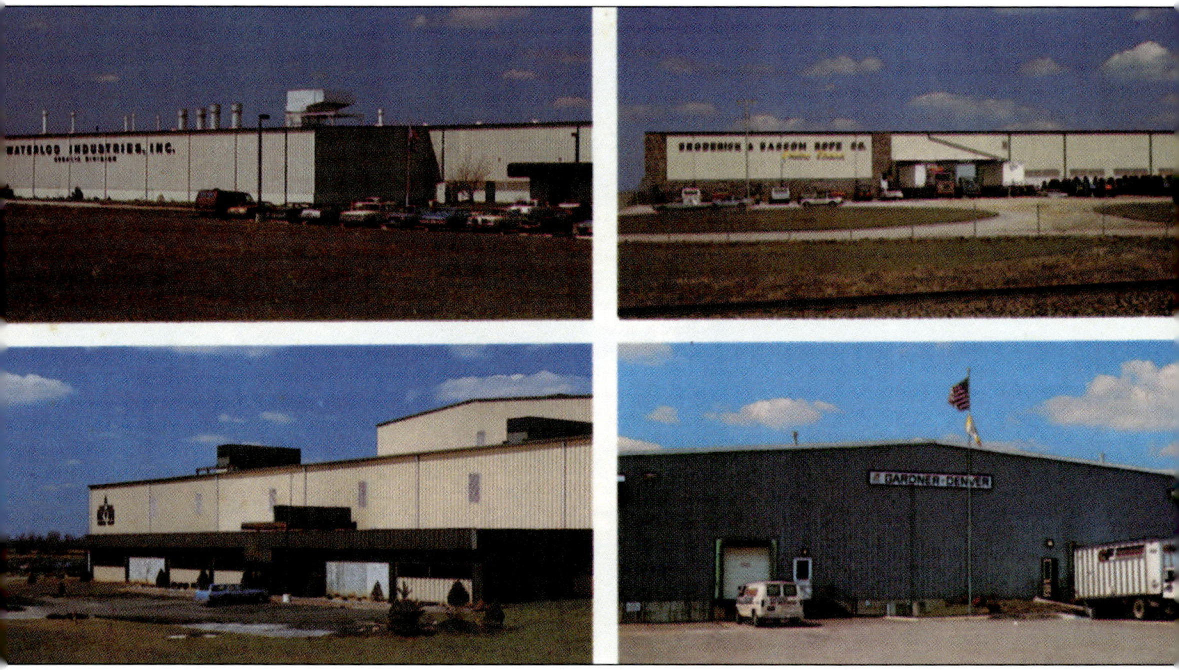

In 1967, Sedalia director of industrial development William H. Hall described Olin Conductors as the "first fruits of the results of our efforts to gain new industry for Sedalia." Sedalia gained more good news in 1969 when start-ups of the Permaneer Corporation and Duke Manufacturing Company were announced, followed by McGraw-Edison in 1974. In 1978 alone, the city added three new manufacturing plants, creating more than 1,000 jobs: Kelsey-Hayes, Waterloo Industries, Inc., and Alcolac, Inc. Pictured around 1983 are, clockwise from upper left, Waterloo Industries, Broderick & Bascom Rope Company (now WireCo WorldGroup Manufacturing), Kelsey Hayes Company (now Maxion Wheels), and Gardner-Denver (now Gardner-Denver Machinery, Inc.). (Courtesy of Sedalia Area of Chamber of Commerce.)

Five

MAKING MEMORIES

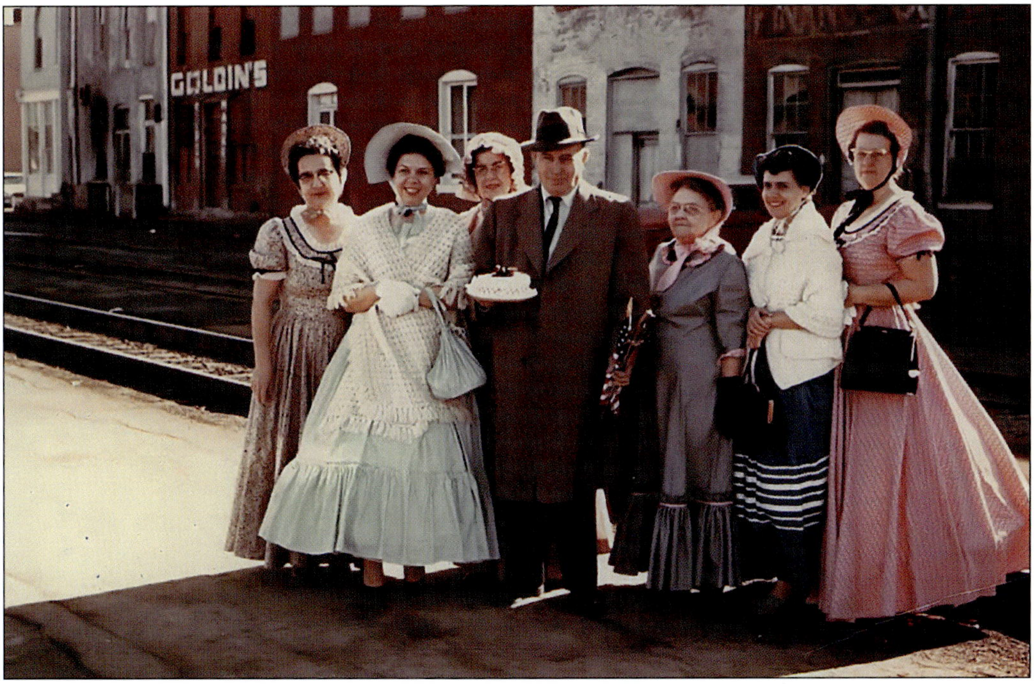

In 1961, Sedalians gathered where the first train had rolled through town a century before. They celebrated the railroad, but more important, they celebrated the spirit of Sedalians who had been making memories for 100 years. Holding the anniversary cake is Leslie Hale, author of *Sedalia Missouri: 100 Years in Pictures*. (Courtesy of Millicent Hale.)

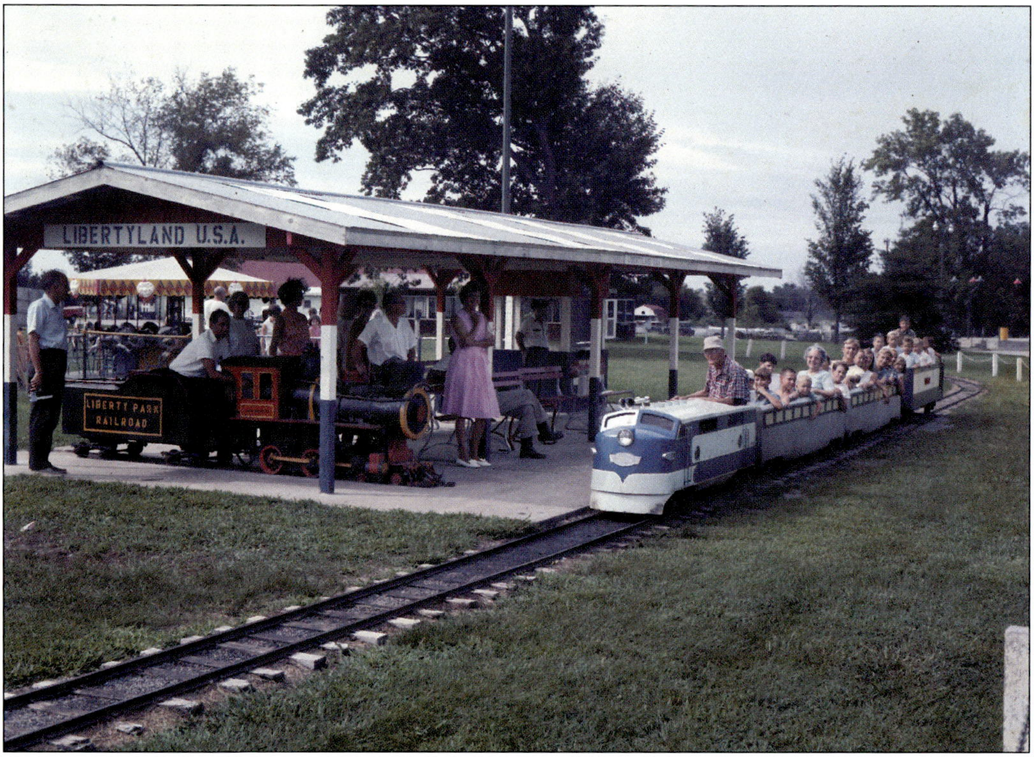

Since Sedalia is a railroad town, trains are a star attraction at Liberty Park. Roy Elliott operated the miniature steam engine (left) during the early 1950s. After his death, his widow sold the train to the City of Sedalia. The Missouri Pacific Railroad donated its *Baby Eagle II* (right) to the City of Sedalia in 1963. Constructed in 1960, the *Baby Eagle* is a reproduction of a Missouri Pacific locomotive.

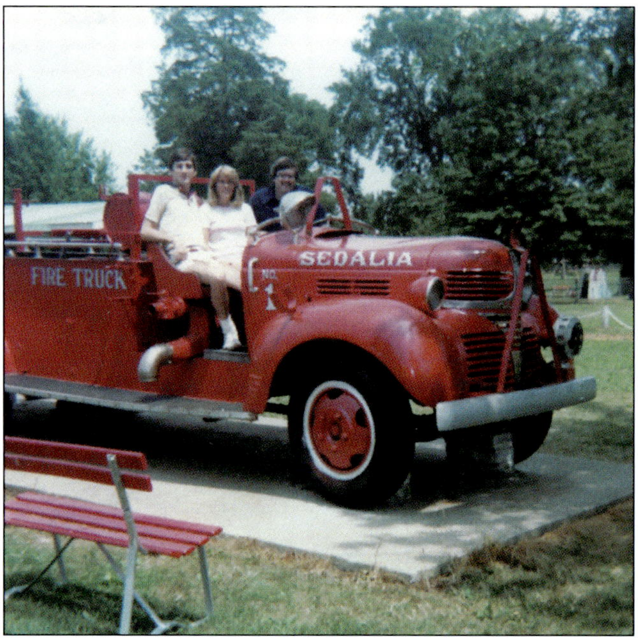

In 1940, Sedalia introduced its "Bullet" fire truck, named for its speed and maneuverability. Chief John Lueck and members of the fire department constructed the truck on a two-ton Dodge chassis. Leslie Hale applied gold-leaf lettering and decoration. In 1963, the truck was retired to Liberty Park, where it became a popular attraction for visitors, such as the Taylor family, pictured during a reunion in 1978. (Courtesy of Tom C. Taylor.)

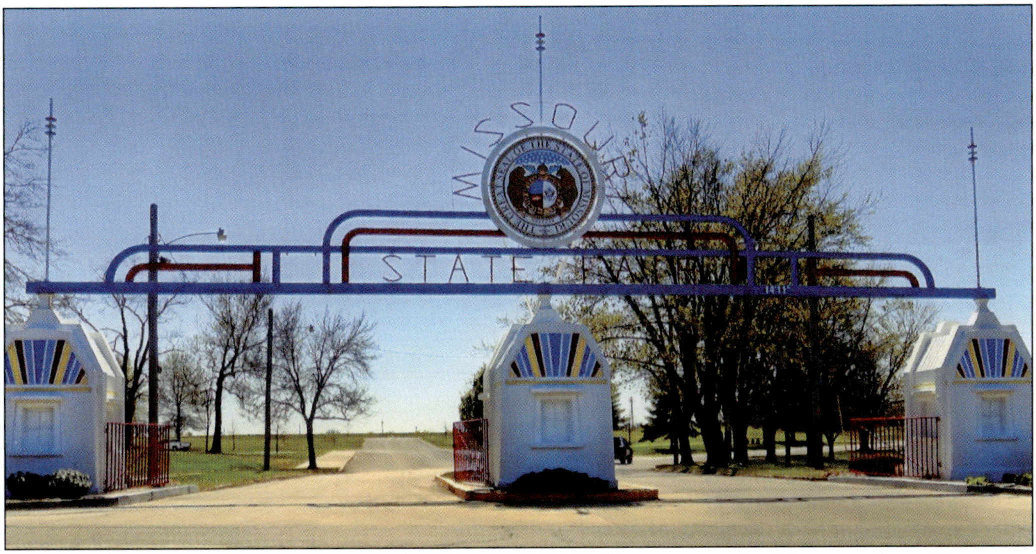

This Art Deco gate on West Sixteenth Street has greeted visitors to the Missouri State Fair since James Keens was given 30 days to build and complete it in 1939. Keen and his crew were paid $2,000 for their efforts. The first fair was held on the Missouri State Fairgrounds in 1901 and has been held annually except 1943 and 1944, during World War II. (Courtesy of Randy Kirby.)

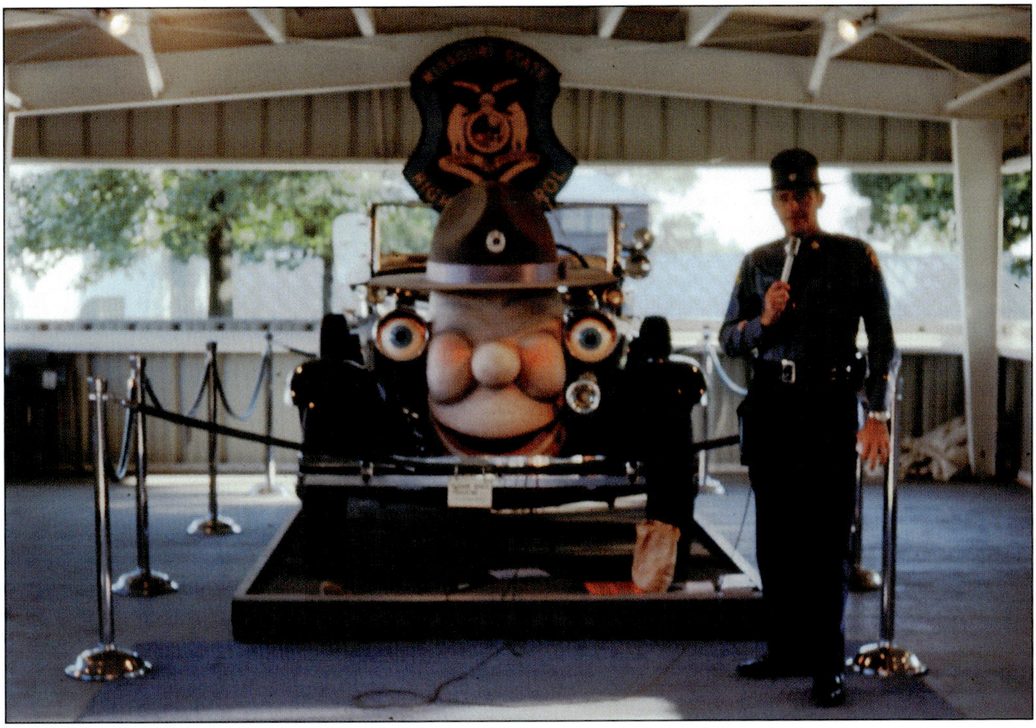

Otto the Talking Car has been a mainstay at the Missouri State Fair since 1969. Based on a 1931 Model A Ford roadster, the Missouri State Highway Patrol's exhibit is located in the Highway Gardens. Otto provides information about traffic laws and safety, punctuated by blinking his eyes, blowing smoke, and blowing his horn. Sedalia native Jim Watson, who served with the Highway Patrol from 1965 to 2000, is pictured with Otto in 1976. (Courtesy of Dr. Steve Carr.)

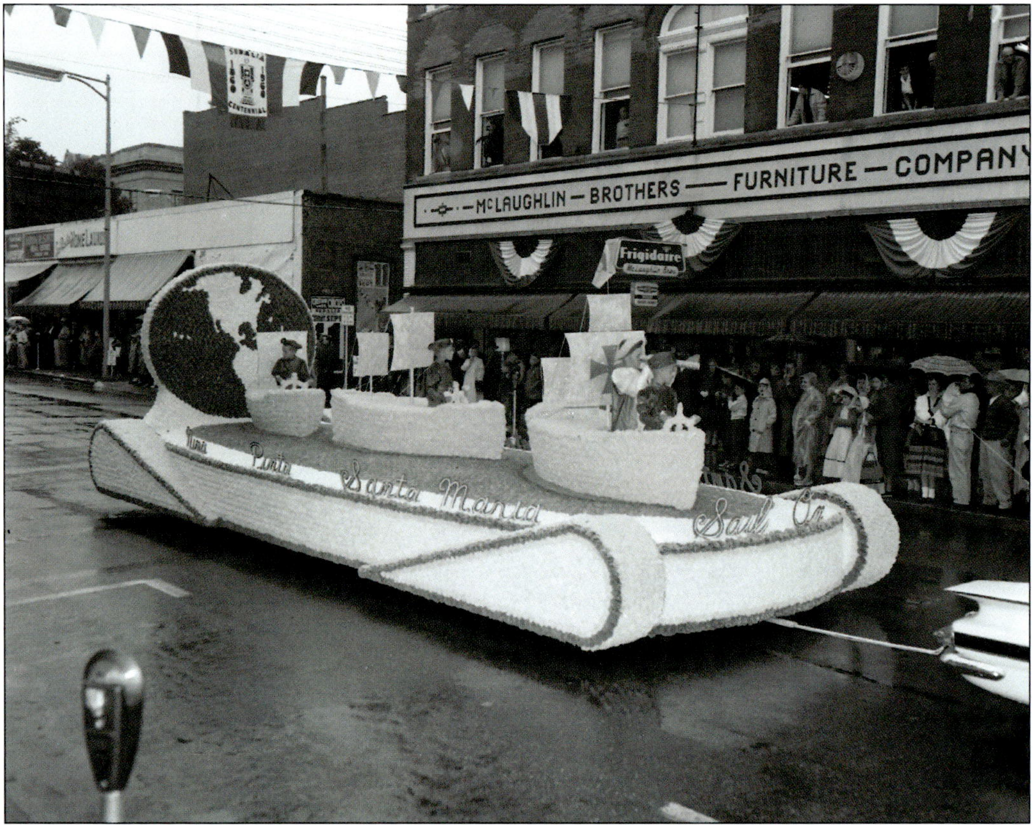

Sedalia's centennial celebration in October 1960 featured the Wheels of Progress Parade, the largest procession in Sedalia's history. Torrential rain did not stop more than 50,000 spectators from viewing the procession that took an hour and 20 minutes to pass any given point. The grand champion float by the Rotary Club is pictured in front of the McLaughlin Brothers Furniture Company at 515 South Ohio Avenue.

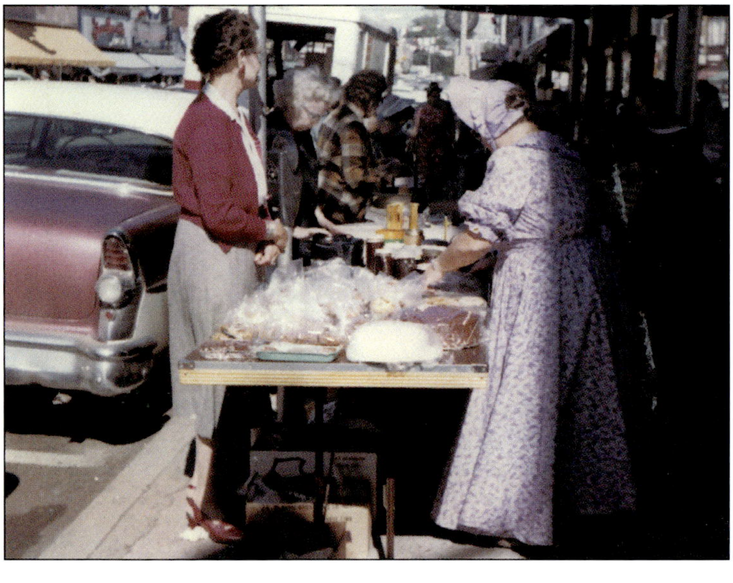

In contrast to the centennial parade, sunny skies dawned on the day of downtown's sidewalk bazaar. Booths representing various organizations offered baked goods and household items, attracting one of the largest crowds of the centennial celebration. Centennial festivities also included a ragtime concert, fashion show, and beard-growing contest. (Courtesy of Millicent Hale.)

A group of beard-growing, law-enforcing men took the moniker "Brothers of the Brush" during the centennial. Being bearded gave them license to fine—and even jail—those who did not grow beards. The Brothers raised $3,500 for the centennial fund by selling shaving permits and taking pictures of "victims" in the jail. The Parkhurst Manufacturing Company donated the jail and trailer for the centennial.

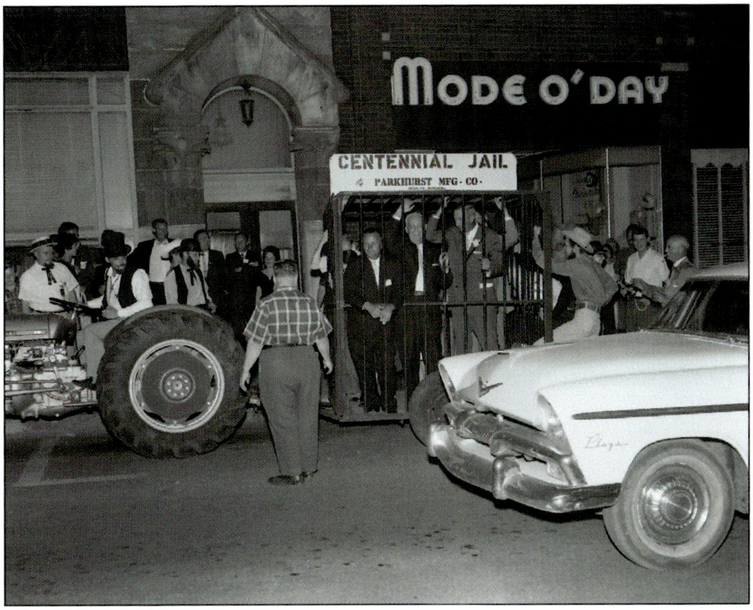

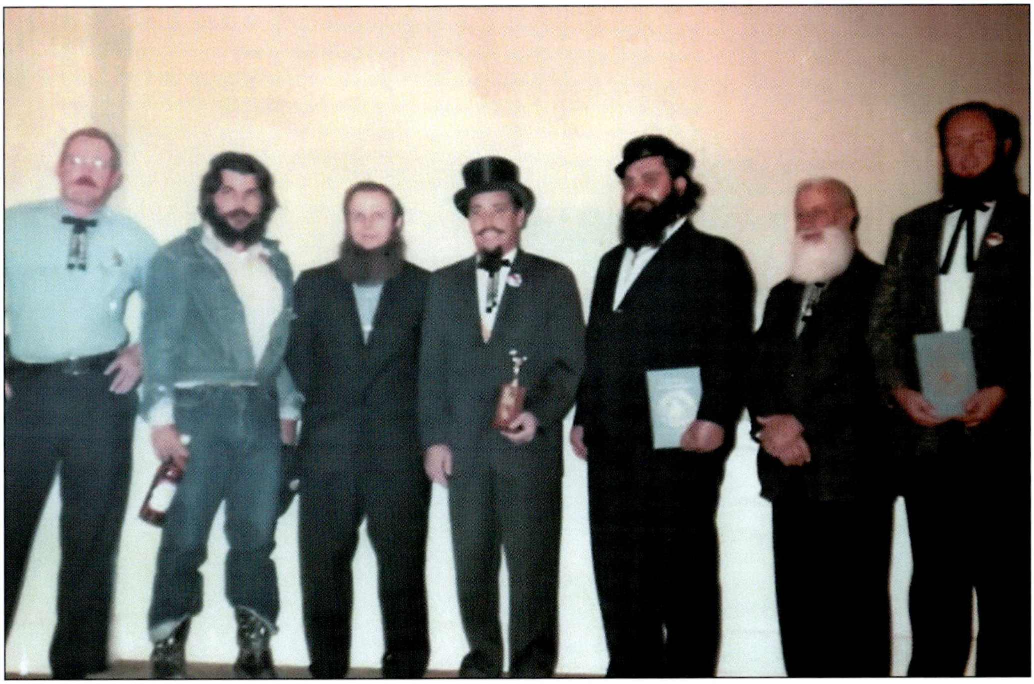

Men began growing their beards in January 1960 for the beard contest. The winners pictured are, from left to right, Bob Bogler (longest mustache), John England (orneriest beard), Tom Darrah (longest beard), Leo Richards (most distinguished beard), Melvin Sylvester (blackest beard), "Frosty" Dill (whitest beard), and C.R. Smart (reddest beard). Most beards were shaved as soon as the centennial ended, with Mayor Abe Silverman being one of the first to shed his whiskers. (Courtesy of Tom Darrah.)

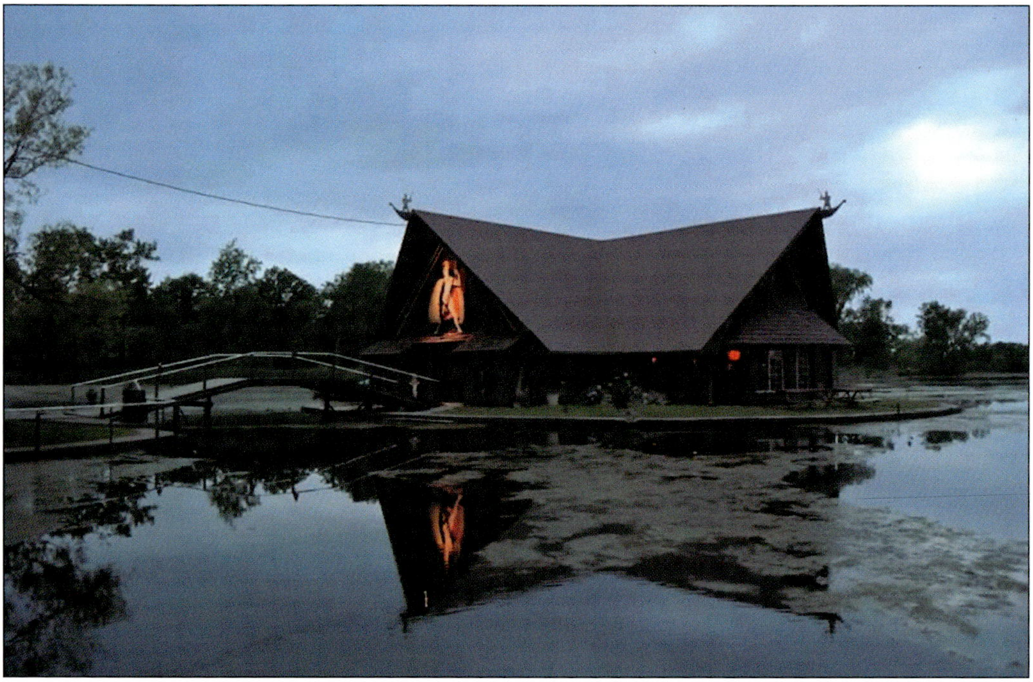

William R. Parkhurst designed and built the Tiki House in 1965. Located on an island on his estate west of Sedalia, the landmark became a popular location for family, civic, business, and social events. Parkhurst founded the Parkhurst Manufacturing Company in 1946. The company remains a leading manufacturer, best known for its farm and commercial truck bodies. (Courtesy of Jon Parkhurst and Lisa Morales.)

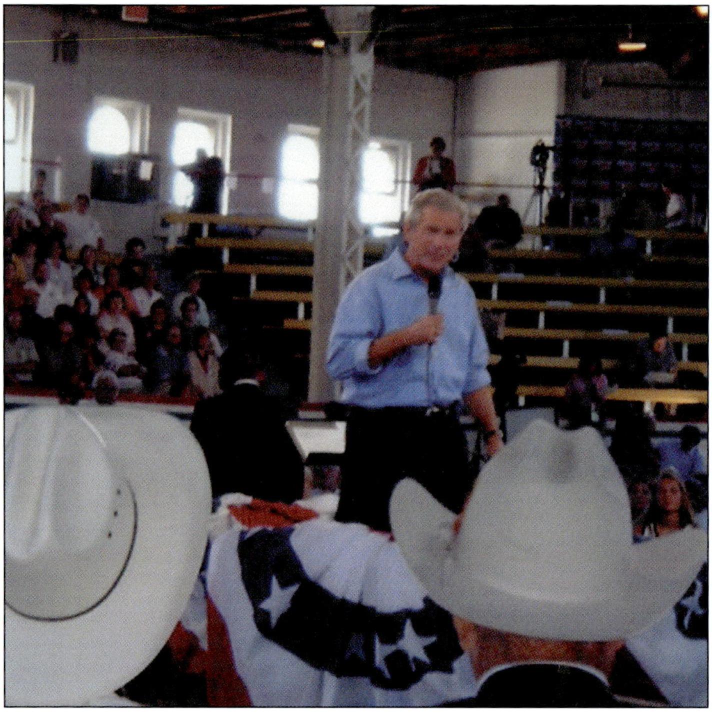

In September 2004, Pres. George W. Bush addressed a crowd of about 3,200 people in the coliseum on the Missouri State Fairgrounds. Bush was one of several presidents who have visited Sedalia during the fair, beginning with William Howard Taft, who attended on Mule Day in 1911. Pres. Harry S. Truman spoke at the annual ham breakfast in 1955, and Pres. Ronald Reagan spoke in the coliseum in 1984. (Courtesy of Elle Wasson Duggan.)

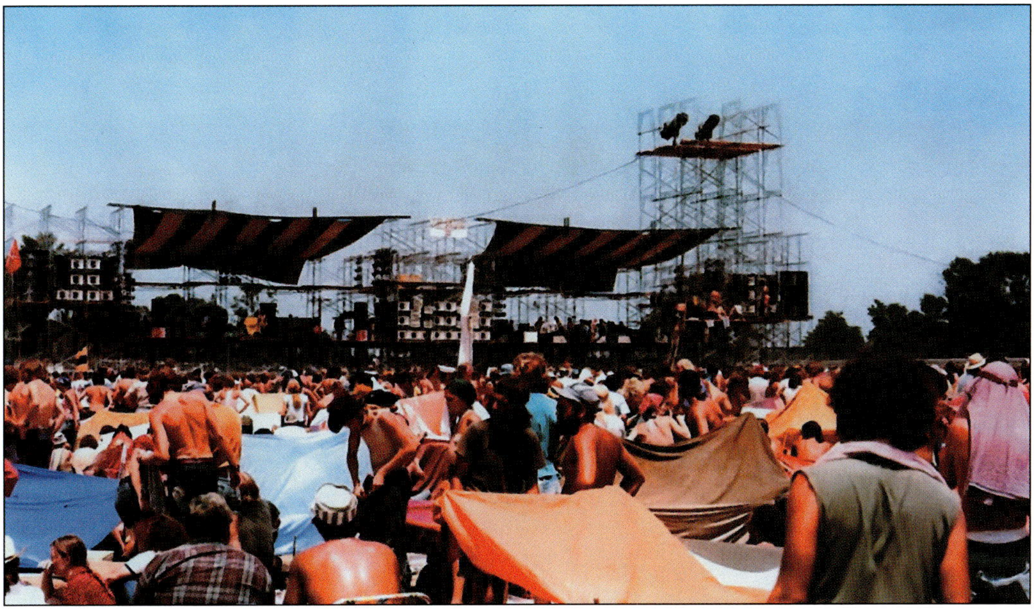

Held July 19–21, 1974, the Ozark Music Festival promised an impressive lineup of performers, including Jefferson Starship, the Nitty Gritty Dirt Band, and Bruce Springsteen. The event made history, however, not for its music but for rampant drugs, nudity, and vandalism. The festival on the Missouri State Fairgrounds attracted around 150,000 to 350,000 people and resulted in numerous drug overdoses and one death. (Courtesy of the Sedalia Heritage Foundation, Ozark Music Festival Exhibit.)

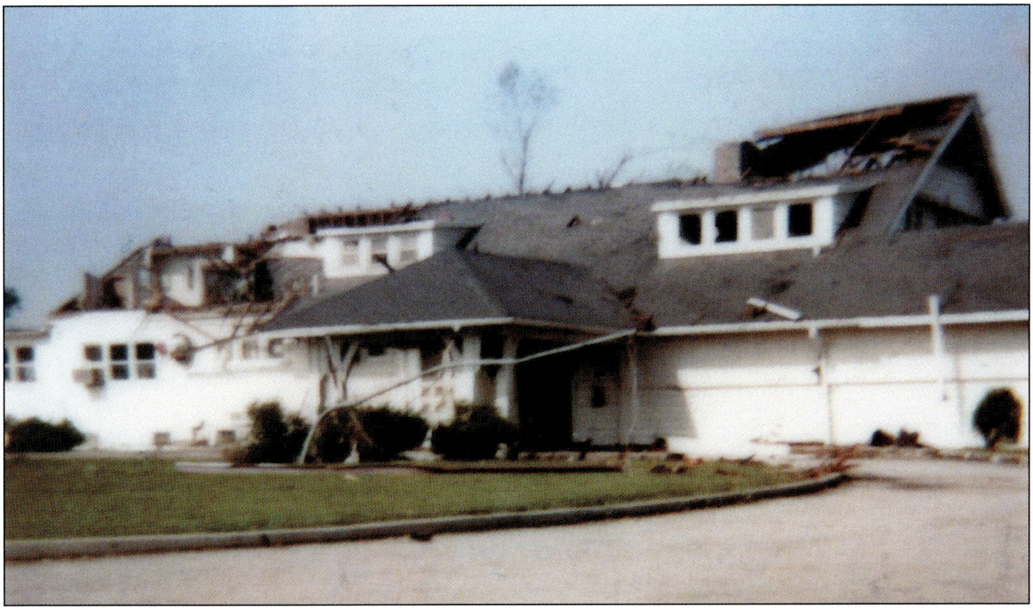

"Sedalia was a lucky town," the *Sedalia Capital* proclaimed after the May 1977 tornado caused $15 million damage to the city. The editorial explained, "Although the damage from the storm was incredible, the really most incredible thing about Black Wednesday was that no one was killed." The storm destroyed 150 homes, damaged 300, and left 1,500 homeless. It also destroyed the Sedalia Country Club (pictured). (Courtesy of Elaine Harvey.)

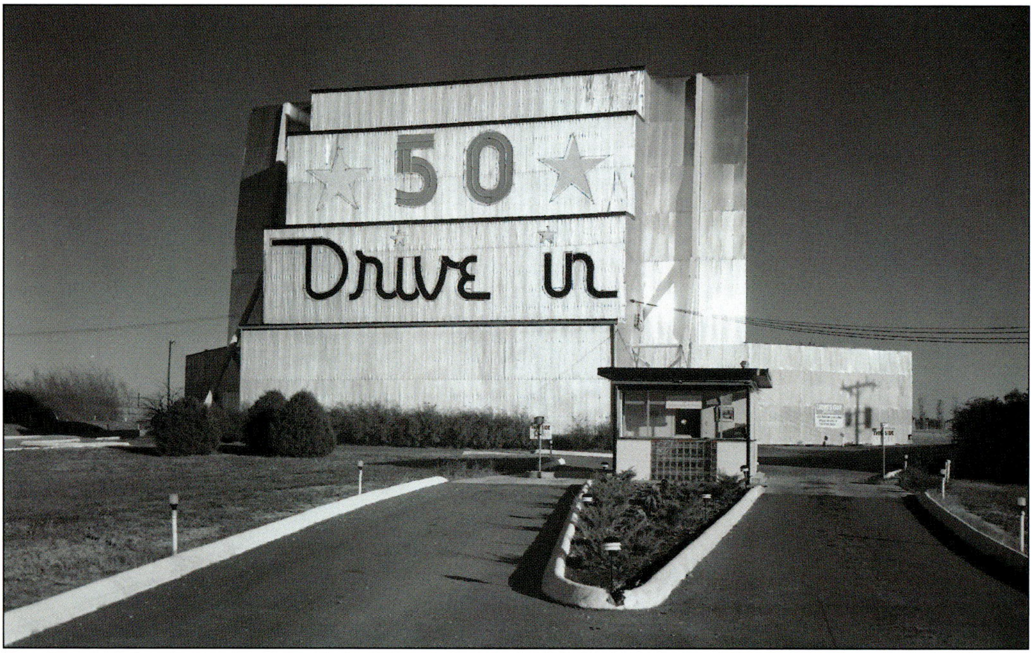

Joseph T. Ghosen offered Sedalians the latest in entertainment when he built the 50 Hi-Way Drive-In Theatre in 1949. Constructed on 15 acres two miles west of Sedalia, the theater provided parking for 500 cars. The drive-in catered to the car culture, offering the convenience of watching a movie and enjoying a snack from an automobile.

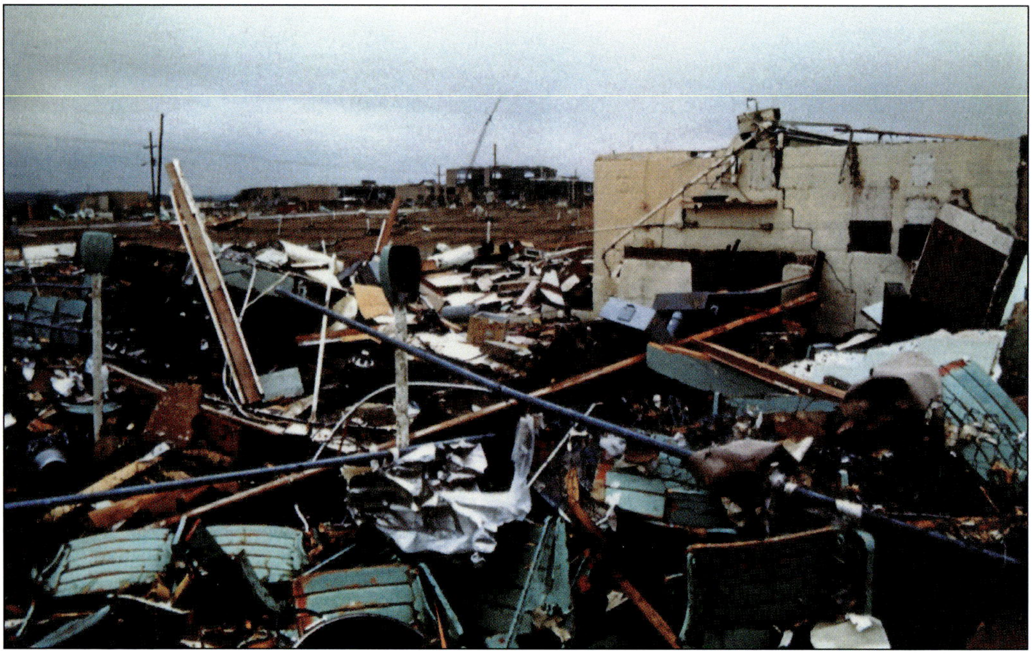

The 50 Hi-Way Drive-In was reduced to rubble by a May 1980 tornado. The storm also heavily damaged the nearby Kelsey-Hayes Company (in background), the Sunset Village Mobile Home Park, and other industrial buildings. The drive-in site remained vacant until J.T. Ghosen's descendants built the Galaxy cinema in 1998. (Courtesy of Tom C. Taylor.)

Built in 1880, the covered bridge over Flat Creek was a beloved landmark, providing an area for generations to fish, swim, picnic, and hike. After arson destroyed the bridge on May 29, 1966, several thousand people paid homage to the bridge's remains, ironically, on Memorial Day. Tom Taylor snapped this photograph while the embers still were smoldering. (Courtesy of Tom C. Taylor.)

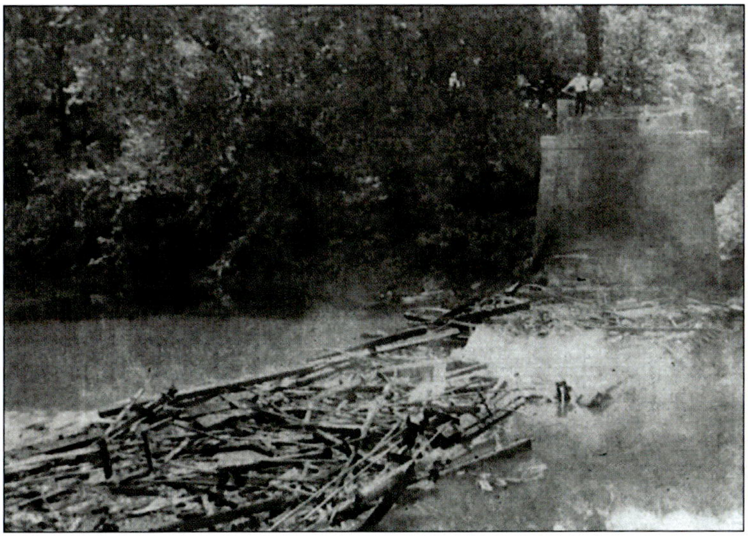

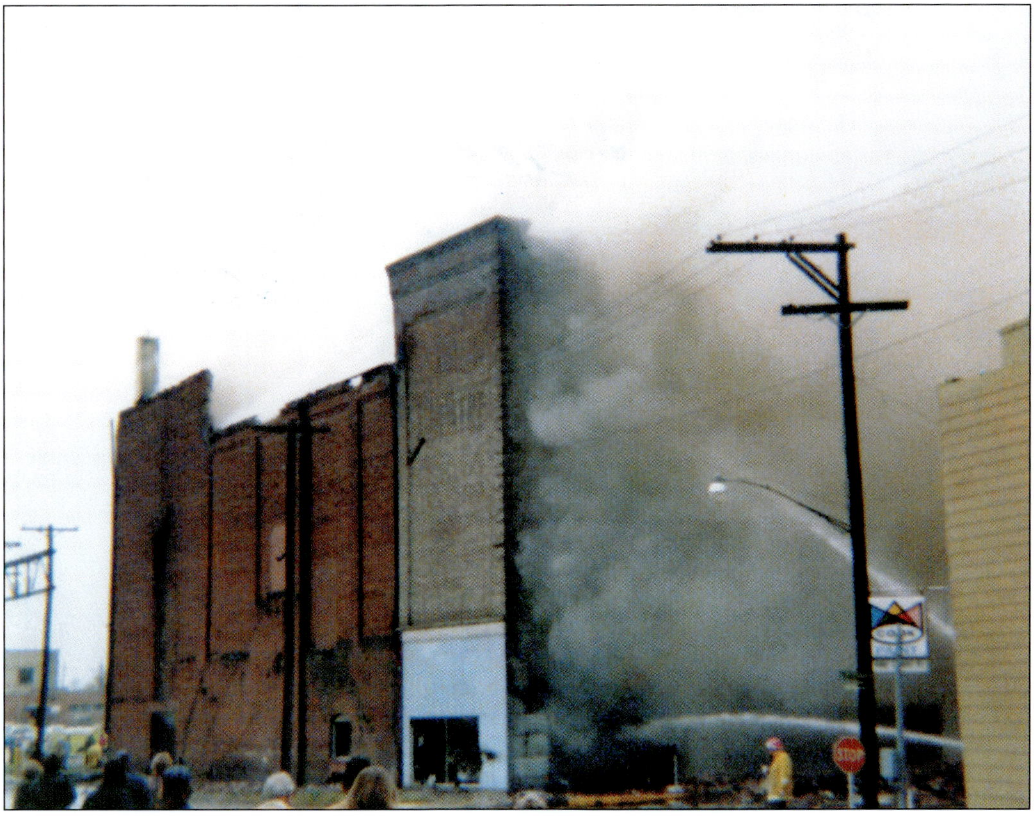

The Sedalia Theatre opened at the corner of Third Street and Massachusetts Avenue in 1905. Built at a cost of $57,000, the theater seated 1,571 people and had the second-largest stage in Missouri. The title of its opening production—*Piff, Paff and Pouf*—also describes its final performance when lightning struck in 1977. (Courtesy of Myrna Ragar.)

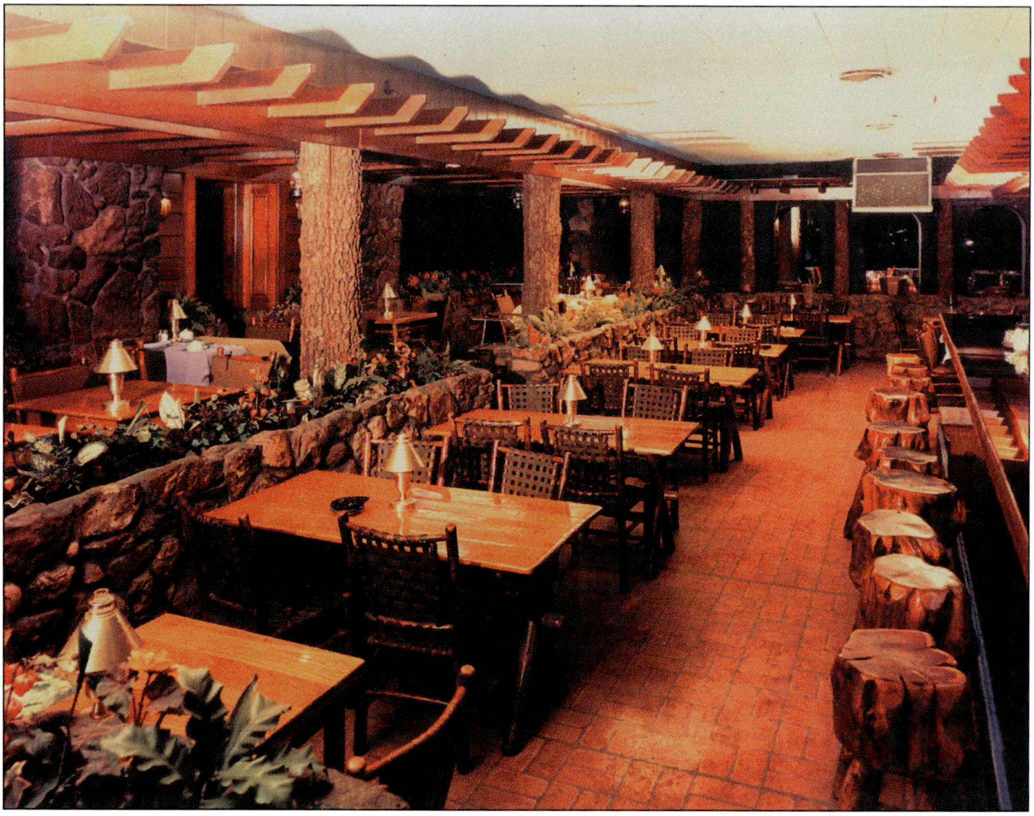

Iva Rice grew up wanting to own her own restaurant. Her childhood dream came true when she opened the Old Missouri Homestead in 1947. She designed and built the restaurant, converting the basement swimming pool of Sedalia's former YMCA to an indoor oasis. She handpicked rocks and used swimming pool plumbing to create waterfalls. The restaurant became nationally known and hosted celebrities, including Clint Eastwood, Gene Autry, Sally Rand, and Brenda Lee. (Both, courtesy of the Rice family.)

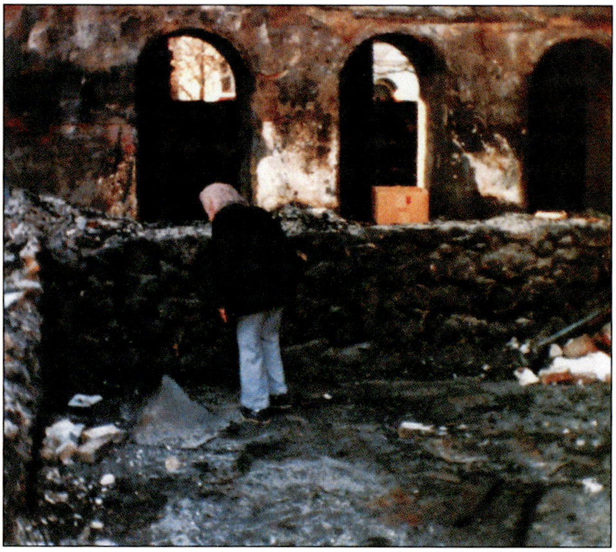

Iva Rice (left) sold the Old Missouri Homestead in 1976. Ten years later, she asked her daughter to take her to the restaurant for what she thought might be her last visit because of her advanced age. She visited the restaurant once more—after it was destroyed by fire in 1986. Bundled up against the January cold, Iva picked her way through the charred remains. All that remained were rocks, the same ones she had handpicked and fashioned into her childhood dream. Iva passed away in 1999, a few months before her 100th birthday. (Courtesy of the Rice family.)

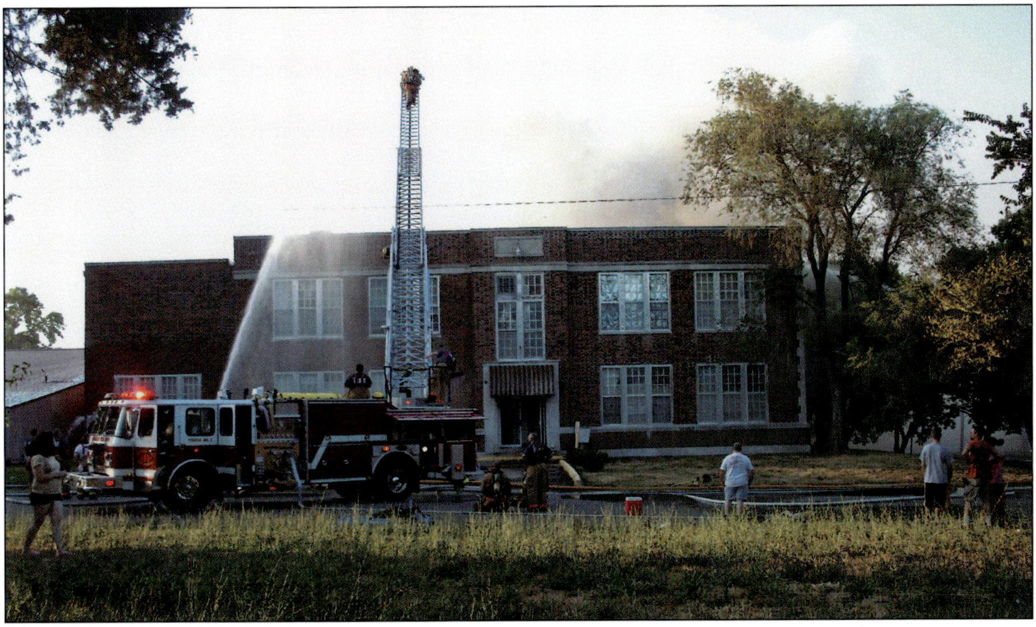

The Mark Twain School was described as a "modern fire-proof structure" when it opened at the corner of Second Street and Grand Avenue in 1928. The new building and furnishings, which replaced the Prospect School, cost $90,000. After it was damaged in a 1977 tornado, the Sedalia School Board sold the property on a sealed-bid basis. It was converted to apartments and remained as such until being destroyed by a fire in 2012.

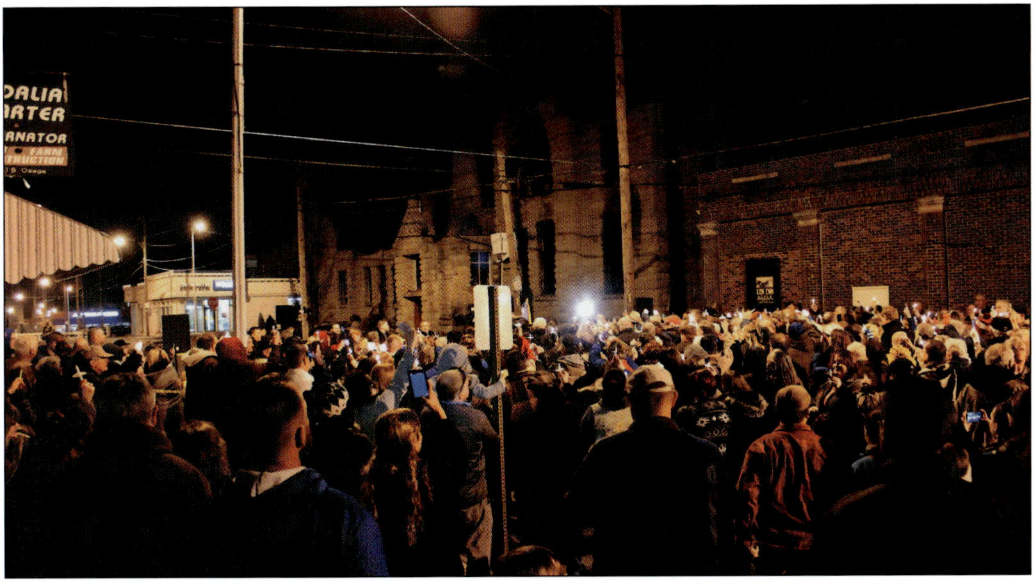

After a fire destroyed the First United Methodist Church in 2016, the congregation and community joined for a candlelight vigil. "Her fired-burned walls will be taken down, but her witness will rise from the ashes," Pastor Jim Downing shared on Facebook. "We know that the church—housed in places made of bricks—is made of human hearts and is filled with God's incredible love. We continue to be the church." (Courtesy of Kevin Walker, Walker Photography.)

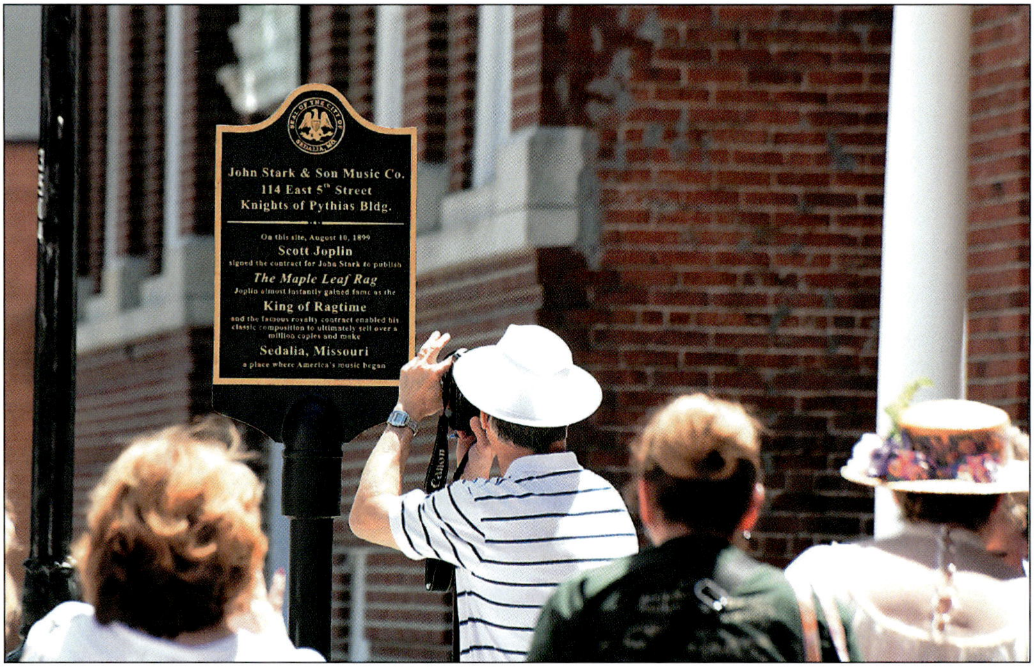

Ragtime enthusiasts paused during the 2016 Scott Joplin International Ragtime Festival to photograph a new marker commemorating musical history. The marker inscription explains, "On this site, Scott Joplin signed the contract, August 10, 1899, for John Stark to publish the *Maple Leaf Rag*. Joplin almost instantly gained fame as the King of Ragtime and the famous royalty contract enabled his classic composition to ultimately sell over a million copies and make Sedalia, Missouri, a place where America's music began." Stark's contract provided a 1 percent royalty to Joplin, an almost unprecedented arrangement for a black composer during that era. Larry Melton (below, left) and many others were instrumental in starting the now annual ragtime festival in 1974 while he was executive director of the Sedalia Area Chamber of Commerce. Melton is pictured after the commemoration ceremony with Kyle Stark, great-great-grandson of John Stark. (Both photographs by Faith Bemiss, courtesy of the *Sedalia Democrat*.)

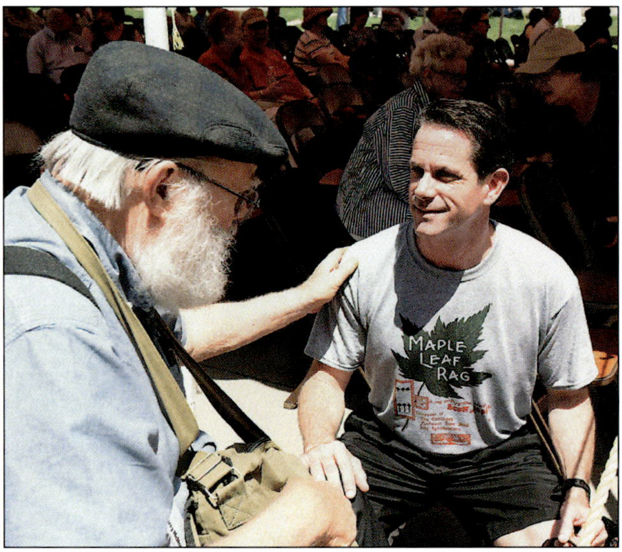

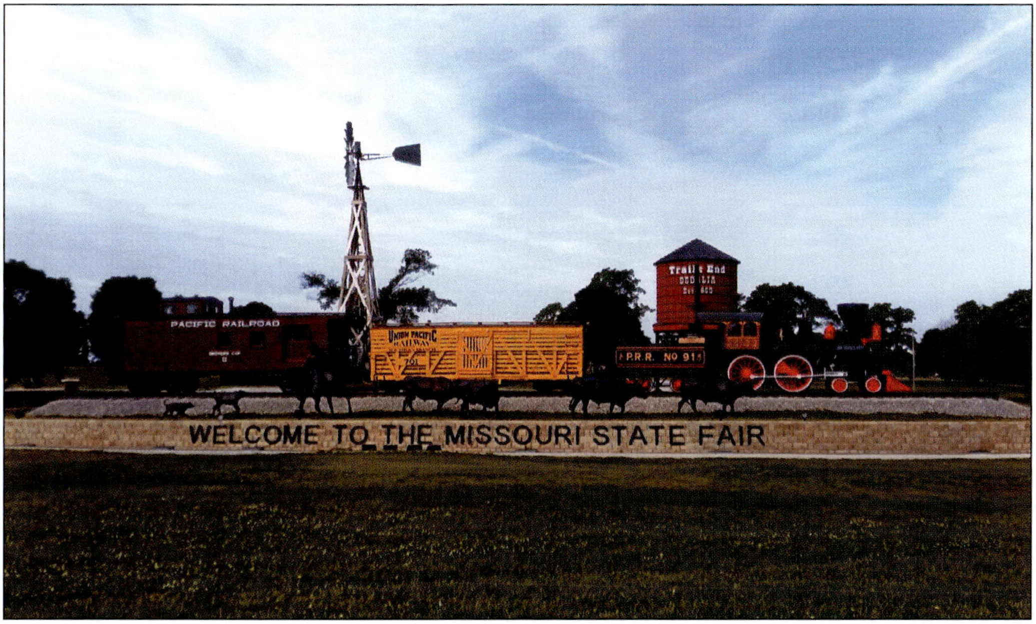

The Trail's End monument celebrates the spirit of cowboys and the role of the railroad in founding Sedalia. It features bronze sculptures by J. Michael Wilson depicting a cowboy with his horse and dog herding five longhorn cattle along the Sedalia Branch of the Shawnee Trail. The monument also includes a full-size replica of an 1865 steam locomotive with functional smokestack, headlight, bell, and whistle, along with a cattle car and drover's caboose. A water tower and windmill complete the scene. The monument dedication in 2015, which included the largest all-equestrian parade in Missouri history, was filmed and later broadcast on RFD-TV. Dale and Liz Yelton were cochairs of the privately funded grassroots project. The Starline Brass Trail's End Plaza is located on the Missouri State Fairgrounds, at the corner of South Limit Avenue and West Sixteenth Street. (Both, courtesy of Jack Slocum.)

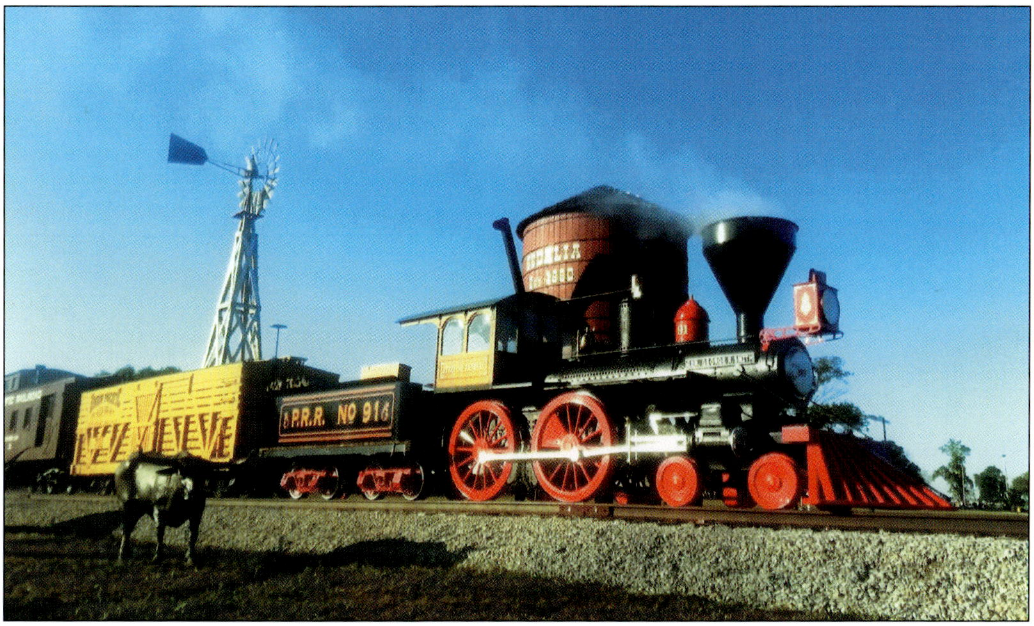